Mrs. Parsons

Dyrbington Court, or, The story of John Julian's prosperity

Mrs. Parsons

Dyrbington Court, or, The story of John Julian's prosperity

ISBN/EAN: 9783741170805

Manufactured in Europe, USA, Canada, Australia, Japa

Cover: Foto ©Andreas Hilbeck / pixelio.de

Manufactured and distributed by brebook publishing software (www.brebook.com)

Mrs. Parsons

Dyrbington Court, or, The story of John Julian's prosperity

DYRBINGTON COURT;

OR,

The Story

OF

JOHN JULIAN'S PROSPERITY.

BY

MRS. PARSONS,

AUTHOR OF "EMMA'S CROSS," "EDITH MORTIMER,"
"MRS. MAITLAND," &c. &c.

LONDON:
BURNS AND LAMBERT,
17 & 18, PORTMAN STREET, AND 63, PATERNOSTER ROW.
MDCCCLXI.

DYRBINGTON;

OR,

THE STORY OF JOHN JULIAN'S PROSPERITY.

CHAPTER I.

DYRBINGTON.

IN a southern county of England there is a parish which we will call Dyrbington. There is a village; just above it, a short way off, is Dyrbington Court; and close to the house is the church. The church is the same, exteriorly, as the church of the sixteenth century; and the village lies nestling beneath the shelter of an amphitheatre of hills just as it lay in those better days. The Court-house of Dyrbington is not the same. A new house, only as old as the Dutch King William, stands where the Catholic home stood; the change of desolation has come upon the church, and the coldness of unbelief upon the village—which is the least that can be said.

The church must be looked at more closely.

There is a nave, a principal chancel, and two aisles, thus giving three places for altars. When the old house was standing and Sir Henry Dyrbington and Dame Dorothy, his wife, were living in it, the two altars in the aisles were called by holy names. The south aisle was called after St. Katharine. And the north aisle was chosen by this same Sir Henry and Dame Dorothy, and Parson Fitzhugh, the parish priest, for the use of a chantry, which they determined to found. So that was called the chantry chapel of St. George.

Sir Henry endowed the chantry chapel with money to maintain a priest to say daily Mass there, for the souls of the members of the Guild, living or dead. Land was severed from the Dyrbington estate, and called, as it is still called, the Chantry farm. It was stocked by the knight and the priest with cattle and sheep. The altar was rebuilt, and very richly furnished for the glory of God, and the good of man; and a house in the village given up to the chantry priest, "*Sir*" John Stukely, as he was called.

The chantry was for the good of body and soul. There was no Poor Law in those times. From the chantry funds the poor were provided for. When the world would no more support them, they sheltered beneath the care of the great St. George, and found food, clothing, and soul's safety there. The villagers all round enrolled themselves members of the Guild of St. George, and scores from the great neighbouring sea-port of Watermouth belonged to St. George. They never thought of burial-clubs, nor of sick-clubs either— St. George was enough.

By the eve of St. George's day, the adornments of the aisle were completed; the altar was up, the new vestments ready, and the deeds of endowment: and the Bishop was at old Dyrbington Court-house ready for the morrow. The church doors were open. Crowds were flocking in, and passing out quietly. Hundreds of hearts were filled with love and thankfulness to God for this gift from Mother Church. On St. George's day, at eight o'clock, the Bishop entered the church for the consecration of the altar of St. George. Let one thing be remarked particularly. At the offertory, Sir Henry and his wife walked up to the altar. They, on their knees, made their oblation. It was a parchment, signed and sealed, endowing the chantry; and Almighty God was there begged to accept it at their hands. And this appalling addition followed: "But if any man at the instigation of the Devil shall at any time sacrilegiously spoil Almighty God and this church of these our humble offerings,—Then, as far as in us lies, do we attach a curse to that sacrilege until restitution be made."

Bountiful refreshments, and merry sports upon the village green followed in the afternoon. And when the people assembled, one man only seemed untouched and coarsely indifferent. His name was long remembered—it was Snigge. An archery butt was set up on the green, and the prize of a fat porker was to be his who best hit the mark—not a very valuable prize, but the villagers might have defended it, had they known how, by the parsley crown, which was worth less. The parish rector, Fitzhugh; the new chantry priest, Stukely; and Sir Henry and his wife were on the green to see the shooting, and they had been welcomed there with shouts of the heartiest satisfaction. Snigge, alone, did not lift his cap, nor give them shout or smile; but Sir Henry spoke pleasantly to him. He was a fine stout fellow of about thirty. And when the other marksmen had tried their skill, he stepped confidently forward and hit the centre spot of victory. Every one felt that he would have liked some one else to have done it,—for, said many voices:—" He is out of the Church,"—and others:—" He is not of our Guild."

We must now go on twenty-five years.

The chantry had done its work well. The sick had been relieved; the poor helped; the aged pensioned; the dead buried; and the faithful departed remembered. Among the last were Sir Henry and Dame Dorothy. They lie in the chantry chapel, and you may see their monuments there, still asking for prayers. Parson Fitzhugh is dead also. He died before Sir Henry.

And Sir Henry had him laid before the high altar, and over him is the still beautiful brass, which the good knight placed there, and which represents Fitzhugh, vested for mass, and holding the chalice between his hands. And so the stones cry out, and bear witness of the past. Sir Henry was succeeded by his brother John—and now the bad times are come. He did all that Henry VIII. desired. Then came Edward VI. And an act was passed on the 6th December, 1547, which transferred to him three thousand religious foundations, that is, all that then remained untouched. This doomed our chantry.

But John Dyrbington petitioned to divide the spoil with the king. And on condition of his carrying out the king's wishes immediately, the petition was granted. Snigge was a great man with the new Lord of Dyrbington, and glad was he to spread the news in the village. The fatal news fell as a deep sorrow on all hearts. They were panic-struck, and miserable; full of fear for the future, and in terror at the present. The chantry chapel was *their own*. A hundred tongues said—"Impossible—*it is ours.*" Hundreds more felt that it was *not* impossible to rob God's poor, and held their peace in bitterness. And the poor were robbed.

There came a day—people knew what was to happen—the chantry aisle was crowded to suffocation, for every parishioner, able to attend, had thronged into that narrow space to assist at the last Mass to be offered in their chantry.

John Dyrbington came, and a parson,—alas! he showed himself to be a bad priest,—who was now to be the parish priest; and this man began to say Mass at the high altar. The chantry Mass ended a little before the Mass at the high altar. The people still lingered, and Sir John Stukely, having laid aside his vestments, was before the altar of St. George, kneeling in prayer. Sir John Dyrbington stepped from his place in the choir to Stukely's side. In a voice which was remembered by all who heard it to the last day of their lives—a voice not exceedingly loud, but yet at once so loud, and of such a tone as had never before been heard within those walls, he addressed Father Stukely and the people. He said that by the king's orders they were dispossessed of their chantry; that the possession thereof had been granted to him, and his heirs, according to his highness's laws ecclesiastical. The priest remained on his knees while Sir John spoke. Then he got up. The people pressed forward. "Where is your warrant?" said the priest. "Here," said the knight, showing it, and offering it to him. Stukely read it in silence. Then, looking at Sir John, he spoke aloud, and all the people heard him. "*I* have never acknowledged the king to be supreme head of Christ's Church. But I have lived here, and used my functions as a priest, within this Church of England, though separated from the See of the blessed Peter. I have done this thing, hoping for better times. I now confess, my beloved people, that I have done wrong in as far as I have owned in any way the evil that has happened to us, and in token thereof *I do this*"——he tore the parchment in two pieces, and dropped them on the pavement. There was perfect silence for a moment. Then Snigge moved forward as if to seize the priest. Several voices exclaimed—"Run for your life." A little lane was opened amidst the crowd for his passage. Making one act of reverence, he passed through the people, reached the porch, and was gone.

The people all went out, striving with each other like creatures scared, and left the knight in possession. All the altar furniture, the chalice and paten, copes, chasubles of gold and silver, purple, red, green, and black; stoles, maniples, crosses; treasures of finest linen, damasks, and laces,—with thuribles and incense boats, a goodly store!—these things, the land, the stock, the farm buildings, the money in store, it was all the knight's and the king's. The larger share belonged to the Court-house—and with it the spoliation curse.

Stukely was seen once more by his beloved people. He was seen at his execution. One young girl, called Kate Frampton, who lived to the last year of Elizabeth's sins, saw him die, and went blind upon the spot. Maddened by grief, she beheld the martyrdom. She spoke to Father Stukely, who gave her his blessing, and a crucifix. She saw, gazed without flinching, and then saying, "The flames, the flames—they go into my brain piercingly," she became sightless. People cried out, "All ye Holy Popes and Martyrs—St. Peter, St. George, pray for him!" He smiled in his agony, which was long, and went to his reward.

So the Protestantized church of Dyrbington has no brass to Father Stukely. But the family of Frampton kept the crucifix. And we shall see it again.

CHAPTER II.

WATERMOUTH.

OUR readers are, we hope, sufficiently instructed in Dyrbington past, to come down to something more near to Dyrbington present.

Let us come down to the beginning of this century—to the time of our many naval and military victories—to the time which, until present experience taught us a different language, has been called "the time of the war."

Watermouth is not the least like what it was when its inhabitants served God, and loved Him instead of money. But it is a very prosperous place. All its old Catholic charitable foundations have been swallowed up by men like John Dyrbington. As you walk about you see old carvings, old archways, worn remains of canopies at street-corners. These things tell of Dominicans, and Franciscans, and Benedictines,—of churches, and hospitals, and of other holy places which went when Mass went. The Watermouth people are proud of their ruins. They show them as curiosities, and take some sort of care of them, and can tell you, any one of them, which stable or waggon-house was the chapel of St. Nicholas, and how many churches have been destroyed, and what a lovely place for summer pic-nics the prior's hospital has been proved to be. And they are particularly proud of a great beetling rock, which juts out into the sea, and which is still called St. Julian's—of which you will hear more.

Watermouth is an old borough, with large Docks, and a very prosperous trade. It is thought a good thing to be born here a freeman. And there remains, out of a hundred rich Catholic charities, one school, where the sons of her freemen may get a very good education at a very trifling expense. Now, if you, my reader, are in fancy treading the intricate streets of rich, prosperous, powerful Watermouth, I may ask you if, near the densest part of the town, yet standing alone, and looking forth upon the far-spread sea, you observe a small house entered by a low archway?—Listen. You will hear the sound of a workman's hammer. It is John Julian at his work. You shall hear his history.

In the good Catholic days there stood on that great rock a chapel called St. Julian's. You approached the rock by a bridge, wonderfully wrought, and skilfully thrown across the river, that there fell into the sea and that now fills the docks, by the Benedictine monks. Here Mass was said for sailors. Here a light burned to warn vessels from that dangerous headland, called the Dead-man's Point. Here the sailors thanked God for safe returns, and here they prayed for blessings when they went to sea. It was small and substantial. But it was glorious inside. Thank-offerings had enriched the chapel, and added a small house or rather room to it, for the monks to occupy when bad weather, or the good offices required at times of shipwreck, kept them at St. Julian's. It was built with great skill. The waves beat against it, and it stood their fury as firmly as the dark rock which sprung from the far clear depths for its support.

The spirit of sacrilegious spoliation neither forgot nor spared the chapel of St. Julian. An old parchment tells that "one of those Dyvil's worshippers and workmen, called Snigge, of the parish of Dyrbington was foremost in the work." It goes on to tell us that, in consequence of the part he took in destroying this place, and appropriating a good store of its treasures, a curse cleaved to him; and that drawn, as people thought mysteriously, to the spot, he came in after years to the ruins, and set up a cooper's shop there; that he was never married, but took an orphan nephew to live with him; that he lived and died there; but that on people coming to bury him, his body was no where to be found—many said his master had fetched it. Others fancied that some, who remembered how he had treated the chapel, had cast his corpse into the sea—however, there was no Snigge. The orphan boy was liked; and when a man he removed into the town. The people had always talked of *"going to Julian's"*—and they said so still, after the young man's settling in the town —till at last he got the name of Julian, as did his children after him. The Julian, whose hammer might be heard early in the morning and late as the light allowed, was the seventh generation from Snigge, the spoliator.

Julian was a man of sixty-five years of age at the time of which we are writing. He was of a very singular appearance. His figure was bowed, and his eyes always sought the ground. He was of very large stature, and very clumsy form. But, to make amends, he certainly possessed extraordinary mental powers. People were superstitious about him—thought him a sort of prophet. And people had never done talking about him. Was he rich—was he poor? Generally there was an idea that he hoarded, and was a miser. He was certainly a remarkable man. But so his father had been—and his grandfather—all the Julians had been remarkable men. Julian was odd. He lived in the past. He was born an antiquary. He knew something of Latin, for he had been at the freeman's school; and he had almost unheard-of powers of walking. As soon as he could leave his work, he started on a walk. He had mapped out every estate for twenty miles round, for that was a thing he loved greatly to do. Speak of a field, he could tell its owner; of a tree, he would find you its age and measurements; of a house, he knew all its history, and the lives of all who had dwelt within its walls. And the Watermouth neighbourhood was tempting to an antiquary. There was unclaimed land; old houses; magnificent wood; extra-parochial districts, where a race of people lived like outlaws, and poured down upon the resentful inhabitants of industrious and respectable Watermouth in times of distress, and supplicated, or terrified them out of large measures of unwilling alms. It must be confessed that Julian had no dislike to gossip with these people; and that with one family long resident in the forest country, he had a sincere friendship. These people, who were called Norwood, had a very aged woman among them—a hundred years old, they said—and though usually accounted mad, Julian could gather from her much of the past, and during the whole latter part of her life, he had been very tenderly kind to her. Julian's wife was an extraordinary contrast to himself; small, fair, rosy; of a very sweet countenance, and with a loving smile, and a gentle voice. Julian was very proud of her. "She is of Dyrbington," he would say—"the last of the Framptons there." And this was true. She was of that Kate Frampton's family of whom we have been writing; and she possessed the crucifix given to the former Kate by

Stukely. She understood her husband, and was very happy with him. She even liked his ugliness and oddity; she was a little proud of his being so different from other people.

But Kate Julian's greatest joy was in her children. Edward was the most promising boy in the freeman's school. He was eighteen years of age, and was reading to gain a scholarship and be a great man, as his mother hoped, at Oxford. Anna was fifteen, a slight girl, fair, and golden-haired; and so gentle in her pretty ways, that no one would have guessed at the spirit of power that dwelt in her young heart. No language can describe the joy of Mrs. Julian when she had these loved ones about her, of an evening, when the work was done. There was a remarkable room in the house—a small sitting-room above stairs, and it looked, by an oriel window, out upon the sea. It was a magnificent view; and Julian's seat, which was a carved oak chair, high-backed, and surmounted by the Dyrbington arms, stood in the space formed by the jutting window. There he gazed on the sea, spreading far till it seemed to meet the sky. His eye dwelt on its calm, smooth, silvery glitter; and watched its sparkling expanse, ever varying, as each dimpling wave wore a smile which brightened beneath the sun, and changed, and grew again, and sparkling went and came, till gradually subsiding into stillness towards the evening, it seemed, to Julian's eyes, to draw its dark-blue mantle over its sunny face, and calmly wait for night. And sometimes from midday to night would Julian watch and gaze, and think what lay beyond that far-spread ocean; whether indeed the shores of the far-off lands were spread with pure grains of gold and precious pearls were found among the sea-weeds. But of these thoughts he never spoke. His tidy little wife, who honoured and loved him well, used not to disturb him in these moods. She would lay her tea-service as quietly as possible, and give him his meal on a small table, whose ancient form matched with the Dyrbington chair. Then Julian would throw off his meditative mood, and the old cabinet would be unlocked, and the carved oak chest opened, and if a friend were by, he would display his treasures—and always first, the crucifix. "It was preserved by one of my family, whose name I bear," Mrs. Julian would say. "She kept it when things were upset in the troublous times." But what things were upset, or even when those "troublous times" were, Kate did not know.

Notwithstanding young Edward Julian's goodness and cleverness, his father certainly loved Anna best. He liked to have the gentle girl always by him. Through whole days in that busy shop, and long evenings in that quiet chamber, that little Anna was by her father's side; sometimes, when he was gazing on the sea, looking steadily, softly, almost sadly in his face, as if her eyes were fixed by fascination there, and could not be withdrawn. He liked to have her by him, but he never invited her to follow him, or recalled her when she left him, or took any tender notice of her when she was by his side. But as he plied his noisy work, and the child pursued her quiet occupation, he would sometimes for an instant stay his hand, and, without looking round, say "Anna?" And when she answered "Here, father," the work would speed on, with its brisk dulness, till the same incident occurred again and again, and the hour of the evening meal tolled out from the church close by. And then Julian would cease working, and turn towards the house, never noticing the child, who still followed, as if drawn by a strange sympathy to devote herself to him.

CHAPTER III.

ANOTHER FREEMAN.

LORD WESTREY was the pride of Watermouth, as his father had been before him. He had a house in the town. He did not live there, but he would never sell it. That great high old dingy house was the place of his birth, and there also his children had been born.

Lord Westrey lived at his wife's place. He had married the last heiress of the old Catholic house of Lullingstone—they were cousins of the Dyrbingtons—and at Old Court, Lullingstone, he had lived ever since his marriage with Lady Westrey. The place was a noble one, and such as is never seen except in England. The house stood on a spacious terrace cut from the sloping side of a sunny hill. And trees, the growth of a century, crowned the hills and enriched the valleys for full four miles till the lands of Old Court, Lullingstone, joined themselves to Dyrbington.

Mary Lullingstone was an orphan. She had been brought up in that ancient home by a sister of her father—Mrs. Margaret Lullingstone. And who would pass Mrs. Margaret by without comment or commendation?

She is living at this time of which we write, though not at Old Court. Very few people ever see her. To say that she is generally believed in, as a living fact, would best describe the little that is known of her. But Mrs. Margaret had been like a loving mother to Mary. Old Court had never lapsed from the faith. The Lullingstone share of the strong heart and willing arm which Mother Church asks from her children had now devolved upon *one*—and that one was a woman. The good aunt watched the child bud and blossom, and she made her take her place in the world, blushing and trembling, but yet right well. And then Mary married a Protestant. Mrs. Margaret went to a house her father had settled upon her, called St. Cuthbert's, and spent her life in prayer and pious works. Lady Westrey's picture was taken on her marriage. It was hung in the library, where a portrait and a bookcase divided the long lengths of wall. Perhaps this picture is a little old-fashioned in our eyes, even for those days. But there she stands, in white satin falling in heavy silvery folds upon the ground; one tiny foot on a footstool; a white lily in her hand, which is crossed on her left arm. There is a dreamy wondering look in the face, which is that of a girl of nineteen. Almost a touch of sorrow, and almost a touch of fear is in the eyes; and yet about the mouth there is the decision of the mind made up. Mrs. Margaret stayed in the house to receive the bride and bridegroom. She received the first Protestant lord of that place, and went her way in sorrow. Yet she liked Lord Westrey, and thought him an honourable man, as he was. But still she went her way in sorrow, and in prayer. She could only pray in one way—that one might preserve her faith, and that the other might receive the grace of conversion. And being an extremely old-fashioned person, she did not pray the less earnestly, because the latter was perhaps the most unlikely thing in the world to happen. One thing only did Mrs. Margaret say when she heard that, in the event of an heir, he was to be brought up a Protestant; she said, "Oh! cruel to the memory of the past!" And the words struck severely into Mary's heart.

But Mary was young, and she hoped—hoped that if she had children, she should, somehow, keep them hers; and she was in love—and so she married Lord Westrey.

Only eighteen years have passed since that wedding-day. And the beautiful woman of thirty-seven is not now very like her picture. She is very beautiful, gentle, stately,—like a swan in her movements; in her character, like soft music of full chords, *very* soft, yet quite distinctly heard, without a doubt upon a single note.

She has suffered a martyrdom in that eighteen

years; a martyrdom unseen, unacknowledged, neither comprehended nor believed—a martyrdom than which no pain could be more acute, and of which it was impossible to complain. It was the disappearance from around her, and about her, of the faith of her ancestors, the being *alone* as she only could be—the punishment of starvation on her soul. She had nothing to complain of. Lord Westrey was the most loving of husbands; a man of bright spirits, and great activity of mind and body; very fond, and very proud of her. She knew that she was the joy and gratification of his life; but the atmosphere of religion was gone. Did she want to see a priest? Oh, of course. Had she any idea where there was one? Did she mean to wait till they went to London? Perhaps she said that she had better go to St. Cuthbert's for a few days. O not that! It was really true that Lord Westrey could scarcely bear her out of his sight. What was home without her? Can't you have him here? You can do what you like, but don't go away. And she would not go away. And little difficulties would arise. And she would wait till she went to London. Yet, now and then, somebody—it was not generally known who he was—would be seen passing through that long gallery with that beautiful lady by his side, or Lord Westrey himself, with a brilliant face of courtesy. He went out unattended; he came generally unannounced, for Lady Westrey would loiter on the terrace expecting him. And that was all that was seen of the Catholic faith.

The trial of such a state of things was over now —over, *because she was accustomed to it.* She had a daughter, more beautiful than herself at that daughter's age, and called after her. Mary was sixteen years old; and the mother's prayers had prevailed for her first-born—how glad she was to see a girl—she was a Catholic. The only other child was a boy; one year younger than Mary. Lord Westrey, when he took him for baptism to the Protestant church at Watermouth, called him Lullingstone, out of compliment to his mother.

Mary Westrey had had, or was having, what more modern mothers would call a very odd education. She had always been at home, and had never had any other teacher than her mother. Now, Lady Westrey living "in the world," as it is called, had duties belonging to her position. Lord Westrey had to sit in parliament. He went largely into society, and led a busy life. He had often proposed that Mary should have some accomplished person to be always with her in her mother's absence; but that mother had never consented. She felt that she had hold of that child's soul. She would not even divide the care of that precious treasure. And she had to teach Mary—and who else could dare to teach her?—to pray for her father and her brother. She had to teach Mary that it had been ill done to marry a Protestant. She had to be perpetually bearing witness against herself, with a wife's and a mother's devotion, still, and unceasingly strong in her heart. Who, but herself, could undertake such a work as this? So Mary was left to her mother, and her mother's maid, a descendant of the old Catholic Wyches of Dyrbington, and the only servant of the true faith in the house. It has been said that Mary was beautiful. It was a fact not to be questioned. It was the beauty of jet-black hair and soft eyes, a fair complexion, perfect features, and a tall slender form. She could speak and write French perfectly. She knew a good deal of Latin. She could paint, not because she was taught, but because she could not help it. It was another language to her. She did not read much. Are you saying "How dreadful!" dear reader? Please to recollect how little there was in those days to read. Do you think that the "Delicate Distress" books of only a few years ago were good books for such a girl as Mary Westrey to read? Please to recollect that if Catholics don't write stories, it may be just as well for Catholics not to read any. Mary did not read as you and I read. But she read devout writings of holy English priests, and lived as she read. Again and again she read, like daily food, and pondered and prayed, and grew strong, in a still, calm, noiseless way. However, if there were not story-books for Mary Westrey, it was a day of good talking, and Mary was an excellent listener.

She had learned elsewhere—in the sanctuary of her mother's room—what enabled her to distinguish gold from rubbish. She stored up the good things that were said, and forgot the foolish ones, and she learned to think. Music she loved, and she played; but not for exhibition. She could repeat what she had heard; and, as it were, tell things new from her own heart, with her hands on the keys of the organ in the hall—that was all. And her mother had stored her with *real* history—the *truths* of the past. In these things, and in the contemplation of her mother, was her whole education.

Mary's love for her father was a different thing from her love for her mother. He was her delightful companion, her perfect knight. She gloried in the applause he won. When he openly admired her, she felt that she was beautiful, and was very glad of it. But when her mother smiled upon her, she never had a worldly thought. It was like the sun chasing away such damps and mists. Soul spoke to soul. And side by side their hearts were open before Him who sees in secret, and judges thought. That mother was heaven on earth to the young girl. She could admit no one to the knowledge of it. It was too great for words.

Lullingstone had been very delicate from his birth. Mary loved him tenderly, and nursed him. Though only a year younger, he was a child compared to her. The boy had been born in the great house at Watermouth. A sudden illness had reduced Lady Westrey to the point of death. There was no nurse for the young heir, and the child was pronounced too weak to live. Anna Julian was two months old. Mrs. Julian offered to bring her child to Lord Westrey's house, and take care of Lullingstone. The offer was accepted, and Lord Westrey always said that his only son owed his life to Kate Julian. Lord Westrey became Anna Julian's godfather. He had known the Julians all his life, and had always respected them. Now he would be theirs, and their children's friend as long as he lived. All this pleased Kate Julian, and it strangely gratified her husband. His eyes were always on the future. There were untold hopes in his heart. What would come? What wonderful things would years bring with them? He loved Anna better than Edward, because she was a link between him and the great.

CHAPTER IV.

HOPES.

Deep down in John Julian's heart dwelt hopes too powerful for words. The love of power, riches, and station which had tempted his ancestors to sacrilege, was firmly rooted in Julian's soul. It was the origin of all his oddness. It was that which led him to ponder on the past, and to see, in the passing away of many, the possibility of the elevation of himself. He always expected that some great change would come. It was an hereditary feeling. His father and grandfather had lived and died, loving, longing after, and expecting the power and distinction which had never come. It was like a disease, of which he preferred not to be cured, which was an occupation to him. He loved gold with a love which lay too close to his soul to be spoken of. Only to his little daughter he would utter mysterious hints; and when he saw Lord Westrey at his door, and received his kind greetings, and saw Anna stand by Lullingstone's side—then he thought, and thought in time became belief, that if his child had wealth, the hope of his heart might come true. On summer evenings the Westreys would ride to Julian's on their ponies. There was a long line of hard beach to which a narrow lane led them from Julian's house, and there Lullingstone used to ride his pony up and down. And Mary liked the sea-shore and the sands; but sometimes she would stay on the high ground and look out on the sea, while her father chatted with good Mrs. Julian, and Edward stood by her pony's rein. Mary would talk to Edward about the school. "So you are going to College?" she said, one day, and smiled as a woman might smile on a child, though she was nearly two years younger than Edward.—"You are going to College?"

"If I gain the scholarship—and I *shall* gain it," said Edward, enthusiastically.

"Why, Edward, you will be quite a gentleman," said Mary, a little thoughtlessly, as she felt a moment afterwards.

Edward's downy face became rosy red. He looked down, but spoke bravely:—"I shall be Edward Julian, as I now am. I shall not be better as a well-educated man than I am now as a well-educated boy."

Mary knew more about it than Edward. She had looked upon the world, of which he had only heard the murmur from afar. She walked by right, with gentle steps, in paths towards which he would toil with his young life's best strength. It passed through her thoughtful mind, and she said, "I beg your pardon, Edward."

She could not help respecting the triumph she had imagined. The youth looked at her, respectfully, yet wondering. But she was gazing on the broad waters, and did not observe him.

Edward Julian was a wonderful boy. He was more than clever; more than strong in mind, of quiet thought, and bright imagination; he was more than industrious, more than ambitious, more than courageous, more than persevering. He was pure-minded and honourable, and full of good desires and love of virtue. His whole religion lay in his mother and Lady Westrey. He had no defined ideas about articles of faith. He saw no difficulty in the fact of his heroines being of different religions—they were the romance of his life. He felt that his mother was always right. There was a sincerity, an openness, a frankness about her—she was patient, kind-hearted, and of an extraordinary cheerfulness of disposition; and her son was like her. But he went beyond her. He had aspirations of his own. And once, when Lady Westrey was pleased with something that he had said, and called him to her, and, holding him by the hand, looked into his face and said, "Dear boy!"—then he felt more than he could ever have told, and more than Mrs. Julian could ever have comprehended. It was as if, at that moment, he had vowed a vow to raise himself, to be sought after, to be the learned, the accomplished Edward Julian. He would not forget his early life: it should be known and told, but only to add to his merits. And he became ambitious for his sister. He wanted her to feel as he felt. He wanted her to be within Lady Westrey's influence. So Edward toiled, and no one doubted about his success. He toiled generously, not ashamed of being a working man's son, and not discouraged by it—not flying from himself, not wishing to get rid of Edward Julian, but expanding the character of Edward Julian into all that Edward Julian might be.

Lullingstone Westrey had a tutor—Mr. Parker. He was very fond of Edward, and encouraged him, and assisted him in his studies. And Edward was often allowed to spend whole days with Mr. Parker and Lullingstone.

And Lady Westrey used, by numberless attentions, to distinguish Mrs. Julian, and she was very kind to Anna. She would make Mrs. Julian bring her daughter to Old Court on her birth-day, and on her foster-brother's birth-day, and they all drank tea together in Lady Westrey's room.

Sometimes John Julian walked to Lullingstone to bring his wife and child home; and then, occasionally, he did what perhaps he enjoyed more than any thing in the world. He paced up and down the terrace with Lord Westrey while he waited for his wife. It is true that Lord Westrey enjoyed this also. He liked considering character:—human nature is very interesting to some people. It was to Lord Westrey. He encouraged Julian to talk by praising Anna, and speaking of the time when he was a boy in his father's house in Watermouth. And Julian did talk; and Lord Westrey used to get into wonderful puzzles. He could not understand Julian; and got thinking to himself:—"How could such a being as this persuade that pleasant, excellent, pretty, simple-minded, sensible little Mrs. Julian to marry him? How strange to see such an odd creature with that promising son and that gentle golden-haired daughter?" These questions Lord Westrey could not answer for himself. The fact was that Julian, as he walked there, talked like a man in a dream. He spoke from within—from that heart of wonder, and hope, and mysterious belief in *something*—he could not tell what. He spoke from that deep, fixed, interior intention which passed over intervening obstacles, and rested on the future. He intended to be great. How? He could not tell. It was like a superstition. He was old; but it would come. He should see it before he died. In the mean time he contemplated the only great man he knew, or could speak to, with wonder, interest, and even curiosity. No wonder that the great man could not understand him, and was sometimes guilty of thinking that, but for Mrs. Julian's love and reverence for him, he should guess him to be crazed.

In the same spirit Julian took his long rambles about the neighbourhood. He had sat in the hut of the forest-settlers, and listened to stories of sudden success as a child drinks in a fairy-tale, with that strange belief in his own destiny strong within him; and thus thinking and feeling he would visit Dyrbington. It was a strange place now—bolted and barred, with windows shut and shutters never opened. Julian was always in his very strangest mood after his visits to Dyrbington. He would work no more for a day or two afterwards, sometimes; but sit gazing from that oriel window, as if he could read his history upon the sea. It happened one evening after such a ramble, that Julian's eye caught, far in the offing, an approaching sail; he watched it at first out of idleness, and then with the interest that grew out of the fact of a large trading vessel nearing the port. Groups of men and boys on the cliff and sea-beach, watching her with telescopes, caught Julian's attention. The evening advanced. The vessel gracefully bore her steady way towards the land. The sun was down, but the moon's rays were on the water. What an unearthly thing is the broad moonlight on the spreading sea! A whiter light and a deeper shade fell on the gathering groups. Julian joined the watchers, and heard that she could not come in that tide, and that people had gone out to her. Silently, slowly, he paced up and down, yet in his way joining in the general interest. At last, almost all were gone home, and Julian, as he, too, returned, heard some one say, "Good night, Julian —good night." The tone of the speaker was that of surprise.

"Good night," answered Julian, coldly, strangely; his whole self absorbed in thought. Then came a playful "You are very late; *you* have no interest in her."

Julian stopped suddenly. He was silent for one moment. In that moment he took quick note of what he saw:—a merchant of Watermouth, called Seaforth, with his tablets in his hand and a thick roll of paper. There was thought upon his face, but benevolence and joy also. Julian looked at it, and read in its lines success. To the question asked in friendly merriment—"*You* have no interest in her?"—he answered, "No; but I wish I had."

In those words the secret of his life—the secret of his fathers' lives—had escaped. His earnestness made the merchant start: he had spoken from the depths of his heart. Mr. Seaforth paused. He remembered the gossip of Julian being rich. He felt that it was true. Taken by surprise, he spoke hurriedly, "I am going to fit out a privateer, will you"—"Yes, yes!" exclaimed Julian.

"You should be prudent," murmured Mr. Seaforth, still strangely considering. "Your children"—"But it is all for them," gasped Julian. "But how much?" he went on—"Oh, sir,—Mr. Seaforth—don't keep me waiting—how much?" He grasped the merchant's arm in his hurry, and looked imploringly in his face. Heaven's light never showed a countenance of more anxiety, or more earnest entreaty. There was something terrible in it. Half repenting, not knowing what to think, but strangely influenced by the sight before him, Mr. Seaforth said something of which Julian only caught a word or two—"Two or three hundred—equal to that." "More, sir, more," whispered Julian, his voice almost gone, under the awe which overcame him, when now for the first time he spoke of wealth. "More, sir, more; say thousands—yes, thousands—two or three; or, or,"—Julian gasped, and said again, "two or three, or MORE;" and the last word issued like a half-suppressed cry; the secret of his inmost soul was escaping with it. Mr. Seaforth jumped back, and uttered an exclamation of surprise. It was involuntary. But, immediately taking Julian's hand, he said kindly, "You shall see me again about this." He passed on, leaving Julian in the still moonlight, alone on the sea-shore, wrapped in an unutterable surprise.

There, in the silence of thought, Julian remained some time; and when at last he gained by slow steps his own door, it was with the sense of being an altered man. The present, the past, the future, all seemed changed. *He had told it.* Every hope, every sensation, every recollection, ended in that—*he had told it.* That which had never before found words had been spoken, and was known. Again and again his heart seemed to say, *It is told.* Again and again he recalled the short interview with the merchant, and as often as he did so this fact came back upon his mind with appalling certainty. It was not that he repented what he had said; it was not that he regretted never having bound Mr. Seaforth to secrecy; it was not that he wished to conceal any thing from one who had, in the first instance, behaved so generously to him; but the one habit of his life which had never been departed from had that night been broken. He felt as though a link between him and the wonderful past was severed; that that which had made the present as a mystery to many was cleared off; and that the doubts and wonderings which had obscured the future were removed. He was now as other men. He had now no secret: *he had told it.* How those few words had changed him! He could dream no more. He was old to change his life. Could he ply his work and talk to Anna as wildly as the mood suggested now? Might he take those wanderings, and work and bargain for his toil now? Might he now indulge in those endless speculations which had beguiled so many hours sitting in the loved old chair, in the peaceful pretty chamber? Julian was suddenly sad; it was sadness mingled with a sense of resignation. He never doubted of success. He never repented of his confession. He never departed from his resolution. He was sad under a sense of change. "Yet," would he say to himself, "it must be; I always knew the time must come; and how often I have wondered as to how it would arrive. And now it has come. It is past. It is known.—*I have told it.*"

That very night, after he had seen Mr. Seaforth, Julian locked himself in the room of which we have so often spoken, and opened an iron chest which none but himself could open. It had been in his family he knew not how long. He knew not what it had been used for originally. It had certainly come from the original "Julians," on the chapel's site, at the further end of the Old Monk's Bridge. Julian opened the chest and looked on its contents. There it lay—the gold and the silver—old guineas, moidores, and half-moidores, and nobles, and marks;—and the gold was parted off from the silver—heaped up by hundreds it lay; and then the hundreds were parted off in tens. Julian had never added to this treasure. He had taken from it, but sparingly, and when necessity demanded. But he loved the sight of it with that sort of fond, unreasoning love, with which we may imagine one's self to gaze on any wonderful thing connected mysteriously with the past, and over which we alone have power. He gazed and spoke to what he saw, as though it had possessed life and knowledge. "How you first came I know not: yet you are mine. I never thought to leave you to others, as you were left to me. I knew I could not. My family have ceased to be like those of whom you remind me; and it is well, for the times in which we live are changed; but I part from you with sorrow, because you have helped to make me what I am; and I feel that when you are gone, I shall cease in some sort to be what I was—to be myself. You will bring greatness—I know you will; and when greatness is come—when it is mine—when I possess and use it, and it belongs to me, and me to it, then I shall not feel the uncertain sort of creature that I now feel to be,—no more myself, since I told of you, and as yet nothing else—but I shall think of you with gratitude, and possess you again, but in another way. Farewell: go, do your work, for the time is come."

CHAPTER V.

DYRBINGTON AGAIN.

LET us look again at Dyrbington. Green lichen and dark moss grow upon the walls. The windows are closed, and insects build their nests, and make their safe retreat between the shutters and the glass. The last of the Dyrbingtons dwells within. The family after the John Dyrbington who appropriated the goods of the Chantry Chapel and Guild of St. George, rejoiced in a great prosperity. That is, it *looked* like prosperity. There was money, and lands, and good connexions; sons and daughters were born to them. But there was one remarkable thing: how few of the many—the unusually many—who had lived in the house, had been laid when dead in the church. Wherever there was danger or bloodshed, treachery or pestilence, there was sure to be a Dyrbington among the sufferers; and when public calamities seemed insufficient for their punishment, they had fallen on each other. There were strange stories told by the old people then living in the village, and there seemed to be no reason for disbelieving them. The present squire's grandfather was said to have died of a broken heart. He had two sons, the father of the existing "old Dyrbington," as he was generally called, and an elder brother. They unhappily both fell in love with a noble Spanish lady whom they had met in London. They spoke to their father before speaking to her, and he refused his consent peremptorily; threatening them with disinheritance if either disobeyed him. She was a Catholic, and that was the objection urged against her. The youngest—Mr. Dyrbington's father—never saw her again. The eldest saw her, and married her. Believing that he could manage matters with his father, he brought her to Old Court, Lullingstone, where she was received, and affectionately treated. But the father drove his son from his door, and in the bitterness of the moment, the brothers met and quarrelled. They fought, and the elder got a mortal hurt, of which he died within the year. The younger brother was a proud man, and never spoke of the thing to any one but his father, it was said. However, the Spanish lady was a widow, with an infant in her arms—a girl. Her husband lies in the vault; for the father sent for the body when the life was out of it. But he would never help the wife. He went mourning for the rest of his life, but never repented: it was even said that, when in some disguise his son's widow came to the house, he met her in the grounds, and drove her from the place with a whip, if he did not actually make her feel the scourge. She had fled with a loud cry, and an appeal to Heaven for herself and her child. Then the old man died, and Mr. Dyrbington's father inherited the estate. He had married an amiable woman, by whom he had one son, the present squire. His wife died of a lingering illness which no one understood, and he was himself killed by a fall from his horse. The son suffered greatly when the parents died; it was a deeper sorrow than the world could understand; but after a time he rallied, and again became the popular man that he had been before his affliction. He was soon engaged to be married to a young girl of extraordinary beauty and good family, and seemed to be exceedingly happy. He certainly loved her devotedly; but she had only accepted him at the command of her parents. He fitted up Dyrbington magnificently for her reception; and the morning fixed for the wedding, she released herself from Mr. Dyrbington by running away with some one she liked better. He never recovered this. He ceased to mix in society; he discharged his servants; and gave himself up to the vagaries of an unsettled mind. An old woman, the widow of a former gardener, lived in the house; and her son, Reuben, occupied a room over the stable. These were all his attendants. Twice a year, Mr. Benson, a lawyer from Watermouth, visited Dyrbington, and transacted business, as it was supposed, with Mr. Dyrbington. He never saw any of his neighbours, with the single exception of the family at Lullingstone: they were never denied seeing him; sometimes, too, he saw one of that family of forest-settlers with whom Julian had made friends: Norwood had interviews with him, much to Reuben's wonder and a little to old Martha's disgust. But Elias—Lyas, as he was generally called—was a very odd, independent sort of character, and a wonderful catcher of salmon; and but for the pride, proper to an old Dyrbington servant, Martha would have liked him very much.

Martha's work was not very hard. The whole house, except two rooms on the ground-floor, which served her master for bed-room and sitting-room, and the kitchen, was shut up. And it was a strange room in which the strange man sat; books were piled about in heaps; and they were such large, old, heavy books. One table, a great arm-chair which he sat in himself, an old ottoman full of papers—that was all; chairs had to be brought in when Lord Westrey came; and there sat Mr. Dyrbington, always reading or writing, scarcely ever stirring, except to go to bed.

Mr. Dyrbington had just reached his seventieth year. He looked eighty. His face was wrinkled, his eyelids heavy, and his jaw depressed. He had been of a tall and stately figure; but now he was bowed down, and his legs trembled painfully till his knees knocked together. He was almost a skeleton. His long neck was bent, and his head almost rested on his breast, and strange clothes hung upon him, telling how much the withering frame had shrunk since they were new; and Mr. Dyrbington was always cold; his touch was like ice, and his voice shook, and snow-white hair strayed neglected on his shoulders. He was a picture of human nature, tired, worn out, dejected, uncared for, and alone.

Lord Westrey, with Mary and Lullingstone, are now riding across the wild and beautiful country which skirts the forest; they are going to Dyrbington. They have arrived and are close to the churchyard. Lord Westrey pulls up; his eye is attracted by a newly-erected tombstone. A low, merry, chuckling laugh is heard close by, and all three look round. A man in the prime of life, with a deer-skin waistcoat, and short boots reaching to his unclothed ankles, with sun-burnt face within an outline of short, glossy, jet-black, curling hair, looked at them good-humouredly enough. It was Lyas Norwood. "Whose gravestone?" asked Lord Westrey, returning Lyas's smile, for, like every body else, he knew the man very well. "Mine—that is, my father's; I begged it of old Dyrbington," nodding his head towards the house in a way which, though familiar enough, did not seem destitute of love and respect; "and it is the only thing I ever begged of man. But," he added with a grave voice, and a face raised to Lord

Westrey's, "but the old woman—she who lies in the same grave—she who was his mother-in-law—she told me to ask it of old Dyrbington. She was a hundred years old when she said it; I could not but obey her."

Lord Westrey and Lullingstone drew up their horses close to the churchyard wall, and looked more closely at the village-cut gravestone, with death's head and cross-bones, and the record, that Elias Norwood, who had been born, and who had died in a hut in the forest, had reached the age of seventy-five. But Mary's head was raised, and her eyes were on the deep blue of the open sky; and the horse she rode stood still, and Lyas looked at her beautiful face, and wondered why her lips moved. And as the man looked at her he bared his head. For reverence was in his untaught soul, and he felt that Mary prayed for the dead.

Then Lord Westrey and Lullingstone ride on, and Mary rides by her father's side down a wide road, with high thick elms on each side, and Lyas, with a ringing laugh, bounds over the fence and is out of sight. They are almost immediately at the huge doors which open into the back-yard of Dyrbington Court-house. A small door is by the side of the great doors. And this little door is opened by Lyas, who has got on before them. The riders dismount—Mary runs in, and Lord Westrey and his son hold the horses as, one by one, the groom leads them through the narrow opening, and then all are within the walls, and the little door is closed again. They are among well-proportioned buildings, where all things speak of years past, and persons departed with them. But there is no trace of the living—none. They have entered like strangers, for whom no one lives to speak a welcome. But Mary's horse has got loose, and stands at the stable door, and paws with its hoof, as though it knew its way, and had recollections of entertainment served within. And the fair girl laughs, and praises her favourite; and the servant finding the door fastened, runs to the further end of the court, and knocks loudly at the door, by which an inner court which adjoins the house is entered. Having knocked in vain, he calls to some one he hears within, and the walls ring, and in their emptiness echo the name repeated many times before an answer comes. But at last a thin, sharp, aged voice replies, "Who do you want—what do you want, I say? Can't you tell me who you are, before you expect me to draw the bolts? If you want Reuben, he's not far off, and I suppose it's not *me* you're wanting."

The servant makes no answer to the querulous voice; Lord Westrey smiles gently, and Mary's laugh, so full of mirth and happiness, makes music there. But Lullingstone cracks his whip, and cries, "Yes, we do want you. Come, Martha, open the door. We have had a glorious gallop, and the ponies want to get into the stable, and we want to come into the house. So please unbolt and unbar as soon as you can. And here is papa and—" but the doors are opened, and an aged face, whose smiles speak a much pleasanter welcome than the voice promised, is seen, and salutations are exchanged of no cold character. The groom, being possessed of the stable keys, walks off to fulfil his trust with entire satisfaction; and Lord Westrey and his children are soon standing in a spacious and very lofty kitchen, a corner of which suffices good Martha for her avocations. Yes, really a corner. And in this corner there is a small stove, a table, two chairs, a low stool, and such kitchen utensils as may be spoken of as in constant use. And this corner is divided off from the other part of the apartment by a high screen of Dutch stamped leather, every grotesque flower of which is well known to Mary, for she has studied them frequently and very attentively from her earliest years. And now, while Martha is telling her master of his guests' arrival, Mary surveys that room once more. The enormous stone-arched fire-place, long disused, is filled up with branches of very dusty and dingy-looking holly. It is renewed only every quarter, and Michaelmas is very near. And there, really in the chimney corners, are two stone seats, chairs rather, for they have backs and elbows. And by the side of the fire-place, projecting into the room, is a fine stone slab, well smoothed, and supported on stone pillars. But there is something in the appearance of that slab unlike all the other stone in the house. Mary has often examined it by sight and touch. Her fingers wander along the edges, and on the under side she finds small crosses cut near the corners. Her lips move; but no one hears what she says. Martha says: "It was put there for a pastry slab. There's some curiosity about it," she goes on, "but nobody knows what it is now. It came out of the old house, I suppose, Miss Mary." Out of the old church, more likely; for those crosses which Mary's fingers had discovered show that it is an altar-stone. But now the party are proceeding to Mr. Dyrbington's room, and we must go there with them.

Mr. Dyrbington, on his guests' approach, rose from the seat on which, with bent form, he had been sitting, with his limbs drawn up beneath it, and his arms rested on each side of the large volume which was open on the table before him. He raised himself like something unfolding from many layers and coils, and after a moment's vibration became steady, and attained to his full height, and welcomed his visitors with vivacity. But the bright glance, the erect posture, the quick smile lasted for an instant only. Mr. Dyrbington sank into his chair, in an attitude of so great exhaustion, that it seemed as though every joint had instantaneously lost the strength and power requisite to the erect position so suddenly departed from.

The young people were well acquainted with Mr. Dyrbington, and there was not any thing in his present appearance to claim any unusual sympathy. Yet, while Lord Westrey brought a chair forward to his friend's side, Lullingstone could not help drawing towards him with an involuntary desire of rendering support and assistance; and Mary, getting still closer, put her fair fingers within his long large skeleton hand, and looking full into his face smiled with such genuine sympathy and love, that the thin lips and hollow eyes of the old man gave back the expression, and he impressed a kiss on the hand that had so gently sought his grasp with more ardour than was common to him.

"These are the things," said Mr. Dyrbington, still holding Mary's hand, and glancing from her to her brother, while an expression of kindness and animation again crossed his face; "these are the things which keep men young, Westrey; you will never grow old while you have such to look upon."

"I wish they could persuade you that they are worth coming to Old Court to see," replied his friend, with more of solicitude in his voice than was expressed in his words.

"It is enough for me that they come here," answered Mr. Dyrbington, languidly; and then added, after a pause, "here, where manhood grows melancholy, and old age strange, and where only childhood, so wisely ignorant of evil, can look upon me with a smile."

"No man ever had more smiles to his own share than yourself, Dyrbington, in the days when you cared about them," said Lord Westrey; "and not false smiles from hollow friends. You have many now—yes, now; many as firm as myself, though not as bold, because you won't allow them to be so;" and Lord Westrey's voice faltered, for his thoughts had suddenly turned unbidden on other days, to which the present formed a melancholy contrast.

"These are the friends I want," said Mr. Dyrbington, stretching out his arm, and placing his disengaged hand on Lullingstone's shoulder, and again pressing Mary's fingers to his lips, "these are my friends, and perhaps to them I may yet do some good. Lullingstone," he then said suddenly, "tell me honestly—do you like coming to see me?"

Lullingstone blushed deeply at the unexpected question, and Mary's cheek grew as rosy as his own. The boy looked at his father, but Lord Westrey's eyes were fixed upon the floor. He then met Mr. Dyrbington's eager glance, and said, with the mingled modesty and firmness of conscious truth, "Not much, sir."

His interrogator smiled.

"And why not?" he asked.

"Because," replied the boy, "I do not understand you; and you make me sorry for something; yet I don't know what."

"And you, Mary," said Mr. Dyrbington, drawing her closer to him; "*you* tell me, do you like coming to see me?"

Mary's answer was given with more than her usual energy. "Yes," she answered; "yes, very much."

An expression of pain passed across her friend's face, and her father appeared to grow suddenly interested in the conversation.

"And why?" asked Mr. Dyrbington.

Mary replied, "Because I should like to make you glad; and I think I do—a little; and I like to look at you, and every thing about you; and I like to wonder what there is in the house besides this room and the kitchen, and what you felt when you were our age, and who were here when you were young."

Mr. Dyrbington listened to her thoughtfully, and then said: "They are a woman's thoughts and feelings; and so," he continued, looking at Mary, "you think of me, and every thing about me, and wonder why it is—shall I tell you?" But Mary had become alarmed at her own candour; and as she had sought the protection of her father's glance in vain, tears were gathering in her eyes, and she stammered forth—"No, I think not, sir; if you please, I would rather not."

"'Tis the involuntary dread of innocence," said Mr. Dyrbington, speaking softly to himself. "They each of them feel it, only in different ways. Alas! poor Dyrbington, and your unhappy owner!" Then, rousing himself, he said with cheerfulness, "And so you never saw the house; well then, you shall see it to-day. Now, Mary, run to old Martha, tell her to open the doors and windows leading to the picture-gallery, and we will remain there while she opens the other rooms—only what used to be called the state-rooms, tell her; and if she wants assistance, here is one will render it to her;" and Mr. Dyrbington made a motion to Lullingstone to accompany his sister.

When the friends were alone, Lord Westrey was the first to speak. "I am afraid that for these children's sake you have set yourself a hard task."

"Let them learn of me," said Mr. Dyrbington, "that their hearts may remain for ever light and innocent as now."

"Did your honour mean the up-stairs gallery?" asked Martha, entering with astonishment written in every line of her face, and speaking in every accent that fell from her lips.

"Yes, the picture-gallery, at the head of the grand staircase."

Hidden among the folds of her capacious skirt, old Martha held concealed a huge bunch of enormous keys. She now produced them, confessing her ignorance of the locks to which they belonged. "I've wiped them, your honour, they always lie in the oil; but, bless you, never a living creature, unless 'twas the cat, or what she might be after, have been up those stairs since my poor dear old man departed, now six years nearly past. I don't suppose that it's my strength can turn the locks, and it's coming on to evening. It's altogether a a job fitter for noon-day than twilight. And, indeed, your honour, if you'll be advised "—"We will all go together," said Mr. Dyrbington, interrupting her, and casting a smile of melancholy intelligence at his friend. "It is not as late as you suppose, Martha. But you must get a broom and some cloths to wipe the dust; we know not what we may find to soil this lady's hands after such long neglect." Taking the keys, Mr. Dyrbington himself led the way up stairs, and Martha went away to fetch the things required, glad to be afforded an excuse to be in the rear rather than the advance of such an adventurous party. Locks creaked back with a rusty sound, and doors swung heavily on their hinges; shutters were thrown aside, and windows opened, and the soft light of the summer evening poured in its clear full flood. They all stood in the picture-gallery. Mr. Dyrbington gazed like a stranger on the things around him. Surprise was in his face—surprise that he should again behold them, and joy too, when Mary clasped

E

her hands in ecstasy, and thanked him for the sight. But Mr. Dyrbington was little able to bear either fatigue of body or excitement of mind. He sank upon a couch and watched his friend and the children in silence. At last, Martha returned from what were called the state-rooms, and said they were prepared for investigation, and then the party proceeded through them. They were exactly as Lord Westrey remembered them, in all the magnificence of gold and tapestry, with rare cabinets of fine inlaid work, and many pictures on the walls. Old chairs and curiously-shaped seats were there; and some of them were covered with satin, and others with damask worked in silver and gold. On the beds were coverings of the same magnificent materials. The children remarked them in voices suppressed with emotion, so great was their surprise and delight at the costly splendour that surrounded them. "There is more to see," said Mr. Dyrbington, as they passed from these state apartments. "There is more to see, but Martha must first get us a light." When the light was brought, Mr. Dyrbington led the way to a small chamber, which was fitted up with iron "safes," as they are called. He opened them, and showed vessels of silver and of gold, at which even Lord Westrey could not restrain his astonishment. Plates, dishes, cups, flagons, and vessels of unknown use and forgotten shape, were there. Mr. Dyrbington showed them all silently, without remark. After this he led the way back to the gallery, and taking the children by the hand, he showed them the pictures of his ancestors, naming each, and explaining their relationships to each other, and to himself. Then, sitting down and placing the children beside him, he said: "It is now nearly time for you to return home. You must think of me often, and of all that I have shown you. But these things you will never see again. I have shown them now to you, that their recollection may impress what I am going to say upon your minds. Many of those things which you have just admired once belonged to Almighty God. That is, they formed a part of the possessions of the Church. Many of these pictures, many of the most valuable of my books, the costly coverings of some of the beds and couches, the greater part of those gold and silver vessels were, by the unhappy zeal of one of my ancestors, taken from the Church, together with certain sums of money, and possessions in land and other property, and transferred to his own use, and so have descended through many hands to mine; and on that account a sore grief has, from that day unto this, cleaved to this place and to all its owners. Even when their exterior was fairest to the eye of the world there was a blighting canker working its deadly influence unseen. And for that reason this house is shut up, and these fine rooms are deserted, and I am old, and alone, and, as it were, lost among men."

"But if these things ought never to have been here, why don't you give them back?" boldly demanded Lullingstone.

"The answering of that question, dear boy, has been the business of my solitary life," replied Mr. Dyrbington, "and I am not answered yet." Mr. Dyrbington rose in great excitement. But when Lord Westrey advanced, and gently laid his hand upon his arm, it wanted only that slight action to bring him to himself. He walked towards the door, and leaning on his friend for support descended to his accustomed room. "I thank God I am the last, Westrey; the last of our unhappy line," he said. "If I can see no better disposal of the treasure which I, at least, have not dared to squander on myself, I shall, when I die, leave it to those who are His representatives. And *the poor* will not be robbed by the small alms required to support this trembling frame for its appointed time."

CHAPTER VI.

NORWOOD.

THAT night, after Martha had removed what was left of Mr. Dyrbington's evening meal, she said that Lyas wanted to see her master. He was admitted immediately. The two men smiled as their eyes met. It was a smile of mutual trust. And with Lyas it was more. The wreck before him filled him with a tender awe. The man of vigour and health stood gently bending in that sorrowful presence. His bright eye was soft, his ringing laugh hushed, and there was a tone in his voice of respect and sympathy, such as care and weakness demand from ease and strength.

Without speaking, Lyas took from the pocket of a jacket edged with deer-skin, a small, but very heavy packet, and placed it before Mr. Dyrbington. At a gesture from the sad figure whose eyes were riveted on the paper, Lyas opened the parcel and put five short, thick, and solid bars of silver before Mr. Dyrbington.

"You are sure, Lyas, that this is all?"

"Certain."

"It is the same?"

"The very same."

"You saw it done?"

"I watched it from first to last. I stood by the furnace, I saw it all. The whole was broken up—then melted down—then run out, as you see."

"There was no deception?"

"None. And I saw it done not without trouble. The man, as your honour warned me, would have kept them in the shape in which they were."

Mr. Dyrbington started, but Lyas did not appear to notice the movement. He continued, while his hearer, leaning back in his chair, his eyelids shut with a close and continued pressure, exhibited in the workings of the drawn muscles of his upturned face the thoughts which struggled in his mind.

"He bid me say," continued Lyas, in a tone of apology—"It was *he* bid me say—that he could give you money, well nigh double the amount of any which that could be coined into, if you would sell him those things as they are. He said he would as soon shed his blood as melt them down. He said their shape and fashion doubled the worth of the metal, and that he must give money for the next."

"Did you tell him what these vessels were?"

"I did not know," was the reply.

"Ah?—well, now listen to me."

Leaning on the table, Mr. Dyrbington buried

his face for a moment in his hands; Norwood, approaching a few steps nearer to him, bowed his head, and leaned more heavily on the stout oak club which served him for defence as well as support. A soft, earnest expression of attention and sympathy spread over his countenance. Mr. Dyrbington raised himself to an upright posture and said: " Those vessels were given by pious persons for the service of God. And for that purpose they —and other things with them—were set apart, and blessed and consecrated. They were set apart for a certain purpose, to be used for a certain end—and that end was for the good of God's creature, man—for his good, living and dead. Now, in time it so happened, that these brotherhoods were broken up; and these vessels were laid aside as useless in reference to their original purpose, and got to be used for the gratification of the avarice and pride of man. And the curse —yes, Norwood," continued Mr. Dyrbington, becoming greatly agitated—" the curse which was pronounced on such as should divert these properties from those sacred purposes, fell upon those who committed the sacrilege, and passed to their descendants, and even at this moment clings to me."

" The curse !"—exclaimed Norwood, " On you ?" —" does it cling to you ?" Expressions of anxiety and sorrow passed quickly over Lyas's face, untaught as that countenance was to speak any but the language of truth; "on you?"—How gladly would he have added, "No—never—not, my dear master, on gentleness, and benevolence, and meek sorrow such as yours—No, not on *you*;" he could not say so. He looked on the picture before him; the old and miserable man. He saw the trembling of his figure, the quick nervous shutting and opening of the eyelids over the eyes that could not weep. He heard the shaking of the jaw, and the clattering of the teeth against each other: and he gazed the more unscrupulously, because the aged head was bowed on the breast and was lifted only by the hard and irregular breathings, almost like sobs, which were distinctly audible in the otherwise silent rooms. Lyas could not say —"No, not on you"—for he felt he had surely heard the truth.

Many moments passed, many more than those two persons knew of, so deeply was each engaged in his own thoughts, and absorbed in his own feelings. At length the sudden fit of nervousness by which Mr. Dyrbington had been overcome gradually passed away. Again he laid his arms on the table; again rested his head on his hands. "I have—as I believe—told you the truth, my friend," said Mr. Dyrbington, looking again into Norwood's face, and now with an air of heroic determination, as if resolved to pursue the subject, to the justification and explanation of his conduct. "I have told you, *as I believe*, the truth." He spoke with great earnestness, as if he would convey no doubts of his having well reasoned and considered the subject. "And the question of how I may relieve myself from this dread grief has long been a matter of deep thought with me." He paused, but Lyas, with an instinctive knowledge of what was right and respectful, never spoke a word either of sympathy or suggestion.

"To return these things to their original use is impossible, as far as I know, perfectly impossible.

"Still with those vessels intended for pious purposes, there goes a curse. They were not made for man, and man may not use them.

"*He* has told us that He honours poverty, and that we are to consider the poor on earth as His representatives. Now, I cannot give them those consecrated vessels, neither can I sell them, for I believe that whoever possessed them would find them laden with sorrow. Neither can I give them as they are to God. But I can give them to Him in another shape; I can have those very things changed thus,"—and Mr. Dyrbington laid his hands on the bars of silver which lay before him, "and I can part with them for the exact sum which they are worth, and give that sum to God's service through His poor upon earth, and so, if it please Him, allay the evil that has befallen my house."

Again there was a pause, which Norwood would

not interrupt. And when Mr. Dyrbington spoke again, it was to ask a question: "Now that I have explained my reasons, say, will you undertake to do this strange work for me,—will you, by little and little, take all of which I have spoken, to Isaac the Jew's, and yourself stand by, and see that these things are melted in the crucible, and bring them back to me, as you have done to-day?"

"I will," replied Lyas, with a firmness which left no doubt of his faithfulness. Mr. Dyrbington stretched forth his hand, and Lyas grasped it with warmth and eagerness. "My friend," said Mr. Dyrbington, his voice weakening to a whisper; Norwood's bright black eyes dilated with the energy of his heart; he fixed them full on the haggard face which was turned towards him. He did not speak, but Mr. Dyrbington knew that he would be faithful and determined in his service; and affectionate, and willing, and docile in the manner of serving him.

"Strange, that I should find my best friend in you;—one who does not reason with my grief, combat my peculiarities, smile at my weakness, or despise my distress; one who will help me to help myself; who will console me, by assisting in that which alone can bring me consolation." Lyas was not a thinker—to feel was enough for him. He never stopped to consider if Mr. Dyrbington was right or wrong, wise or foolish: he only saw him wretched, saw also what would comfort him, and felt for him, and determined faithfully to serve him. No suspicion as to whether Mr. Dyrbington's feelings on the subject of the sacred vessels were not exaggerated, partaking perhaps of the superstitious, prevented his standing by with patient fidelity, while Isaac the Jew, sadly against his will, performed the task demanded of him. His ready wit contrived means for taking the articles, many of which were large and ponderous, from the Court-house without even Martha knowing that he had done so. Neither did Isaac ever know by whom he was employed. And the metal in its new shape was easily conveyed to Mr. Dyrbington, as we have seen. This service took two years, it is said, to accomplish, and was, during that time, the chief interest of Mr. Dyrbington's life. Many were the walks which, during that period of strange service, were taken by Lyas from his home in the forest to Dyrbington, thence to a dark, back settlement of the Jews in Watermouth, where, with steady determination, he had, at each visit, to combat treachery and avarice with the weapons of stedfastness and honest faith. But he was successful. He trusted no eyes but his own. He fulfilled the promise he had given, strictly and to the letter. No reasoning had any force; all arguments were thrown away; he felt that he, at least, was doing rightly: and having watched the metal through the fire, he received his trust back again, and surrendered it in its changed condition to his employer.

This night, after Lyas had left Mr. Dyrbington, he walked briskly, and seldom lifted his eyes from the earth, till he had passed the open plain, and was within the forest country where his home lay. The green glade opened widely before him, the majestic oaks on each side mingling their branches above his head. Still Lyas walked on, and turned from one glade to another, or pressed his way by a yet shorter path where no glade had been cut, till he again gained a comparatively open place, and still walked on. At last his step grew slower, his eyes were raised, he looked above and about him, and ceased his walk occasionally to listen. The night air was cool and pleasant, but Lyas had reached a place where it had seemed to grow yet cooler, and that suddenly, and on his left a slight white mist arose. The grass was growing rank, and its feathery flowers rose high; the rich green fern waved its jagged branches in full luxuriance, and gave forth its own peculiar scent, as its brown mossy stem broke beneath Norwood's tread. The man was near his home. He had come to a point where a stream was meeting him, and where the lime-rock, rising high, with its bare cold breast turned its waters aside. The stream washed the smooth and spreading base of that fine up-standing mass, whose summit was crowned with an ivy-bound wreath of holly and yew, and then it swept gracefully round, and its current rolled more heavily in its deepened channel for the interruption it had received. Lyas listened. His practised ear had caught an unexpected sound. Presently a figure which had been crouching on the river's bank rose to its full height. Norwood quietly advanced through the long grass, and laying his hand on the shoulder of a fine youth of perhaps sixteen or seventeen years of age said, in cheerful accents of mingled pride and love, "My son! you are fishing late. Do you not find them asleep?" " I think they must be, father," replied the youth, and he pointed to a few fish spread on some gathered fern by his side; "for that has been all my evening's work, and I have not had a single rise for the last half-hour." "And yet persevered with patience?" said the father, and again he laid his hand proudly on his son's shoulder, and met his glance with a smile. "I did not go back," replied Harold; "*you* were not there, so I waited here till you should return." " Thank you, Harold, thank you—and now that I am come, let us go to your mother; she will be expecting me, as you were."

At first Harold appeared preparing to obey his father, but after a moment he hesitated, and then throwing himself on the ground, and leaning against the trunk of a tree that bent over the stream, he seemed to be preparing himself to remain the night out of doors. His father felt a sudden alarm, and sprang towards him in a manner that betrayed unusual emotion, on which the lad raised himself into a sitting posture, and gazed on him with an expression which might have passed for that of boyish mischief, and ill-repressed drollery, or for that sort of contemptuous sarcasm which may be imagined to belong to a rude state of life.

"Harold, what means this? It is time we were both in the house; follow me."

The youth fixed his eyes with a changed expression on his father, and clasped his hands imploringly. "O, father," he exclaimed, "why *there?* I have fought with my strong desire, and I cannot overcome it; let me go."

"Go,—go, my son—where?"

"Away, away from the woods, and the wild country, away to the houses of men."

And now both father and son betrayed the strongest emotion.

"Away to the houses of men," cried the boy again, and rose on his feet with one light spring, and threw his arms in the air, and all the animation of ardent hope spread over his features,— "away, father, away from this uncivilized life; away to where men meet and herd, not with the wild deer of the chase, but with their own kind. Father, I can live among these things no longer— away, I say," and the boy almost screamed as

again he cried—"Away to the houses of men."
And the words found their echo, nearer than
among the distant glens, which indistinctly gave
back the cry; they sank into Norwood's heart,
and involuntarily his lips repeated, but slowly,
sadly, and softly—"*the houses of men.*"

The words were spoken in a scarcely audible
murmur, but Harold's heart in its turn was
touched. He jumped forward, fell on his father's
breast, and heart throbbed to heart. But Harold,
still firm to his purpose, whispered, or rather sobbed in his parent's ear, the reiteration of his wish:
—"Father, let me go,—let me go."

Unnerved, and overcome by this unexpected
request, Lyas, unable to speak, leaned sorrowfully
against the trunk of a tree. Words were dropping
at intervals and incoherently from Harold's lips:
Lyas heard some of them; they comforted him.
"Father, dear father, I love you—I love you
dearly, most dearly. Father, believe me, I would
rather have died than have grieved you thus.
Oh, I love you! But what I am to do—what *can*
I do? O father,"—and the choking sobs made
the voice inaudible. Then nothing was heard but
the unequal breathing, and tears dropped heavily
from the boy's cheek to the father's hand which
he held within his own, and fondled in his breast.

"O Harold, you do not know what you ask—
how much it is to ask of me, how little it is of
gain for yourself."

But the boy answered in reply: "When I saw her,—O, how lovely!—so good, so beautiful,—my heart became filled with the thought of her. I must go, for I love her."

Lyas answered quickly: "Fear me not, my son; tell me your heart—you love?"

"I do," replied Harold; and all excitement passed away, and he appeared as grave and recollected as his father. "I do."

"And her name? How is she called?"

"Anna Julian."

"Anna Julian! my son, tell me all. How do you purpose to accomplish what looks to be impossible? You have had your thoughts; explain them to me."

"It is not impossible," said Harold. "Her father has been here this very day. The old man likes me; we have talked much together. He told me to-day that his son had gained the honour —what it is I know not—for which he has laboured so long; and immediately he will have to leave his home and go to some far-off place, where more learning is to be acquired, and where possibly he may henceforth live. He, therefore, will never follow his father's trade. But when I asked the old man if he were going to give it up, with a son prosperous enough to support him, as I supposed, he replied, that though his arm was growing stiff and his heart was unwilling, and his thoughts were fixed elsewhere, he yet must continue his trade, that it must not cease, and that he rather required to increase his gains, than to trust to another, or content himself with the little he could safely call his own. And then," continued Harold, "the old man sighed and looked unhappy, and the heart that loved the daughter could not but feel and throb for him."

"Go on," said Lyas, with interest of a sort that he had not shown before.—"Go on."

"This is what you must do for me," said Harold. "You must go to Watermouth to-morrow; you must offer me to Julian to learn his trade; I shall not have much to learn; and to work for him, and bring him as much custom as quickness, good-will, and industry can procure. And he shall not pay me money; but he shall give me food and lodging in his house, and treat me respectfully, as my father's son; and when I am worthy of reward, I'll ask it of him."

"I will do this," said Lyas thoughtfully. "I will do this, for I see your heart is in it, and it is useless to try to go against nature. But it is a new path and your thoughts are strange. And Harold," he added, with a voice which faltered once more for a moment, "I own it comes upon me as something of a disgrace, to have my son sell his freedom as it were; but this perhaps is in the fancy. It would be a bitter disgrace, and avoid it, Harold, as you would avoid your father's frown, to see you like those among whom your strong heart

F

takes you. They speak, to lie; they move, to hurt; they think, to deceive; they become powerful only to injure the poor; and when they suffer they call themselves under a curse; when they would make restitution they know not how. This, I have seen among men. But you, Harold, listen to the inward voice. Have nothing to do with the evil ways of men, and by that means avoid their cares."

"I have only to do with *her*," replied the youth.

At an early hour, Lyas Norwood proceeded towards Watermouth. He was clad in his usual and somewhat remarkable attire, and bore over his shoulders, by means of his constant companion the stout oak stick, a large basket, which he had himself woven, with the skill in that craft which was usually found among the forest settlers. It was bound round with a portion of net, such as was used for catching salmon, and the larger sorts of trout. The basket had become nearly as well known as himself. This morning, it had been packed with unusual care, and yet there was but one fish to place in it, a large and fine specimen of that peculiar sort of pink-spotted fish which in the forest stream was not uncommon, and called from the time of year at which alone it was caught, the Bartholomew trout. The one, thus carefully placed in the basket reposing on fresh fern and covered with the same, had been taken from the night-nets that morning. Harold had brought it from the river in triumph. "Look, father, the finest I ever saw, will you not go by Lullingstone and sell it there?"

"No, my son," replied Lyas. "We have a friend at Watermouth, and if all goes well, I can leave it." Harold's face blushed crimson. "Let me help you, father." But his father refused his aid, procured his absence by sending him on some trifling but time-occupying errand, and yet had scarcely laid in the last covering of fern, when the boy returned. He then raised it to his shoulders, and on Harold's remarking that the basket lifted as if it was heavy, he turned the thought into a joke and walked off, affecting to stoop under the burthen of the mighty trout, and heartily returning the laughter his drollery produced. The way which Lyas pursued tended to a point from which travellers to Watermouth from various places continued their way together. He had gone but a few steps on this path when he was joined by a man who, from another direction, had reached the point of union almost at the same moment with himself. When Norwood became aware of his companion's presence he pressed on faster, desiring by this means to avoid him; but the stranger, though older than Lyas, quickened his pace, and was soon at his side.

"You are stirring early," he said.

"Like yourself," replied Lyas, casting a scrutinizing glance on the stout-made, active, elderly gentleman, who, with his mild countenance, and neat though poor appearance, might at any other time have excited his interest.

"The early bird gathers the worm," said the stranger, "and you, friend, have an early day's work in your basket, doubtless."

"When *I am* your friend, you may guess at my employment," answered Lyas, in a tone of discourtesy which he intended should put an end to the conversation.

The stranger gave a melancholy sort of smile. "As you please," he replied; "yet I will not say that *I* am not *your* friend."

"We neither of us know either the other's name or business," said Lyas; "and therefore can know neither friendship nor interest, though one of us may not be above curiosity."

Again the stranger smiled. "You are wrong," he said; "I know too much for curiosity."

Lyas Norwood looked at his companion carefully. The plain habit of coarse and well-worn cloth, told only of neatness and poverty; the active step and figure, only of strength and temperate habits; and the quiet manner only showed strength of mind and a serene temperament. Norwood examined him boldly, for he neither turned on one side or the other, but walked briskly on, with the head a little bent forward, and seldom raised his eyes.

"Do you know so much?" said Lyas with a

laugh; "if so, your knowledge should teach you not to annoy one who might prove a dangerous companion."

"Do yourself no injustice," replied the old man: "Elias Norwood was never a dangerous companion to an unarmed, and, as I might now almost say, an aged man."

Norwood started at the mention of his own name; but immediately recovered himself, and to hide his confusion, for the stranger's eyes were for the first time fixed upon him, he affected to have stopped only to made a readjustment of his basket. In doing this he again felt the power of his companion's glance, and, at once displeased and disconcerted, said: "You know my name, good man, and that is more than I desired. Now, either you or I must step on faster, for any further companionship is unnecessary."

"Why so? We are going to the same place."

"And where may that be?" for Norwood felt a sort of fascination, which obliged him to answer.

"To Watermouth."

"Well?"

"To where you will unload your basket."

Lyas laughed loudly.

"That's no answer, master; for we unload according to contents."

"Well, then," pursued the stranger, "your basket contains——"

"What?—I say, man, tell me what it contains, if you can?" and he added, through his clenched teeth, "if you dare."

"Probably," said the stranger, taking purposely no notice of Norwood's last words, and speaking very slowly, while he rather increased the rapidity of his walk—"probably, some of the holy vessels, once belonging to the Church of Dyrbington; or, at least, such like." They had walked so fast, that they had almost reached the town, which lay spreading below them, as, having emerged from the forest they stood on the high open common leading to it. Lyas felt instinctively that the old man durst not so have tempted him had they still been within the forest precincts. But then again, he shunned the thought, as pointing to that which would have been unworthy of himself.

While these things passed through his mind he hesitated, and again the stranger's eye examined him. It was all the work of a moment, and there was no time for any reply. "Farewell," said Norwood's companion abruptly. "We must not enter the town together. Farewell for a short space; we shall meet again at Isaac the Jew's." And having said this, he increased his pace almost to a run, and left the astonished Norwood to his own conjectures.

So amazed was Lyas Norwood that he stood still and watched the hurrying steps of his late companion like a creature thunderstruck. How could he have known, or guessed it? And to what use would he put his knowledge or suspicion? Would he say the like elsewhere? Would the report spread and be carried to Dyrbington, and bring annoyance on its melancholy master, and add to his sorrows, and still further confuse his already distressed mind? These questions, as they arose in Norwood's breast, wrung his heart with anxiety; and he remained standing as if stunned and unable to proceed, or even to move. After awhile he raised his eyes. Far across that spreading plain of downy turf, almost as far as the eye could reach, and close upon its furthest edge where houses began to be scattered and the hill to descend, the figure of the mysterious old man reduced to but little more than a black speck was discovered by the keen eye seeking for him. Lyas walked on, and recalling the words "we will meet again at Isaac the Jew's,"—proceeded towards the town, and that part of it where the worker in gold and silver dwelt.

CHAPTER VII.

HARD QUESTIONS.

Norwood immediately, without any preface, opened his business with "the dealer," as Isaac was commonly called.

"I have brought more silver," said Norwood. "Are you willing to do the work I require to-day? I have come early on purpose; but if you cannot do it now, fix your time, I will bring the things again, and punctually at your own day and hour, whenever it may be."

The dark-looking figure addressed by Norwood seemed to be scarcely dressed, but to have wrapped himself in such articles as, in a hurried transit from his bed to his kitchen, he had found by the way. He only just looked up once, that his eyes might witness to the truth of Lyas Norwood's appearance as well as his ears, and then preserving his crouched-down attitude in the corner of the dark little room, which was almost filled up by a large and massive square oak table, he continued his morning's work of blowing up the fire in a small stove, by kneeling down in front of it, and applying his mouth to the bars. Isaac made no reply, and Norwood standing at the door surveyed the apartment. Immediately opposite to the entrance was the steep narrow staircase which led to the sleeping-room above. It was very narrow and of stone, and wound up in a little tower, which projected from the angle of the room into the court behind. On his right was the window. It was stone-mullioned, and arched, and in the upper part there were small irregular bits of coloured glass which, through the coating of the dust of years, still showed deep tints of purple and ruby. Heavy oak beams showed above where figures were cut of roses and the lily-flower, and curious designs of which men did not know the meaning, and among them still remained the figure of the cross. On the side opposite to the window, and in the furthest corner from the door, was the small iron stove before which Isaac was crouched. The large table, so heavy and so dark with age and dirt, almost hid his bent form from view.

But the Jew rose up with a sudden spring, on Lyas placing his hands on the table and bounding over it to his side. His deep-sunk grey eyes flashed first with alarm and displeasure, and then, as it seemed to Lyas, yet more brightly, with a grim welcome.

"What more? more like the last?—man, let me have it—let me have it, I say; or go, go, and show it not to me; I'll not look on the things, if I may not possess them;" and having read refusal in Lyas's face, he made a gesture as though he would push away the basket which contained the temptation to his avarice.

"You are not to have them," answered Lyas, firmly and quietly, "and you must not see them unless you choose to do the work for which I am here to hire you. I have here vessels of silver, and, as it would seem, vessels of gold. I ask you to melt them down as you did the last. I tell you, that I will stay and see it done, nor leave this place till I can take the metal back again, only in another form. For this I will pay you in money what you demand. Now give me your answer quickly."

"I will not do it," exclaimed Isaac, fixing his gaze on Lyas, and his eyes flashed angry fire: and again he repeated: "I will not do it—I will not."

"Then good day," said Lyas, as he turned round. Isaac, seized with a sudden regret, caught him by the arm.

"Don't trifle with me," he said, "you are going to let me have it. Come, don't trifle with an old man; you shall name your own price, only I must have them."

"Why will you not believe me?" asked Lyas; "You are one of the cities and towns, and I of the fields and forests. My tongue expresses the meaning of my heart—my words and intentions are one.

Cannot you use your gift of speech to express your will? You have said you will not do it."

"But I will, I think I will," faltered out Isaac. "But you are hurrying, Lyas—you never give one time. Here, leave them, and I will do the work; call again towards evening, and it shall all be ready for you."

"I wish that I understood your vile craft myself," exclaimed Lyas impatiently, "and I would not stand here repeating my words again and again. But once more, hear me. I will *not* leave them. I will watch your hands, and narrowly observe your doings, and not think my pledged word redeemed till I have seen the hard substance liquid like the river's stream, and again hardened metal in my hands before the fire has gone wholly out from it. This I will do, and nothing else, and if you were to deceive me, you should yourself answer it to him who sent me. Thy poor body, aged as it is, should appear before him. I would have back the miserable dirt for which you would sell your truth, though your life and mine should buy it."

"Stop, stop," exclaimed Isaac, shrinking away and glad to be relieved from the gaze which seemed to penetrate his very soul. "See, some one comes—Ha!" and a faint look of renewed hope passed across his face as he returned the salutation of Lyas's late companion. "See," he continued, "there is one who will watch my work.

Go, as I said, and when you return, the metal shall be ready for you."

Before Lyas could answer, the stranger had come forward, and replied, "Isaac, that will not do: I know that man. I will not buy that which rightfully he may not sell. Do his bidding, and take your lawful hire. It is the best bargain you will make this day."

"You will not buy!" exclaimed the disappointed dealer impetuously: "Then why mislead me? Why receive my message? Why appear here now?"

"Enough, enough," said the stranger, showing a little of the impatience which Isaac's manner was so well calculated to produce. "Enough; go to your work. This man and I would have a word or two together."

On this, making a moaning sound as he murmured his discontent to himself, Isaac proceeded to collect together some of the utensils necessary for melting down the silver flagons and other sacred vessels which Norwood produced from the basket he had carried, and before half an hour had elapsed he had commenced the work.

While the work of melting the precious metals was proceeding the stranger and Lyas Norwood stood as silent spectators, and viewed the operations of the Jew with an equal, but a very different kind of interest. Lyas thought of Dyrbington's master; and his heart softened as it recalled him, and his frail body, and anxious labouring mind, and sorrowing spirit. And then Lyas thought of himself; an actor in scenes he did not comprehend.

Still he watched the motions of the practised Isaac with a jealous eye. Not so the stranger. Lyas had been so much absorbed in his own thoughts, that he had for a time forgotten his new friend's presence; and now that he looked upon him, he saw a countenance from which he could scarcely withdraw his eyes. As a man looks on a friend for the last time—sees him turn his back, and watches his receding form till it has faded in the distance, and at last is gone—as he looks at the ground where that friend trod, surveys the empty space, lets his eyes wander over the spot where so lately he was seen and which shall know him no more—so looked the strange companion of Norwood's morning walk; so thoughtfully resigned, so contemplatively sad was his aspect. He stood leaning against that firm oak board, and his arms were crossed upon his breast. He leaned as one who could scarcely stand upright; and he gazed on Isaac, as one whose sight was fixed by some fascination to see with pain, what brought him sorrow without hope. At last the work was done: and Isaac, who had never spoken, except in mumblings to himself, eloquent of a savage species of discontent, growled out: "There, will that do for you?" and, without looking up, or waiting for a reply, disappeared, carrying some of his apparatus with him, by a small side door which led into the court.

"Stay, stay," cried Norwood, "your money, man, return."

Isaac thrust in his head, and answered: "Wait till you can touch your ruined riches. I'll be back in time;" and then he disappeared again, and a hollow contemptuous laugh was heard ringing among the old walls, which struck painfully on Lyas's ear, and he looked for sympathy on the stranger. Their eyes met, and the bright grey eye of the old man sparkled the more for a tear which had gathered there, and which now, with a deep drawn sigh, he brushed hastily away. The circumstance could not escape the observation of the quick-sighted Lyas. It stirred up an unusual interest within him. He exclaimed abruptly: "Who are you?" A smile succeeded the tear,— an amused look and a friendly smile—and he answered kindly:—

"It would do you no good to know—perhaps harm. I am one who would gladly be your friend, and the friend of Mr. Dyrbington also, if it might be."

"I have no friend amongst those who practise concealment," said Lyas; "and it looks more like an enemy than a friend to obtain a knowledge of things supposed to be secret; and then refuse to account, either for himself, or his mode of gaining information."

"You are inconsiderate; of what have I obtained knowledge? Question me, I will answer you freely."

"How knew you the contents of my basket?" said Lyas, proceeding slowly to pack it again, and to replace the produce of the morning's net safely and carefully among the fern.

"You should rather have asked how I knew you;" answered the old man. "Knowing you to be Lyas Norwood, and knowing you to be employed by Mr. Dyrbington in the manner we have seen, and knowing that you had appointed to be here to-day, and seeing that your basket was evidently heavier than a fisherman's store would make it—the contents became a matter of easy guessing, if not of certainty."

"And how knew you so much?" asked Lyas; the expression of surprise which had increased visibly on his countenance at every word the stranger spoke, now fixed there. "How knew you so much?"

"When the sound of exultation is heard among the ravenous birds of the forest," replied the old man, "you know that the weakly fawn is dying and exposed; and that the sorrowing mother can neither nourish nor protect it. So when I heard in this place, the note of greedy welcome and avaricious hopes, I knew that the fruits of departed piety was surrendered to the unbeliever's scorn, I was led to imagine to his use, and I was here to purchase it out of his hands, but it seems that I was wrong."

"It is well for you that you were disappointed," said Lyas. "Those things were of no common kind. There was a sorrow about them, and it cleaved to those who touched them."

"Who taught you so?" asked the stranger.

"He who owned them, and had proved the truth of his words—Dyrbington himself."

"And of what use are those bright bars?" asked the stranger again.

"They can become money, you know, and that money can be bestowed on the poor; and Dyrbington says that the poor are here on earth in the great Being's stead, and so in this manner there will be a return made to Him, and the sorrow will depart."

"Wonderful!" murmured the stranger softly. And then addressing Lyas he asked, "Do you understand this?"

"No," replied Norwood, "I know nothing of these things."

"How do you mean? Of what religion are you?"

"Perhaps of none." Then suddenly changing his thoughts to their former subject he said: "But once more about these things. Isaac knew not that they were from Dyrbington, and how knew you?"

"When last you brought such, I was here and saw them, and seeing them informed me. There were marks, and on one an inscription; I knew them in that manner."

"Then," said Lyas gravely, "you know too much, and what you must never repeat."

"You consider me possessed of a secret; a secret which might bring your honour, and Mr. Dyrbington's peace of mind into question?"

"Yes," answered Lyas.

"I am one of that Faith which once was at Dyrbington, and built the church, and blessed the people, and gave great gifts to God," said the stranger. "For *my* hands those gifts bring no sorrow, for I can use them as *they* designed who gave them."

Lyas listened with speechless interest, and the old man went on: "When *that* religion was departed from, and these things which belonged to its service were desecrated, then the priests of that faith were persecuted and slain; and the sorrow arose of which you have just now spoken. But still, in this land, in retired places, under various disguises these priests of the people, and keepers of the ancient faith remained, and I am one of them. If you ever are in trouble, such trouble as leads you to think of me, then go to St. Cuthbert's; and if I am alive you will be brought to me. But it may be," continued the speaker, "it may be that I shall not be there; that I shall be gone. In that case do not regret it, it will make no difference to you. Another will see you;

another whose love may be greater, whose hopes may be more fervent than mine, and his powers less limited. Tell him your heart, You will find a friend."

He did not wait for an answer, but left the room. Lyas stood for a moment, then followed him to the door, but no further. He saw him mingling with the ceaseless throng, and soon lost sight of him. Then Lyas discharged his debt to the thankless and discontented Isaac, slung his basket on his shoulder, placed the precious metal safely about his person; and full of his own thoughts walked away.

CHAPTER VIII.

HOPES AND FEARS.

The time fixed for Julian's interview with Mr. Seaforth arrived. He felt himself to be another man, and with the feeling of change there mingled some little sensation of awe.

He had often, very often, from youth, through manhood, almost to old age looked on that hoarded treasure, and felt, and believed that one day great things would come of it. And now the thoughts, the fancies, the belief, the wondering of years—of all his life, and of the lives of others, how many he knew not—which had been so long gathering, so privately nourished, and preserved as secret with such wonderful success, had all suddenly been brought to a point. In a few months he should be another man. But in the meantime he suffered an oppressive sense of living under a disguise: a feeling which had never occurred to him, while the gold had remained a secret in its hiding-place. But now, that he had told it, that he was the acknowledged possessor of wealth, he felt that there was a something inconsistent with his character in appearing as the poor labouring artizan; and so for a short time, Julian remained even more closely at home than usual, and his wife wondered at his silence, and so also did Anna, but happily they each recollected that he might be anxious about Edward. And Kate Julian shook her head, but with a smile on her lips, and said to her daughter that "father thought more of Edward than he liked to confess."

After a few days, a messenger from Mr. Seaforth's office placed a note in Julian's hand. He received it, and trembled. The words, "you are to call this evening," were delivered in evident ignorance of that call being required for any thing important. Mr. Seaforth's house was a large dwelling in an open part of the town. Though it faced the street, gardens and shrubberies spread away behind to some extent.

Mr. Seaforth was also a banker. The bank was the adjoining house. Julian was soon seated in the merchant's private room.

"If I am to assist you," said Mr. Seaforth, "and if you are to profit by my assistance, there ought to be all possible candour. I assure you, I advise it, not more for my own satisfaction than for your benefit, and I may add, that you shall never repent trusting me—may I ask you some questions?"

"Whatever you like," replied Julian. Still he said to himself—"the time is come;" and he had no desire to make any mystery or concealment to a man whom he regarded as the agent of his future fortunes. Mr. Seaforth therefore pursued his interrogations in a very business-like manner.

"This money has descended to you?"

"Yes—through several generations."

"Where do you keep it?"

"In the iron chest in which it came to me."

"How much of it do you desire to invest?"

"All of it."

"What may the amount be?"

"I cannot tell accurately—a large sum."

A declaration so opposed to the merchant's habit of life made him to pause. But the first look of surprise was followed by a smile, and he went on. "Gold?"

"Yes, most of it, but silver besides."

"And you still like to join me in fitting out this privateer?"

"Yes."

Again there was a pause, after which Mr. Seaforth said—"And you wish to be a merchant?"

"Yes," answered Julian. "If to be a merchant is to be possessed of wealth, and power, and station, I do wish it."

Julian had bent forward towards his host, all the deep intensity of his feelings betrayed in his countenance. He did not, at that moment, hear the same door by which he had himself entered suddenly opened, and only recalled his stedfast

gaze of inquiry on hearing a voice exclaim,—
"Hold hard, there, I say, hold hard. What;
wealth, power, station!—wind, tide, and good luck
—like that, do you?—Why, yes, and so do I.
Shake hands then, friend, for there's something
that's alike between us."

Julian jumped from his seat, and Mr. Seaforth
with less expression of surprise rose also. "Ah!
Ralph," he exclaimed sadly. Then with an air of
vexation he shook his head reprovingly. But the
new comer only laughed more loudly.

Ralph Seaforth, the merchant's brother, had
been the commander of that very ship which had
brought the merchant and John Julian into such
happy relations. Julian, on learning this, looked
at the new comer as one mysteriously connected
with his destiny. Though Ralph Seaforth was
intoxicated, and Julian detested drunkenness and
all approaches to it, he yet looked at him with a
sort of respect, feeling that he was there to take
part in those measures which were to end in the
gratification of all his ambition had ever desired.
His heart forgave him his follies, and extenuated
his vices, and regarded him as an actor in a great
work, a tool to be used, a help in the path of
prosperity, a means towards the attainment of
entire success. So when Ralph offered his hand,
Julian accepted it; and when again his rude
laugh rung around, and he reeled back and could
with difficulty recover his balance, and laughed

again to see his brother, sorrowing and mortified, sink back into his chair, Julian did not feel that disgust which he would have felt under other circumstances, but rather a solemn sense of the necessity of bearing all things, not only with composure, but even willingly, out of respect to the cause which was worked by means of many hands, and various kinds of help. Julian offered his chair to Ralph, and was bringing one of humbler sort for himself. But Mr. Seaforth got his brother out of the room. The fact was, that Ralph was a thoroughly abandoned character; and Julian knew it. But his mind was so fixed on his own future, that he was willing to get over all obstacles, and to respect Ralph Seaforth, if Ralph was to command the ship that should make his fortune.

As Julian approached his home, after his interview with Mr. Seaforth, every thing seemed bright to his mind's eye, as if no shade of sorrow or sin rested upon earth. Ralph and his intemperance were forgotten, and once again the cloudless sky, the soft moonlight, and the expressions of joy which belonged to that evening when he had spoken to Mr. Seaforth on the beach rose up before him. His own success was even surer in his thoughts than ever; and he trod the threshold of his home with a firmer step than common, almost with an air of pardonable pride. Edward stood at the door. "My son," he said, "you are going to feel the sweetest thing that man can feel—*success.*"

"Ah! father," replied Edward, "I have only made the first step yet. So much more seems to lie before me to be done, that I can scarcely think of the past—the future so overwhelms me."

"The future will be like the past, my son," answered Julian. "Man shapes his own fortune, and you possess qualities which may ensure you yours. Be true to yourself, and fortune will be true to you."

And now Anna bounded out to her brother's side, and placed her arm in his, but looked in her father's face. "Lyas Norwood is here," she said, "he has waited some time to speak to you."

The father looked on the two children for a moment; he did not usually show much tenderness towards them openly, but this evening restraint seemed to have left them, and there was an anxious tenderness in his ardent gaze. But he said no more, and entered the house.

There stood Lyas. Mrs. Julian had accepted his gift, and the fish had been dressed for supper. A tempting table was spread, and Lyas was pressed to partake of the meal. But he refused. "My visit here, this night, is chiefly on business," he said. In few words, and with less embarrassment than might have been expected, he made known his boy's wish to change his mode of life, to learn a trade, and settle among men. Then he offered him to Julian. Julian without any hesitation refused the offer.

And now, there was a great deal to be done, for Edward was going immediately to college. Congratulations on his success poured in; and when Lord Westrey called, and praised him, and Lullingstone shook him heartily by the hand, and said: "Why, Edward, we shall be at college together— I am going next year;"—there never was a happier youth than Edward Julian. Mary Westrey was there too. She stood so still and silent, looking on all about her as if it was a moving picture. Mrs. Julian smiled and wiped her tears at the same time, and almost laughed from nervous excitement when she received Lady Westrey's affectionate message. But soon, she turned aside, and recovered herself, and curtsied again, and smiled on Lord Westrey, and said: "My duty, if you please, to her ladyship, and I hope I shall not grow too proud."

Edward bounded to his mother's side, and flung his arms round her, and gazed in her face so lovingly, just for one moment before he released her, that all admired him. A thought just gleamed through Mary Westrey's mind, and brought a bright light into her earnest watchful eyes. "I am glad, very glad indeed," she said; and the boy blushed, and stammered, and left the room. Edward went to college, and Mr. Parker, who loved him, went with him.

And on the very day that Edward went, the vessel sailed with which went Julian's hopes of fortune. No wonder that, between events of such interest, Lyas Norwood's disappointment was forgotten. All was full of hope, and more, even of certainty. One thing only had struck Julian with an instant's sensation of regret; he scarcely knew why, but still he felt a little sorry on finding that Captain Ralph was not the commander of the ship—that he would not sail again for a few months; Mr. Seaforth said so, and so the thing passed. Julian had lurking feelings of one man's luck exceeding another's, and high ideas of the captain's qualifications in that particular. But be that as it may, when Julian watched the swift-sailing "*Sarah*" wind her way among the forest of masts in the well-filled docks, he felt a little regret that the captain on her deck was not Ralph Seaforth.

It must be explained here that Ralph Seaforth had quarrelled with his brother. That is, he had quarrelled with him as seriously as was possible, considering that all the bitterness was on his own side. Ralph Seaforth was a miserable drunkard, whose incorrigible wickedness in many ways had at last worn out his brother's charity. He would not employ Ralph any more while he pursued his present course of life. He had often threatened —the threat was now fulfilled. And this quarrel concerned Julian, for Ralph was persuaded that he had supported his brother in his determination. Untrue as this was, it bore Julian bitter fruit. Ralph Seaforth was his enemy.

Let us now return to Harold. He was not discouraged; he determined to persevere; indeed so strong were his feelings, that he could not have done otherwise. "He will not take the rude, untaught, and perhaps, ignorant boy," Harold said. "That is the reason; that *must* be the reason; for the good man is kind, though strange and rather rough, and has always loved us. I will overcome this. What he will not teach, I will attain of my own genius." And Harold, whose resolutions were never made in vain, kept his word. In a few weeks, he had taken some specimens of his first success to Julian's house. He was always kindly welcomed there, and now his industry was praised, and he received all the encouragement he desired. Julian gave him some general instructions; told him where the best materials were to be purchased; once even sent Anna to show the youth the way; and also lent him tools. Harold was happy, and bent all his energies to improvement in his trade. Thus passed weeks, and months, and autumn glided away, and the cold of winter came. Thoughts, but they were very heavy ones, were crowding on Julian's mind. The *Sarah* had been expected, but she had not appeared. Surprise had grown into doubt; doubt into fear; and fear was now passing into the certainty that she was lost.

Julian had never communicated the fact of his interest in this vessel to any one. Mr. Seaforth had not departed from his usual rule, never to talk of the affairs of any one connected with him. Julian's venture was known only to himself. There, in the projecting window of the pretty parlour, he would sit looking on the sea, and wondering on his fate. After he had seen the *Sarah* sail so merrily out of the harbour—after he had seen her fairly out of sight—lost in the horizon, and said farewell to her in his heart, he had not frequented his shop as diligently as he had used to do. He fulfilled orders, but when the last firm-bound vessel exposed at his shop door for sale, had found an admiring purchaser, no other proof of his industrious labour had taken its place. When the first doubts about the vessel arose, they did not much affect his mind. Julian had felt too certain of success to abandon his belief very suddenly. But one night after this, he met Mr. Seaforth, and they had spoken a few words together; few as they were, they made Julian feel the terrors of suspense,— not yet, however, could it be said that he feared. After this, the work of his shop became still less agreeable to him, and Anna first observed that her father seemed restless and disturbed. She was loving, and young, and she did not like to remark it to her mother, least of all did she dare to speak to Julian himself. She took her work and sat alone in the deserted workshop, and when she saw her father enter, tried all her little arts to draw him to his former habits. Sometimes Julian tried to begin something, but nothing seemed to answer under his hands, and he would leave the tools in disorder, and wander out. In his wanderings he sometimes reached Norwood's hut, and there would sit in silence for long periods of time, watching Harold, who, glad to display his ingenuity, worked on, insensibly producing the effect he desired on Julian's mind. And so Julian went on through dreary weeks and dreary months—what a dreadful winter time it was! His little stock of money was dwindling away. Disappointed customers ceased to come with their orders to a man who was never ready to supply them. On Mrs. Julian's face a sorrowing wonder crept. She felt alarmed; she knew not what to do; and womanhood's cares gathered round Anna's heart.

Still Julian wandered in his lonely way, for whole days absent from home. And still he turned his steps, most frequently towards Norwood's home, to see Harold work, and watch him as he carved the wood about him into living forms. It was very clever, and Julian knew it; but he never said so; he only sat and stared with a sad face of interest. There was always the unanswered question at his heart—where is the *Sarah?*

He was returning home one day in this wretched mood when he met a weeping child—she was starving. He gave her money and food, and asked her name, it was "Anna." He startled, trembled, and walked on. A hard shower of rain came on just as he was entering Watermouth. He stopped beneath the shelter of the porch of a tavern. There came rude sounds of drunken mirth. Julian, always abhorring such scenes, was leaving the place when he heard his own name—he paused —it was Ralph Seaforth, saying how Julian had ventured his all in the *Sarah*—the "old miser's all," it was called—and how, because his brother had prevented his taking the command, the *Sarah* had gone "ill wished" out of harbour, and that she was undoubtedly lost. And they talked rudely of the pretty girl, his daughter—but Julian could hear no more—he rushed away. At a corner of a street he met Mr Seaforth. "What do these rumours mean, sir?" said Julian, immediately commencing on the subject uppermost in his own mind.

"It is the most extraordinary thing—left long ago—that is on the point of leaving, when we heard; no account since—nothing positive—only a vessel was seen by an Indiaman lately come into —— evidently in distress—I don't know what to say—I am very uneasy—and I feel more for you—indeed, believe me, more than for myself."

Mr. Seaforth left him abruptly, and Julian walked on. The odious echo of that rude man's voice, was still in his ears;—the starving child was before his eyes. His wife—his Anna—Julian's heart did not dwell upon himself. His folly in being negligent of his trade! He was not really poorer. He had still a little store, enough to meet emergencies. He had never wanted more. But he must work.

Anna was standing by the door when he got back, evidently lingering for him. He spoke to her fondly, and she with equal fondness returned his greeting.

"I have been absent many hours" he said. "Have any customers inquired for me?"

"Yes, father; several,—and," said Anna with a little hesitation, "and seemed disappointed not to find you here."

"I have been very idle, lately," replied Julian smiling, "but will my child collect my tools, that I may work hard to-morrow?"

"Dear father," answered Anna, jumping by his side for joy; "every thing is ready for you, and I waited there so long to-day, thinking you might come back!"

"Did you, dear one?—God bless you, child—good night."

The following day, as soon as the light permitted, Julian was hastening across that open country towards Norwood's home. The morning was piercingly cold, but Julian's step was quick, and his warm heart was full of affectionate resolutions and generous thoughts. He did not feel the cold of the outward air, and in the vigour of his healthy resolutions he had lost the chill which had fallen on his spirits the evening before. He was soon standing before Harold. He said; "Harold, what I once refused, I now come in a wiser mood to ask for. Will you come to me, assist me in my trade, preserve it, enlarge it? If so, agree with me now on the subject of your hire."

Harold heard him with a flashing eye, which grew brighter at every word, But at the last, the red colour rose in his cheek. "I will not sell my labour to you," Harold said. "You shall treat me not as a servant, but as a son. Then I will come. When I have learnt all, then, if you desire me to share in your profits, we can speak of it—but not now. These were the terms my father offered, and I will not change them."

"Keep to them if you will, then," answered Julian. And Harold's hopes were fulfilled for the present, and his ardent spirit looked gaily on the future.

After his morning's meal Julian went, as of old, to his labour. His favorite Anna was soon in her accustomed place. The chips of wood which fell about him she gathered and threw, from time to time on the fire; and the bright blaze and the merry crackling sound that issued as it rose were pleasant incidents. Julian looked round upon his child, and when their eyes met they smiled—their hearts were more glad than they had been for many a long day past.

Anna's needle plied more quickly in its silent industry for the active sound of her father's noisy work. She did not think of the past, and its inexplicable sensations of sorrow and anxiety, but only of the present moment and its happiness. She thought, too, of Edward, and of the Christmas time without him; for Edward had had his parents' leave—and Lord Westrey had advised them to grant it—to accompany Mr. Parker on a visit to his friends; and she was very proud and glad on Edward's account, and not anxious, for she knew the greatness of his heart, and felt—yet did not know what she felt—the nobleness of her own. Harold lived in the house with them, and immediately he became an object of interest to Anna. She could not understand her brother's cleverness, but she could understand Harold's. He would try to carve a chair like that from old Dyrbington Court House. He cut Mrs. Julian a brooch of white lilies from a piece of ivory. He had a gift in his hands, and they were never unemployed. It was her life to watch him, to praise him, and to help him where she could.

Of an evening Harold sat filing and chipping at a little table of his own, and Anna read aloud. She read books lent to them by Lady Westrey.

H

When night came Harold showed Anna his work, with graceful diffidence marking his bronzed cheek. His flashing eye watched her as she examined what he had been doing; and when her bright look gladdened him Mrs. Julian herself could not help admiring him.

Anna knew that she was first in Harold's thoughts, and it changed her life—it added to it an unutterable joy: she would have liked those days to last for ever—she did not know how to call her feelings by their real name. But Harold knew; and he was patient;—patient, as all people are who are in earnest; who hope, expect, believe, and yield themselves in undoubting faith to an influence they feel to be good.

Harold was the most diligent of workmen. He did not work like a servant, but like an artist who pursues a fancy of his own. It soon appeared that his hands could form any thing that his heart desired; and Mrs. Julian told Lord Westrey of his genius.

Lord Westrey took back a bunch of lilies carved in wood to show Lady Westrey. Lady Westrey thought it a wonderful thing for an untaught youth to have accomplished; and she drove with Mary to Watermouth to tell Mrs. Julian what she thought.

"I will buy this," said Lady Westrey, "if he will allow me."

Mrs. Julian blushed. "Ah!" she said, "that is an odd part of Harold. He won't sell any thing. He says he could not work for money. But if you, Lady Westrey, would be humble enough to accept it—now pray do, madam—and forgive my pressing you—"

"Yes, mamma!" said Mary. And Lady Westrey, smiling, said she would take it, and that she could send him something at another time.

"I could not sell a picture," said Mary—"I know I could not, unless it was the will of God!" Mrs. Julian smiled. "What shall we send him, Mary?" asked Lady Westrey.

"Books, tools, any thing to help and encourage him, but nothing to repay him—let us go to the work-shop." Lady Westrey looked towards Mrs. Julian as if asking leave.

People were not in the habit of refusing any thing that Mary asked. Principally because her requests were never wrong; but also because of a certain sincerity that mingled with her thoughtful manner and gentle ways. To anybody else Mrs. Julian might have spoken of the disorder of the place where Julian worked, but she never mentioned it to Mary or her mother. She went first and asked them to follow her.

Harold was modest and blushing, and very happy. Anna was happy too, and very proud of Harold.

Mary Westrey stood by Harold silent and with her eyes full of thought, as he answered her mother's questions, and showed her all she asked for.

When silence came she said, "It is not enough." Harold started; she had uttered what he felt. His heart knew that there was more, but he did not know how to get to it. He fixed his flashing eyes on her quiet, beautiful face. She said, "Can't you draw?" Harold threw back his head, and pushed the black glossy curls from his forehead. Mary stooped down and took from the floor a bit of charred wood; she turned to the whitewashed wall and began to draw. She took no notice of Harold, but seemed absorbed in what she was about. But to Harold it was like drinking in inspiration. It was wonderful to those who looked on, to see his flushed cheek, and ardent gaze—his whole soul speaking in his face—and to see, in contrast, the noble girl's still, exquisite beauty, as with a bold hand and out-stretched arm she drew upon the wall,—it was within a few days of Christmas,—JESUS, Mary, Joseph, the Stable, the Manger—she had not finished the adoring shepherds, for she was interrupted by Harold falling on his knees.

"You can do it," said Mary, dropping the charcoal—but Harold was gone.

Some hours afterwards, when he returned, he carefully rubbed out every line that Mary had made. "I have learned the secret," he said to himself—"It is all in my heart."

CHAPTER IX.

IS THIS SUCCESS?

JULIAN could not despair. He could not surrender the belief that the gold would return to him. That strange mysterious gold; that sacrilegious spoil of his strange ancestors. How many generations had possessed it! How sure had been the feeling that it would do something—that the hour would come when it would bring to its owner all that he desired! Julian could not despair. He could not think that that old iron chest was for ever emptied of its treasure. At the bottom of his heart there was a fixed belief that it would—almost that *it must* come back. Still Julian sat in the long evenings in the quiet chamber that looked upon the water; and shading the lamp-light from his sight, he would gaze on the waves as they reflected the star-light, which grew brighter and brighter in the frosty night. Then he would after long watching turn his eyes within, to that iron-wrought chest, now emptied of its store. Recollections would crowd upon his mind, memories of words which had hung on his ears in childhood; and he grew to know more of the history of that gold than he had ever felt to know before. The chapel of St. Julian had yielded something towards its increase, but its sacrilegious commencement had been made of things pilfered from the chantry chapel of St. George, at Dyrbington. It had produced its effect. Its influence had wrought actively on Julian's ancestors, and on himself, and this Julian knew, and felt that the treasure was not like common gold; it would not now sink and die, and become powerless, and no longer shed its strange influence on man; as if that, which had been devoted to His service by pious acts, and the Church's blessing, *could not* be inactive; but if prevented from its course of good, must then perform that other part, and be a curse, if not a blessing. But ever, and ever, his heart repeated —*it is not gone*—it is not passed away—it will come back!

It had been a dark threatening night, and when morning arrived it scarcely seemed like the return of day, so much was the sky darkened by tremendous clouds, dense, heavy, and unusually black. The wind was blowing in a direction that always betokened storm, and often danger; for any vessel trying to enter the harbour of Watermouth at such times ran great risk of being driven on a sand bank which made shipwreck almost inevitable. The day of which we are writing was one of those which wears an aspect of threatening felt by whatever has life. The cattle seek for shelter though the storm has not begun; the birds are unseen and unheard; the domestic animals refuse to leave the house and seem to look up to man for protection, and man himself feels awe in the consciousness of approaching terror. Julian wandered about after the morning meal as one expecting something. He approached the window, and looked out. Presently his wife spoke.

"It grows darker and darker," she said. "How those gulls and sea-birds cry, and fly in towards the land. There is something awful in the roll of the waves."

"What is that?" asked Julian abruptly, and heedless of his wife's words—"What is that?" He pointed to a dark speck. It was a considerable distance off, beyond that sand bank. Snatching his telescope quickly from Anna's hands, Julian pronounced it in a minute after his first observation to be a boat labouring with the waves and wind, and, in spite of the best efforts of her rowers, likely to be stranded. "They will be lost!" exclaimed Kate, with clasped hands and streaming eyes, for the danger was too apparent to need further explanation.

"Now God help them!" ejaculated Julian

solemnly, and on the whole party fell that awful feeling of bitter danger and sure death near, and themselves powerless to save, or to assist.

It was but, as it were, a few yards of water. But those few yards separated life from almost death. There remains for them but a short time —a short time of living despair.

Strugglers with death! could you have known how hearts on shore yearned to give you safety, could you have known how many hearts, besides those in Julian's dwelling, were wrung in agony as the thought of *their* husbands—*their* children —*their* parents rose within—and one thought more of *their* unfitness to meet that moment which was approaching you—had you known this, your efforts might have been greater even than they were.

It was life's last hazard.

Now, would that they could have known that they were watched for—prayed for—cared for— would that their closing eyes could have seen the light on the good monk's hill—that their strained and sharpened sense could have heard the gladdening sound of that chapel bell—that the rising breeze could have borne them *hope*. But no, those days were gone, theirs was the worst bitterness of death.

Was there no hope?

"Save them!" exclaimed Anna, and falling on her knees, she again said, "Save them!" Who heard her?—Not her parents, she had only spoken their own secret prayer, and they scarcely knew that the bursting thought had found a voice. But another was there—Harold—he rushed from the room. The beach, the cliffs, were in a moment, as it seemed, alive with human beings.

Some strong hearts who felt it more sweet to share danger than to look upon it in inactivity, brought out and manned a boat. Among these men was Harold, the first proposer, the eager hastener of the enterprize. Suddenly there was a cry, and it was passed on from the watchers on the high lands, " There are more in distress—the boat surely belongs to a vessel, on this lower side of the Dead-man's point. If she breaks from her moorings she must be lost. Any moment the rising breeze may tear her away."

Then there were further cries of direction for two or three small fishing boats to be brought on men's shoulders to the top of the cliff, and down the other side by a winding path, to put out to sea, for the small distance between the shore and the vessel, which was almost a wreck, to bring the crew to land. And these directions were followed valiantly. The women worked like men, and the men like giants in strength and activity. But still the chief interest was fixed on the small number of brave men who had gone out to help the boat; but small as their number was, more than life for life was offering.

On hearing of this vessel Mr. Seaforth had hastened to the height from which she was observed, and Julian had instinctively followed his steps. There lay a vessel, hardly kept from dashing on the rocks, her masts gone, and her whole appearance wreck-like.

"The *Sarah!*" cried Mr. Seaforth. And a hundred voices repeated the word.

"How was she discovered?" "Who first observed her?" were questions eagerly asked as preparations for relief went forward.

Lyas Norwood, attracted to the sea coast by its threatening appearance, had diverged from his usual route to the town, and had come suddenly on the sight of the *Sarah,* just as the more restless of the watchers on the beach had climbed the height which united the ridge of rock called the Dead-man's point with the land.

Below the Dead-man's point, there was a dreary looking bay of water, formed, it would seem, by the constant and unavailing efforts of the waves to surmount that steep and rocky boundary, which, jutting out so far into the ocean, had earned for itself its threatening name. It was in this little bay that the *Sarah* was anchored. Only those who knew well that dangerous mooring could have ventured on so bold a measure.

Mr. Seaforth was full of activity; John Julian stood in tranquil wonder; but amid the bustle his absorbed contemplative state was not observed.

Suddenly Lyas Norwood was at Mr. Seaforth's side. "There is another," he said.

"Another? Another? What do you mean?"

"Another vessel. She has tried to turn the point and failed. She is on the rocks, and cannot last much longer. Come to the height and see. There are a few poor fellows clinging to the masts; but the tide is going out, and strongly too. She cannot last. She is going to pieces now. Every wave tells upon her. Are we then to see death before our eyes, and be unable to send succour? Again, again—they cannot battle with their fate. They are worn out. Another, and another is washed off—Holy angels, what a sight! It is maddening to behold it. Ah! a cry —what a note of agony!"

The beholders pressed their hands to their eyes to shut out the terror they could not lessen, and some ran away a few steps, and others turned their backs on the awful woe, and stamped the ground in agony of mind, and a few fell upon their knees, and here and there were seen on stern rough faces hard-wrung tears.

Meanwhile, life was being given back to all on board the *Sarah*. Boat after boat safely gave in its living cargo, and such arrangements were being made as would put the vessel in a position of safety, until she could be brought into the port.

The joyful proceedings now brought crowds

from the beach to the scene of landing; all came but a few; those few whose hearts were with the adventurous in charity, whose fate was not yet sure.

Among those who had collected on the highest ridges was Ralph Seaforth. He was the only one who felt no gladness at the sight of the *Sarah*. He stood angry, disappointed, revengeful; all that had occurred was as plain to Ralph Seaforth as if, there before him, the history of the last few months had been spread out.

The *Sarah* had captured a Spanish vessel, and Mr. Seaforth had just learned that the Spanish vessel was conveying an enormous amount of gold.

Let us leave the bustle and excitement of saving the half-dead creatures from the vessels on the rocks. All is doing for them that human effort can accomplish. Let us leave them and turn to the beach, where multitudes are gathered to welcome the boat which has just brought its burthen to the shore.

There was Anna Julian, and there was her good mother also. And there was every woman and child who had seen husband, son, or father embark on board the *Sarah*.

Of those brought from the wrecks few could climb the steep way to the town without assistance. It was all going on steadily and with quiet arrangement, and purposely with as little excitement and noise as possible. It was well to avoid the trial which loud grief and lamentation might prove to some whose spirit seemed hovering between this world and the next. As silently then as possible, and with all speed, the sufferers were taken to the places prepared for them; and they were conveyed to the town, not by the beach, on which so many were gathered, but by another, rather longer, but more quiet road, through a ravine in the cliff.

Anna had never moved from the beach on which she still stood, and where at last her mother joined her. She had heard of the vessel jammed in among the rocks, beyond the Deadman's point. She knew of the multitude swerving that way; of some returning; of others gathering about them; of the sands being again filled with watchers. But what the senses took in the heart never responded to. It was the boat and its fate that occupied her. The thing doing she knew to be full of danger, but that it was *right*, and that it *must* be done, she also knew— not once for an instant did she wish they had never gone. But out with them had gone her heart; she was standing on the sands, but there —far off on the sea—there, where her eyes are fixed, there is her heart, there is her sense of being, there is her better part, as if for a time the soul had left the body, yet not given it up to death, but left it waiting till it should return.

It was cold, and the wind was rough and boisterous, and the people about her were looking up with anxious faces to the threatening skies. But Anna felt no cold, nor heard the wind, nor thought of where she was.

Every now and then it was thought that the labouring boat had sunk. Shrieks told the heart's dread. But Anna uttered no sound, no, not a sigh; she felt neither fear nor hope; the heart was still—quite still—no passion heaved it—it seemed to have left her—it was out on the sea, where the dark speck on the waters told of the labouring charities of the devoted few.

Some standing by were calculating the time. They were saying how long in fair weather it would take to row that distance. Some said that the rowers had been long, too long, that they had made no way, that they would never reach the perilled boat in time, that they would themselves be cast upon the bar, that they had better never have gone, and that they wished that they had some one with them who would say "turn back."

But not one anxiety passed through Anna's mind. There there was no sense of time, no calculation of danger, no desire to change the past. In a trance-like state of waiting she stood, and still her fixed eyes were on the boat. She scarcely knew where she was, she scarcely heard what passed: she had no thought of her life past, or her life to come; no sense of any thing but of the moment then with her—and not till those brave men had gained their perilled brothers' side, not till the words pealed forth around her, "They return, they return"—not till assurances passed about that the tide would help them; that they were nearing fast; that they were coming on bravely; that danger was over; that they were alive, they were safe—not till then did she hear and feel; and not till they were near enough for her to see *one* who was called the best and bravest of all did she tremble; and not till his feet touched the sand, amid the ringing cheers of those around, did she drop against a friendly rock, and weep tears that would not cease till they had left the long pent-up fountain dry.

The women wept, and the men ceased their loud cheers, to grasp Harold's hand, and tell him that the brave deed was his, for that he had put the thoughts into hearts that would never have dared to attempt what they had accomplished, but for him. The five men saved were all men of Watermouth; fathers, husbands, and sons. The other sufferers were almost forgotten. In that moment of success they would carry the men home in the boat that had saved them. The thought was no sooner spoken than the thing was done. Immediately the boat was raised on men's shoulders, and with cheers and cries of joy, surrounded by almost all the persons who had collected on the beach, the men so bravely saved were borne off triumphantly. But Harold stayed and looked at Anna. He turned from her to her mother. Kate Julian's bright eyes were running over with gladness, love, and admiration. Harold put his hand in hers; she pressed it, raised it to her lips, left a mother's kiss upon it, and said; "Heaven will reward you!"

There was a deep glow on the young man's cheek, and his eyes dilated with a soft and peculiar light. "Let us go home, Anna," he said, "let us go home, Anna!" He dwelt upon the name, it seemed to have a sound upon it that it had never borne before. He did not try to suppress its music, he said it again—"Anna!" She looked up; he saw that she had heard it.

That night Mr. Seaforth had said to Julian that he was rich. "Any position purchaseable by wealth is yours, Mr. Julian. I am glad that such singular good fortune should have fallen on one of such distinguished integrity of character. Not a creature in Watermouth but will rejoice at your success, sir—success! Yes, indeed—great, quite unparalleled success. For myself, I really can scarcely yet believe it. Good night—bear my congratulations to Mrs. Julian—and think of your son! Dear me," continued the kind merchant—"it could not have occurred to a better man. Just the very person to do credit to it. All things in a good train for its right using; I heartily rejoice!" And there, just where Mr.

Seaforth had first heard the secret of Julian's store did they now take leave.

Mr. Seaforth made this a time for insisting on his brother accepting a sum of money enough to secure his future independence. He bestowed ten thousand pounds on Ralph. But when pressed to allow him to take the command of his next vessel, he hesitated, avoided an answer, and when obliged to reply said, that Ralph had so much lost him the respect and confidence of many whose good opinion he valued, that he would not promise to employ him again till there was an improvement in his character and habits.

Ralph heard in silence; he heard, and as he heard he determined in his mind that it was John Julian's respect and confidence that his brother disliked the thought of losing.

He looked upon him more surely than ever as his enemy, and hated him accordingly. Many and bitter were the promises he made that day in his heart against him. And, forgetting that he had no proof to go upon, he murmured to himself; "Well, if I am his enemy, he made me so; he must take the consequences. If he cuts me out of my share of the wealth which he gathers in so richly for himself he must not be surprised to find my hand in his treasures, helping myself in my own way." And then the thought of Anna Julian rose to his mind, and he went away with the stirring of all evil passions in his breast.

I

At John Julian's better thoughts were working in a better mind. Harold was thinking that the time was come for him to say that he loved Anna Julian. And at Lullingstone Lord Westrey heard of the arrival of the *Sarah*, and was very glad. Lady Westrey and Mary were in London. Lord Westrey had only come to Lullingstone for a few days on business. On hearing the news he rode to Watermouth to congratulate Mr. Seaforth. Mr. Seaforth mentioned John Julian to Lord Westrey, and Lord Westrey felt that it was one of those moments in a man's life when he wants a friend.

· He was soon seated in the quiet little parlour with the low window looking out upon the sea.

That cheerful little chamber with its antique furniture, its chair from old Dyrbington, and its now emptied iron chest! How often had Julian sat just where Lord Westrey now was sitting, gazing on the sea, with eyes, as it were, enchained, and his own self stilled, oppressed by a feeling prophetic of what had now come to pass. And now that it had come; now that he was rich, and certain of being richer, there was in his heart a want unsupplied, which money could not purchase. He wanted to be relieved of impertinent gossiping assiduities. He wanted to rise quietly, without any noise, and rude wondering congratulations. All that verged on loud mob-clamour was dreadful to him, even in idea. To him it was nothing astonishing that John Julian should be a rich man.

It was that of which he had thought from youth to age. He had expected it. Yes, for long years he had looked out for the time that had now come; the present was but the realization of the expectations of the past. And he had prepared for it. He had placed his son where he might have education equal to his fortune. He had brought up his daughter with a care which could not be exceeded. He had kept her always by his own, or by her mother's side. He had guarded her from all acquaintances, and he had given her so much education as to make it an easy thing for her to advance to greater things. Had he ever, in any transaction of life, in any calculation that bore upon the future, forgotten for a moment that he must one day be rich—*must* be rich? He heard Lord Westrey's voice, and his heart beat quickly, and freely, relieved immediately of half its load. "Any thing I can do for you? Julian you know how sincere are our feelings of regard for you and your wife, and—"

"Lord Westrey—thank you—hear me"—interrupted Julian; "I am rich, very rich, I never wanted a friend before, but to have one now—and such a one as yourself—is surely all that I want to crown my good fortune. But have you time to spare, for I have much to say?" Lord Westrey smiled. He thought that he had never heard Julian speak so directly to the point in his life before. "The whole day is at your service, if you please," he answered.

"Less than that will do, my lord. But you must hear a long story. First, however, I am rich. Lord Westrey, I am worth seventy thousand pounds, and expect to be worth much more."

Lord Westrey uttered an exclamation of surprise. He had thought of two or three thousand at the utmost. This announcement perfectly astonished him.

"How glad I am that I called," he exclaimed immediately. "Trust to *me*, Julian—keep out of the way of all vulgar harpies. Think of your children—your charming girl, and that fine boy, your dear excellent Edward—seventy thousand! —what a situation for you to be in—I know not what to say, but that I am glad, very, very glad," —and Lord Westrey grasped Julian's hand with true-hearted warmth.

"Lord Westrey, you can be every thing to me and the children that we want," said Julian.

"I will then," said Lord Westrey emphatically.

"But I have always been rich," continued Julian musingly.

"You rich always, what?" Lord Westrey's manner roused Julian from the reverie into which he seemed to be sinking.

"Yes, always," he repeated with animation. "And this is the story I want you to hear—but

Kate must come, she has never known of this store, she—"

"Mrs. Julian never known? A secret store of money, all these years, and your wife never known?—Julian?"

"It's true, my lord; she knows no more of what I am going to tell, than you do."

"What did you do with it—where did you keep] it—how long have you had it—this is the most extraordinary thing, certainly, that ever occurred!"

"I kept it in that small iron chest," said Julian, quietly pointing to where it stood in its usual place. "And I have had it ever since my father died, and his father gave it to him, and so from generation to generation it came on; but the world is different in some things to what it has been—Edward is different to me—things pressed it upon me that the time for the gold lying quiet in its old place was over. And, somehow, I always knew that it would bring riches. I always knew that when sent out it would come back—and so it has. But here comes Kate."

In half-an-hour's time Kate, in Lord Westrey's presence, had heard her husband's story. She heard with astonishment, and a sensation almost amounting to fear. Kate could only weep and wring her hands and sob forth that she did not like this wealth. So, Lord Westrey, having sent away her husband, was obliged to put some facts before her eyes with rather remarkable plainness. They were, that her husband was decidedly what the world would call an odd man; that, nevertheless, his children were now raised to a position in which they would be remarked upon by the world—not always the kindest in its judgments; and that the happiness and success of her offspring depended upon herself. Kate heard, and felt that all she heard was true. It was not a case in which there was any choice allowed her. The thing had come—the time had arrived—certain responsibilities were hers, and she was lifted to a place which she must fill, and on the discharge of her duties depended her children's happiness, almost their respectability. "Perhaps," Lord Westrey had added, on saying this, "perhaps this is putting the case in its utmost strength; Edward could no doubt get on by himself, and Anna might be driven to assert her rights; but let me say, that you will teach your children a bad lesson if you teach them to do without you. Great as the exertion may be you are capable of being all that they will require, and that is what you must set yourself to be. Lady Westrey will be all that an affectionate friend can be, but *you* must be *yourself*—not what you have been, but what you now are; and let me add one thing more, and I say it without flattery, there never was a woman better calculated to meet the responsibilities of an elevated position. You have but to think of how much depends upon you, to accomplish it all with admirable ability and grace. There never was any nonsense or pretence about you. You have quietness of mind, and courage, and a plain straightforward way of seeing things—" Mrs. Julian was smiling through her tears. "There," continued his lordship. "there, you will have accustomed your mind to all these changes in half-an-hour, and by to-morrow morning no one will know by Mrs. Julian's manner that her husband had ever a less balance at his banker's than he has at present. You must think of telling your boy now," said Lord Westrey, when Julian returned.

"I do not wish, my lord, that he should know all that I have been telling you about that old gold in the chest. It is, I think, sufficient for Edward to know that I had money, and used it, and that it has multiplied to that which I now possess. The secret of the long-descended store is safe with you, my wife, and Mr. Seaforth. And I think it had better never go any further."

"You are right," said Lord Westrey, after a moment's thought. "Yes, you are right. I think that it will be best to tell Edward in this way. You continue your connections with Mr. Seaforth?"

"Yes," said Julian, "I reserve thirty thousand pounds for my wife and children, and the rest, with the exception of two thousand, to meet the expenses of my change of position, is to remain in Mr. Seaforth's hands, to be used again. This was his own suggestion."

"Very well; quite right and judicious," said Lord Westrey. "Now let me advise you about Edward. Let me send Mr. Parker to Oxford. He can take a note from you, and another from me. Edward must be told that you have made a beginning of unexpected success; so much so, hat you are going to leave your present abode and commence another style of living. By the by, where will you go? Edward ought to be told all at once, I think."

"Your father's favourite spot, Mayfield, is empty," said Julian. "Your steward told me a short time since that you wanted a tenant."

"The very thing for you," exclaimed Lord Westrey. "I shall like extremely to have you there. And a prudent choice too," he continued smiling, "you may do the place justice on eight hundred a year."

Mayfield stood immediately on the outskirts of the town, on the road to Dyrbington.

"Then," continued Lord Westrey, "Mr. Parker is to tell your son that you are going into Mayfield immediately, and that, on his return in summer, he will find that place his home; and"—Lord Westrey paused and laughed—"and *if you can afford it*, a horse for him to ride will be in the stables. Ah!" he said, and laughed again, "we have to be very careful with these youths; they know so little of money that they are led to believe what the first extravagant fellow they meet with tells them, and half ruin us before we know that they have ever dared to change a guinea without a sigh. Ah! Mrs. Julian does not believe a word I say. Well, but I shall do as I have said; and now let us leave Edward; he will do well enough, I dare say, and speak about the other—about Anna."

Mrs. Julian's face was lighted up by a sweet tender smile; but over Julian's countenance there passed quickly an expression of vehement interest which only by a strong effort he controlled. "She is almost sixteen," Julian went on in answer to Lord Westrey's inquiries. "She has had some pains taken with her; not that she has been to any school, I was afraid of her making acquaintances. She writes an excellent hand, and as to reading—you know the books that Lady Westrey has, at various times, bestowed upon her; history and biographies: well, the volumes are not many, but she knows them almost by heart—I think that there will not be much trouble about her English education."

"You must let me tell this to Lady Westrey, and when you have heard what she advises, you must agree between yourselves whether or not you will abide by her decision."

" No fear of that!" ejaculated Julian.

"Then," said Lord Westrey, "we have now got full instructions for Parker; and as soon as I get back to town I will send him down to Oxford. Do you want me to do any thing more for you? Have you told Anna?"

"I shall tell her to-night," said Julian. And then, after more thanks, and more assurances of kindness, Lord Westrey departed,—Julian feeling that his visit to them had not been the least wonderful of the events that had occurred, for it had led to the education of his darling Anna being placed in the hands of the very family into which—the whispering voice within never quite pronounced the thing that might be.

The evening came; a calm, still evening; for the late storms had spent their strength and had left nature again to her repose. Within the house the mother's quiet step was heard as she went about her household work.

As yet there was only the knowledge of change in that mother's breast, there was no visible token of that which had come upon them. As it had been a month before, so was it then. The same neat, matronly figure, in the sad-coloured gown and fair white apron, laid the neatly-spread table, for their usual meal. And still the slight, graceful figure of a young girl came and went, passed and repassed, assisting in the household work. That fair girl in the dark winter dress lit the fire in the grate, which her own hands had that morning brightened, then ran down to the kitchen, and brought thence the steaming kettle, and having, with her mother, concluded the usual arrangements, disappeared to come again, with washed hands, and blooming face, and glossy ringlets parted on her fair young brow, to wait her father's entrance.

Perhaps the operations had been conducted rather more silently than usual, and perhaps the mother's eye had oftener wandered to her daughter's form, and had longer rested there. We dwell purposely on this evening, because there were hearts from which its memory never passed away. We like to think of Anna in her humble, but not degrading toil; we like to follow her to her small chamber, and see her as she made her simple adornments, because we are soon to take leave of such things, and to see them no more.

When she returned to her mother Harold was in the room. Four days had passed since the shipwreck, and to all they had been days of less labour than usual. Anna and Harold had been a good deal together, and to their mutual pleasure. It was not that Harold talked, and made himself what is commonly called an agreeable companion to Anna, for he said very little; neither was it that Anna talked to him, for she was seldom inclined to speak when he was by. But it was, that in his presence there was an influence which she felt, and in which she rejoiced; an influence which produced pleasure, that was called forth by nothing else. And now that she saw Harold, her cheek blushed brightly, yet she advanced to him with a radiant smile. "I have not seen you all day," she said.

"I have been with my father," he replied.

They were simple words, yet Kate looked up anxiously. She looked at Harold. He was standing gazing with a frank smile on Anna. A sudden sense fell on Kate's mind of his uncommon beauty, and of the charm with which his peculiar manner invested him. She had always known, as she afterwards said, that "he was not in any thing like a common youth." One moment told Mrs. Julian the truth. One look at her dear Anna's blushing cheek as she met Harold's eye a second time; one other look at Harold, over whose face each feeling of the heart passed always in the unchecked freedom of the innocence which dares be bold, and where she had never seen the passage of a thought that required rebuke,—and Mrs. Julian knew all.

The door opened, but no one saw it—Julian entered, but no one observed him.

"Harold!" exclaimed Mrs. Julian—there was a nervous tremor in the tone, and it thrilled through Anna's heart with a terror hitherto unknown—"Harold!"

"Yes, yes," he answered, and advanced to her, "you too have loved, and you know——"

"Hush," said a voice deep and low, stifled in

its strength by the very intensity of the feelings that produced it. "Hush," cried the same voice, but all ungovernably loud, and more terrible than if it had gathered power from anger, for it was the cry of a heart troublingly gazing into the depths of despair—"Hush!"

It was Julian who spoke. All were silent—he advanced slowly, and as if a sudden palsy had robbed him of his strength. Anna and her mother looked and trembled; but Harold knew no fear, and spoke again: "I ask," he said, now addressing Julian—but again came that one word "Hush!"—as if Julian could say no more. There was a moment of terrible silence. Anna stood, the picture of meek stillness; her hands clasped, her figure drooping, her slow tears falling without sob or other sound.

Harold with anxious gestures advanced to Julian. He evidently knew nothing of what was meant. He looked at him most lovingly, gently grasped his hand, and in soft and tender, yet inquiring accents said, "My friend?" The words recalled Julian to himself, and to a recollection of the character with which he had to deal.

"Yes, Harold," he answered; "but *her* friend too!"

The youth gave a start, and then answered with a look of joyful acquiescence.

"Her friend too," repeated Julian; and still

holding Harold's hand, he advanced to his daughter's side. "Anna," he went on, "I had something to tell you to-night, and when I entered the room just now, I had come to tell it. I will tell it now, before Harold, for it concerns us all. It is a matter of great moment, Anna; unknown to your mother till this morning, when I told her before Lord Westrey."

Anna looked up into her father's face. Her interest was awakened, but on her gently-tinged cheek the large tears still lay.

"I have become, my child, unexpectedly rich; yes, Anna, rich, very rich, with expectations of being yet richer; so that my children must take their place among the higher ranks of life. Mr. Parker is to be sent to Oxford by Lord Westrey's kindness, to tell your brother. It will be necessary for us to act consistently, and we shall immediately leave this house; we are going to live at Mayfield. Lady Westrey will point out the best way of fitting you for your future station in life. At your age the ways of cultivated society are soon learnt, and such accomplishments as are required will not be difficult of attainment. I should have told your mother and yourself what your possible position would be before, had not the affairs in which I have been engaged been attended with such risk."

Anna turned her still pale face away from him,

and fixed her eyes, which had lost all expression, on Harold. He answered her look with one of earnest stedfastness. All trace of the open ardour of unconcealed affection had passed away; and in its stead there was that which spoke of long endurance and patient hope. Not a word did he speak; but he never took his eyes from the object of his powerful love. Still he looked at her, as if the longer he looked the surer he was to see her again, and never lose her more; still he looked, as if the feeling of certainty grew upon his soul as he gazed.

Then for a moment he turned to Julian and extended his hand; it was grasped with a pressure intended to convey something of the mingled emotions in Julian's breast. Then to that good mother Harold turned, and his heart of honest courage trembled as he looked at her; but he quickly grew strong again. It is the knowledge of faithlessness that makes man fear. Harold knew not what faithlessness was. His heart was only conscious of fidelity. He did not offer his hand to Kate Julian—he saw her mother's face of tears and smiles, of love and sorrow blended, and he laid his head for one moment on her shoulder, and threw his arms around her with a son's embrace. In another moment he was at the door, and stopping for one last look.

Still Anna's full sad eye was upon him with the calm gaze of a statue. But at that very moment there were rushing thoughts within her breast as if another self was imprisoned there.

"Stop him! he must not go!" said those agitated thoughts. "Give him one glance; speak but a word; advance a single step; oh! stretch forth your hand only, and all will be done," urged wildly that imprisoned self; and still went on: "He goes; the time is passing; another moment and it will be for ever too late; the wealth that raises you, might it not raise him? The influences that are to fit you for another station, would they be powerless upon him? Now—this instant—he goes—oh, one effort!"

But though Anna's eyes were fixed where Harold stood she did not see him. The rushing thoughts and wild inquiries within were answered by a vision which seemed to hide him from her sight. There was the log hut in the forest; and there was a mazy sense of something that had conveyed her far, far, far away from it all. Between her and them there was a sense as of boundless space. The sound of work and toil had died away; the ear could no longer catch the voices it had known before. But suddenly that vision passed, dispelled by a short sound. Anna started—saw things in their reality once more—it was the closing of the door that she had heard, and Harold was gone.

And long years afterwards she was glad that it had been so. With a fervent thankfulness, impossible to describe, she was glad that that involuntary whirlwind of passion had found no vent—she was glad that he had departed without a word, look, or sign—with no other encouragement than that which his own brave heart afforded to itself.

CHAPTER X.

A NEW WORLD.

THERE was much to be done. Lord Westrey put Mayfield into what would be called in these days "ornamental repair." Lady Westrey wrote long letters about Anna; and Mrs. Seaforth having volunteered the assistance of her experience, had been admitted to the family councils. It was determined that Anna should go to a lady living in France, with whom Lord Westrey had placed two wards of his, for their education. Julian was sorry to lose his child, even for a time. Mrs. Julian's heart trembled at the thought of a foreign country, but Anna herself seemed to like the plan.

In the house at Mayfield there was noise from workmen's tools. Painting had been done, papering was going forward—the busy sounds of polishing bright floors were heard, and the luxurious carpets were ready to put down. Yet, notwithstanding all this bustle, one part of the house was already inhabited by Mr. and Mrs. Julian, their daughter and their servants.

The old house had not been left without a pang. Mrs. Julian had shown that she felt more than the others. When the moment came for her to go, to leave that place, not as one who is to return again, she paused by the door, and stepped back involuntarily, and placed her feet again within its threshold. The possible contrast of the unkind future and the kindly past shot through her soul with lightning vividness.

The week passed on. Lady Westrey proposed that Mrs. Herbert, a friend of hers who lived in Watermouth, should bring Anna to London, to meet Madame Lefranc. This offer was gladly accepted. No time was to be lost. Anna and Mrs. Herbert arrived at Lord Westrey's—and what a new world opened to her! Her father had done a good thing for her. It was a fine thing to have such happiness within reach. But in her heart there always lay an unanswered question—Where was Harold?

The voice was never strong enough to urge Anna to do any thing to get that question answered. It never suggested to her to ask her father, or speak to her mother. She had the strongest feelings that she would rather not do either of these things. She did not wish Harold to be spoken of. She did not wish to be obliged to speak of him herself. She dreaded the record of an opinion, or the expression of a feeling on either side.

Anna and Madame Lefranc were charmed with each other. Such feelings of sorrow as had come over her when parting with her parents, all fled away when she became known to her future instructress and friend. And when Lord Westrey told her they had sent for her brother to spend a couple of days with them, before her departure, her happiness was at its height.

She had so often been to Lullingstone Court with her mother, and had so often played on the lawn with her foster-brother and his sister, that as a little child she had not felt the difference in their respective positions, and now that she had passed childhood, something had happened;—the effect appeared to be a sudden disappearance of the space dividing the families, as much by Lord Westrey's act, as by her father's good fortune.

The days were fresh in Anna's recollection, when her mother had very often lectured her on the impropriety of speaking to her playfellows as if they were her equals, and calling them simply by their christian names, days when she was very small indeed, and when Lord Westrey had often interrupted her mother by saying, "Never mind, never mind, good Mrs. Julian, there's time enough for that!" Those days were fresh in Anna's mind, and the intervening time seemed to have dropped out of remembrance. Again, in the simplicity of childhood, she seemed to be their equal; and she looked on her foster-brother Lullingstone as if some real relationship existed between them. "I wonder," said Lullingstone one day, "I wonder if I am as clever as your brother Edward was at sixteen. What do you think, Anna?"

"Indeed I cannot tell; you know I cannot possibly be able to tell you; I don't know any thing about Latin."

"Of course you can't, I wish all girls learnt Latin. I'm so glad that Edward is coming. Edward often comes to see us; does he tell you, Anna?"

"Yes; he always mentions Lord Westrey's favours when he writes to my father."

"That's a very formal speech, Anna. Do you really think Edward's coming here a *favour?* You know that he is getting on wonderfully—shall you think it a *favour* if he takes the highest honours?"

"I don't know," said Anna."

"If he had been stupid, and vulgar, and conceited, and—and ugly, perhaps that would have made a difference—what would it have been then, Anna?"

"Oh, a great favour, I am sure," said she, laughing.

"No; not a favour at all—only a piece of folly in papa, that's all—a piece of inexcusable folly; that's what I think."

"Well, perhaps so—yes, I think so too."

"It's always folly to have any thing to do voluntarily with any body you are ashamed of. That's a rule," said Lullingstone boldly.

Anna said nothing. Presently Lullingstone began again: "Anna, how much older are you than I am?"

"Five weeks, I think."

"Oh!"

"What are you going to learn at Madame Lefranc's?"

"All that I am capable of learning."

"Do you like learning?"

"Yes; very much."

"What languages are you going to learn?"

"Only French at present, at Madame Lefranc's; but I shall not give up learning when I leave there."

"That's right; but why only French?"

"Lady Westrey says that I shall not have time for more."

"Mary says that you have a beautiful voice."

"Madame Lefranc thinks that I may sing well if I am taught."

"Do you know Caroline and Jane Eastner?"

"No."

"They can't do any thing."

"Oh, don't say so! neither can I."

"But they can't learn."

"Perhaps you'll say the same of me when I come here with them at Midsummer."

"No; you are Edward's sister."

"Well?"

"He knows you, and he said you had great abilities."

"When?—to whom?"

"To Mr. Parker, when papa sent him to Oxford the other day. Did not Edward begin to teach you mathematics?"

"Is Edward anxious that I should get on?"

"Yes, very."

Anna was silent; she meditated and was pleased.

"I will never marry any one but a clever woman," was Lullingstone's parting remark.

The day fixed for Edward's arrival came, and he came with it. Anna had not seen him for several months; he had grown, and improved in person and manner.

Anna was delighted with him. She thought him the handsomest—except Harold—the handsomest person she had ever seen. But this exception was made to herself, she never uttered Harold's name, and was very glad that Edward did not ask after him, or make any mention of Lyas.

Edward had not spent Christmas at Watermouth, and so he had not seen Harold as an inmate of his father's house. He had heard of his father taking him, and had felt glad of it at the time; but other things had removed the remembrance of Harold from his mind, and now he did not ask about him because he did not think of him.

The moment of Edward's arrival was one of general joy in the house. Mr. Parker and Lullingstone had been expecting him for full half an hour, and the stopping of a hackney coach at the door had made Lullingstone exclaim, "There he is; there's Edward," and forthwith rush to meet him. Lady Westrey smiled, and looked in her sweet placid way towards Anna, who was standing up irresolute, and listening. Then came another cry from Lullingstone, "Yes, yes; here he is—it is Edward—here he comes." And then Anna bounded out to meet him, and embrace him, in the ante-room.

The brother and sister had never met more fondly, and never so admiringly; and one, at least, felt the full importance of the prospects opening around them. Edward had had a short, but a sufficient acquaintance with the world, and he well knew the value of the wealth his father had gained for him. He had felt that the life of a struggling man was before him; and though, full of youth, vigour, and spirit, he had always assured himself that the struggle would be successful, he yet had known enough of pain, and enough of ambition to feel how sweet it was to be thus carried on by a high unexpected wave to fortune. When thoughtful and alone it had wrung tears from his boy's heart to think of this happiness. And now he was again in his kind patron's house, with, if possible, a freer smile, and a firmer foot than before. He was no longer the being toiling for bread, but one who pursued distinction for distinction's sake, and loved learning for itself.

"Don't you think your brother very much improved, Anna?" said Mary Westrey to her that morning.

"I admire Edward so much; how bright-looking he is," said Anna frankly.

Mary raised her large dark soft eyes slowly from her work; they fell on Anna for a moment, and were again withdrawn. "He is very handsome," said Mary.

"Oh Mary," said Anna; and the roses were very bright in her cheek.

"Isn't he?" asked the other, again speaking in that quiet way.

"Well, yes, I suppose he is."

The next morning the two girls were assembled in what was called the inner drawing-room; Lord Westrey was there reading the newspaper; Lady Westrey was in her dressing-room writing letters. The two boys and Mr. Parker had not been seen since breakfast. It was raining heavily, and the atmosphere was so dense that a lamp had been lighted. At last Lullingstone came in, all excitement, with some papers in his hand. "Look here Papa. See—Edward has done this beautiful passage of Shakspeare into Latin, which Mr. Parker says is splendid. I proposed his doing it in joke, because I thought he couldn't do it, and he did it directly. Mr. Parker is quite delighted, I assure you he is, Papa." Lullingstone was most energetic in his manner, and Lord Westrey, smiling, took the paper from him; but Lullingstone had more to say: "and see here Papa, I brought this to show you; here's that pretty song that Mary sings—isn't it a wonderful translation?" Lord Westrey took that too, and was just murmuring: "Extraordinary—really very clever—the most interesting youth altogether that ever was met with"—when the boy in question entered.

"You young rogue, you've run off with my property?" he cried, springing over certain intervening sofas and chairs, and pouncing upon Lullingstone, who laughed heartily, and made signs to his father to secure the papers.

"Catch him and punish him, Edward: I allow no thieves here," said Lord Westrey pocketing the manuscripts, and rising to effect a safe retreat. "Punish him as he deserves Edward, I leave him to your mercy," and so saying, Lord Westrey left the room; and Lullingstone, having escaped from Edward's hands, tried to go after him, but was turned aside at the first bound, upon which followed a game of flight and pursuit, first about the room, which made the girls laugh heartily notwithstanding the peril with which it seemed to be attended, and afterwards still further continued into remote regions, till Lullingstone throwing his arms round his friend announced, with a triumphant laugh, that his father had had the papers all the time.

"Please to forgive me for having taken such a liberty with your song," said Edward Julian to Mary Westrey that evening.

"Did you like it very much?—I don't recollect you ever saying that you admired it."

"Possibly not," said Edward. He spoke the words in an odd dry sort of way, which made Mary look at him.

"But you did like it—and very much?"

"Yes, very much; more than I ever liked a song before. I liked it all, words, and music, and —and—every thing."

"I will sing it this evening," said Mary.

"No—no, thank you,—don't sing it," said Edward abruptly. Mary again looked up into his face.

"Why not?" she asked.

"Because Lord Westrey has that paper, and if you sing the original it might bring notice upon us—I beg your pardon—upon *me*."

"Yes, yes," said Mary.

Edward knew what he was doing perfectly well. He had known it a long time. He was in love with Mary Westrey. He knew that she was already admired in that great world on which he could only look from the threshold which, as yet, he had not crossed. As yet—he said the words to himself emphatically. He who would marry Mary Westrey must not look to bring her down from her own station, but must, like a conqueror, win his way to her side, and of his own right meet her and win her as an equal. Edward had thought it all over again and again, and he knew that it was this that he was doing. He knew that his life was wrapped up in the hope before him. He knew that for it he lived, and for it had developed in mind and feeling. He knew that it was in obedience to it that he had toiled, and that to it he owed such success as he had already had, and should owe all that was to come. He knew also that he might be disappointed—that he might be simply too late; or that he might speak and be rejected, be told that his love—surely love so strong, so sure, so true, and so courageous, should meet a better fate—that his love could never be returned; and he felt that such an end would break him down, ruin him, perhaps be his death. Well! He could not change his views, or moderate his hopes. He loved; he loved with all his soul; with an energy that united the ardour of youth to the strength of a man. It was the fruit of the man's mind and the boy's heart that belonged to him.

The time came for him to go, and he went,

leaving Anna, who was to remain two days longer. Edward looked upon Anna's visit to the Westreys as the first acknowledgment that had occurred of the power of wealth. It had been a great happiness to him. As to Anna, she liked to be a gentlewoman, and to look forward to the ten thousand delights that life seemed to offer her. New thoughts and expectations crowded upon her when alone—when the day was over—when the time for thought was come—when all was quiet, and she was alone with recollections of the past. And always, in those peaceful hours, that unanswered thought would arise of *Where is he?* and mingle with the new ideas which occupied her mind.

CHAPTER XI.

ABSENCE AND MEETING AGAIN.

NEITHER Julian nor his wife had forgotten Harold. Unknown to their daughter they had each been at different times to Lyas Norwood's house. But they had not seen Harold either time. Julian had been the first to visit them: he had gone the day after Harold's departure. As he neared the dwelling he had looked out anxiously, hoping to see him: but only Lyas stood outside the house, and he, not a little to Julian's relief of mind, advanced to meet him.

"Never mind it; never mind it, Julian. I try not to mind it myself—why should you care?"

"I loved the youth," said Julian.

"Yes, I believe you did; I believe you do: but not as his father loves him, Julian; and yet I—*I* tell you not to mind."

"Where *is* Harold?" asked Julian.

"Gone," replied Lyas, abruptly. "Gone." He seemed suddenly affected.

"But where," repeated Julian. "Tell me where

he is. Tell me something about the youth, Lyas. Tell me, or I shall be miserable. I loved Harold, but I could not give her to him; think, Lyas——"

Lyas started. "He did not ask her of you, did he?"

"No; but had our circumstances been as he supposed, he would have looked forward to the day when he might have asked for her. I told her how things were before him, and he went away."

"And departed in friendship?"

"Yes more, God knows,—in love."

"Then all is right," said Lyas.

"He must hope no more," said Julian with solemn emphasis.

Lyas bent his bright black laughing eyes on Julian, and gave him a moment's silent gaze, as if he would carry his scrutiny to the farthest depths of his heart, and bear that independent merriment along with it.

"He must not hope! *you* tell *him*, tell *me*, tell *any* man that he must not hope! Tell the glorious sun to warm us no longer with his beams. Tell him as he now pursues his way to the summer's highest point, to go back in his career, to sink again to his lowest state, to rise no more; never again to gild our days, and warm our bodies, and rejoice our hearts; and when *he* obeys you, then tell *man* not to hope."

Julian repeated his question concerning the youth.

"He is gone," repeated Lyas in answer to the request. "He is not here; you cannot see him—he is gone."

"But where? Where is he gone?" urged Julian.

"He is gone," said Lyas, "far off—away into the world; away into the midst of that teeming cauldron of life; away in the strength—Oh Julian—in the strength of his *Hope!*"

"You have done wrong," exclaimed Julian hastily. "That youth gone, and alone! You don't know what may happen to him! And you will not tell me where he is?" urged Julian for the last time.

"I don't know," said Lyas: and turning from his interrogator he walked slowly towards his house. Julian returned to Mayfield.

Julian and his wife worked busily at Mayfield. They were to see their children in July, and desired to finish their arrangements before receiving them. The Westreys had remained in London for masters for Mary. They were returning to Lullingstone the first week in August, and it had been arranged that Anna and Edward were to meet again in London at their house, and that Anna was to return to Watermouth with them.

As the time approached Edward felt full of home thoughts. Over and over again he read his father's and mother's letters. They were so happy in their improved fortune; and all things belonging to their new station seemed, from the first, to have come so naturally to them. This thought could not but have occurred to Edward, and he entertained it willingly, as a strong proof of the natural superiority of those he loved.

His mother told him that a horse had been provided for Anna, and another for himself. He already had heard from Anna of her having a riding-master. He thought often of the pleasure he should have in riding about with her. Then he heard that his father had hired a groom, a young man highly recommended by his last employer, and all the more acceptable to Mr. and Mrs. Julian, because he was the son of one of Lord Westrey's grooms, and one of the Wykes who were formerly of Dyrbington. And many other things were said, and many additions to their comfort were recorded; but all was said, and this did not escape Edward's quick mind, with such modesty and simplicity, and with so deep a sense of the pleasure and advantage that would arise to their children, that as Edward read, and re-read, it was always with increased admiration.

"Oh blessed home! Oh happy Mayfield!" he would exclaim, "yours are the thoughts and associations to live among. How easy it seems to be grateful, good, and happy, when I think of you!"

At the appointed time Anna Julian arrived

again in London? Jane and Caroline Eastner were with her, and they were escorted by Madame Lefranc, who was not a little proud of her last pupil. There was such a welcome, with such scarcely suppressed astonishment at Anna's improvement in every way, and congratulations such as only very tender friends can venture upon, that the young object of so much interest could only answer by tears. She stifled such demonstrations of joy and gratitude as well as she was able, and succeeded pretty well for some time; but it is on record that in the evening, when she sang her last song to Madame Lefranc's accompaniment, and Mary Westrey, overpowered by surprise and pleasure, exclaimed, "Indeed, mamma, it is wonderful!" such a torrent of tears burst forth as could not be suppressed; and that Lady Westrey carried her off to her dressing-room, and praised her, and fondled her, and bid her weep as long as she liked, and kissed her very often, and finally shed tears for company. Then there came a night of peace, and a morning of brightness, and Anna rose early, thankful and happy.

It was quite true that Anna was greatly improved. Not five months had elapsed since she had left the friends who had now welcomed her, but it seemed as if a full year's work of change had been wrought upon her.

Edward was delighted. She submitted very readily to be catechized on what she knew, and took all criticisms in good part. It was pronounced that Anna could not draw, and that to devote any more time to that accomplishment would be only wasting it. But this was the only thing in which she had not succeeded. She was declared to have a decided genius for languages, and her singing was singularly beautiful. It is not surprising then that Edward was delighted. Even Lullingstone put her through a species of examination, conducted with all his boyish quickness, and tenacity of purpose, and at the conclusion knew not which to admire most, her good humour, or her knowledge of such things as she had studied.

All looked forward to the time of leaving London, and seeing Old Court Lullingstone again. At last the day of departure came, and the journey was accomplished, and all arrived at Lullingstone. Lady Westrey had asked Mrs. Julian by letter whether she would like to be at Lullingstone to receive her daughter; but the alternative that had been offered was accepted, and the morning after Anna arrived, she was sent to Mayfield under a promise that when her parents could part with her she should return.

And now it was Anna's turn to be surprised and delighted. Her father and mother looked the same as ever, only her mother's dress was richer in texture than it had been before. Perhaps some change had come upon her father in this respect, but if so, it was so slight as scarcely to be observed. He was, compared with Mayfield, very much what he had been compared with his old home, and Anna thought that she loved him the better for it.

As to Mayfield itself, the most fastidious could not have found much to blame in it. There is no describing the joy that Julian and his wife had in beholding their children at this time. Such feelings are perhaps the nearest to perfect happiness that are allowed to earth. That tall, great, ungainly-figured man would limp about near Anna. The power of speech seemed to be almost gone. It had never been his way to say much when he was pleased, and the greater his happiness the less he could talk about it. And thus in a state of silent jubilation he would follow his daughter about, and contemplate her as if she had been some rare thing never seen before.

"You must get a piano-forte for me, father," said Anna; "do you know that I can sing?"

"You shall have it, my child. Do you sing *well*, Anna—are you admired, my child?"

Anna laughed, such a light happy gay musical laugh, and threw her arms round her father, and held up her sweet face to him for a kiss, and said, "Oh yes! dear father: but *you* must admire me. I can't be satisfied with any thing else."

That evening Mrs. Herbert came in, "just for one hour," to see Anna after tea. And soon after her arrival Mr. and Mrs. Seaforth appeared, "just for a few minutes," and for the same purpose. Mrs. Herbert had been asking Anna some questions about her studies, then she asked her if she would sing to them, and Anna did so. The room was a very good room for music, and the exercise of the voice was easy in it; moreover Anna was in good voice and in high spirits; she knew that she had loving judges, and so was not nervous; and she wished to please them, and so did her best. She sung a glad-sounding, joy-inspiring melody. It stirred the souls of her listeners to drink in the rich full notes of her trained and flexible voice. And when she ceased there came a burst of praise, with which her light laugh mingled in all the unaffected joy which the easy exercise of an unfailing power gave to her. Only Julian did not praise, yet none had listened with such a hushed spirit as his. He murmured to Mrs. Herbert, who sat beside him: "Does she do it well?" and when her soft answer came, "Beautifully, excellently! I am surprised and delighted;" she, only, saw the look on that father's face. How glad he was!

Then came another day, and Anna and Edward must try their new horses.

"Come, Ned, get your sister on horseback, and mount yourself, I want to know how you like my choice. I used to think that I knew something about a horse. Will you take Michael Wyke with you?"

"Oh no," cried Edward "we will go by ourselves. But this is only our second day at home; you must not expect us to go far. But we will try the horses. I long to do that. And do you know, father, that often at College after receiving your and my mother's kind letters saying how much you had provided for us, I used to sit still, and fancy the delight of seeing you again, and of riding about with Anna, and feeling so proud of her, and so thankful to you."

"Good boy, good dear boy," said Julian, stroking his son's head as he used to do when he was a child. "But there is more to come yet, Edward. Our stores are not all opened yet I believe. But may heaven bless you, my son; and now go; hasten your sister; I want to see you."

Edward and Anna were soon mounted.

"They are beautiful, beautiful," he murmured, as his glance followed them. His heart beat against his gaunt form as they passed on to the entrance-gate. He could see them go through it. Some one outside opened the gate for them, and he heard Edward's voice thanking him, and Anna's head was bowed, and her face was turned so that her father could see it, and he felt almost jealous of the bright smile that dwelt upon it.

Julian hurried on to see who the person was on whom these recognitions had been bestowed. The person proved to be Ralph Seaforth: he advanced

up the drive to meet Julian. Julian felt vexed
and troubled.

"I came on to congratulate you on the sight
that has passed by me," he said, in accents far
more bland than his usually were. "Really, Mr.
Julian, people may talk of money if they please—
but *they* are the things to be proud of. I consider
your son Watermouth property. I always say that
he is our show boy. The school may well be proud
of him. But strong wits and such a figure don't
often go together. He is the handsomest young
man I ever saw."

"I have no fault to find with Edward,—a good
boy, a fond, affectionate, dutiful boy, Captain Seaforth. He's an excellent boy; and his mother and
I are thankful for him."

Julian had turned towards the house, and now,
by the side of his slow-moving, shuffling figure
walked the guest whose presence was certainly not
desired, and whose strong, powerful, largely-de-
veloped and upright form, with a scarcely per-
ceptible swagger in the gait—for Ralph was trying
hard to do the gentlemanly—offered an extraordinary contrast to Julian's appearance. Julian,
because he felt a little annoyed, bowed his head
lower on his chest, and bent his knees more than
ever. So they advanced, each in his way, till
they reached the turf before the drawing-room
window. There sat Mrs. Julian, very calmly busy
at some household sewing. She spoke to the

Captain and asked if he would come in. But Julian had seated himself, not very ceremoniously on a garden sofa which stood by, and Captain Ralph chose to remain with him.

It was a sweet home-scene to look at. The sun's rays lit up all around them, but was screened off from themselves. There was the bright green close-cut turf, and some trees of majestic growth beyond. In places the turf had been removed, and large beds of flowers had been made, and there they now spread out their rainbow colours, and gave forth that delicious scent only known to summer.

"How beautiful this place looks, now that it is kept in good order," said Seaforth.

"Yes," said Julian, growing very thoughtful.

"Though almost in the town, you seem, when here, to be quite in the country."

"Yes."

"And so quiet."

"Very."

"It looks so happy." (No answer.)

"You ought to be the happiest man in the world." (Silence.)

"I don't think that you have much to wish for."

"Ah!"

"What a glorious day this is!"

Julian looked up to the unclouded sky, and down again.

"I am thinking of buying a little property something like this."

Julian gave an excursive glance around him.

"I suppose my brother told you that he has given me ten thousand?"

"No, he didn't."

"Well, he did. He does not want me to go to sea any more, I see that; in fact he told me so; but I must have a little more, and so must work a little longer. Besides, I am a lucky captain. I have been in a thousand dangers and never brought any loss to my employers in my life. That stupid milk-and-water fellow, Brown—he was a great loss to both of you, notwithstanding the gain."

"I can't help that—I am contented—the Browns come in here sometimes, we know them. I like the family—steady, quiet people; I like them very well."

"However, as I was saying, I want to buy some nice little place, and turn steady and quiet myself. People get tired of a wild life after a time. I am tired; I think of settling down."

Julian gave an approving nod of his head.

"My sister, Mrs. Seaforth, encourages me greatly. She says I shall make a good fellow with a little more of her teaching; what think you, Mrs. Julian?"

The window had been opened high, so that Mrs. Julian had heard all that had passed. She had also heard before of the talked-of amendment, for Mrs. Seaforth, good, kind woman, was a believer in it, and looked forward with great satisfaction to its consummation. She argued with herself, that as her husband and herself had no children, it would be such a nice thing to see Ralph, who had long been nothing but a trouble to them, a reformed character, and steadily settled, and married to some good woman, and having a family out of which they might choose an heir. She was such a loving, kind-hearted woman, that she could hope and believe any thing that promised good, even to that most unpromising saying, that "a reformed rake makes the best husband."

Mrs. Julian made the best reply she could. And then after a rather prolonged silence, all at once Ralph made a sudden start in conversation, and began to say how he had seen such trees as one fine specimen from Japan growing in its native clime: and then followed lively accounts of hair-breadth escapes, and droll adventures, so graphically told, that in spite of themselves, the listeners were interested. And this seemed to be all that he had in his mind to accomplish that day, for he then rose to go; and Julian shook hands with him, and Mrs. Julian gave him a sweet gentle smile, which encouraged Seaforth a good deal in more ideas than one.

CHAPTER XII.

POSSIBLE TRIALS IN SIGHT.

After a day or two there came an invitation from Lullingstone to Edward and Anna. Lady Westrey had written to Mrs. Julian, and put it to her to decide whether or not the parents would accompany the children, and Mrs. Julian had answered Lady Westrey, that they would not now. "At present," said Mrs. Julian, "Anna is a child, and she cannot need my care: should she ever need it, I shall at that future time be perhaps better qualified to give it." So Edward and Anna were to go alone to Old Court Lullingstone. Anna had got so accustomed to her friends in London, and there was so much love among them, that this visit had no terrors. The carriage stopped, the grey-headed butler opened the house-door, the young folks bounded into the hall with a "How do you do, Thomas," and an answering, "Very well, thank you, Master Edward," and to Anna, "please, Miss Julian, Hester is waiting to show you to her ladyship's room." Then came dinner: and when all were previously assembled in the drawing-room it was found that Lepard Eastner had arrived, that he might see something of his sisters during the long vacation; and that there was another unexpected addition to the party in one who had hitherto been known to the Lullingstone family only by name. He was a young man of five-and-twenty, and of rather singular appearance. Tall and very slender, of a dark and pale complexion; every feature was handsome, but placed in that head each one wore the appearance of being larger than it ought to be. This made the singularity of his looks. The high-bridged nose was too prominent, the forehead too high; his eyes were too full, and too large, and his mouth too wide; he looked as if he had too many teeth in his head, and they were too long and too white. But about the mouth, and forehead, and eyes there was great beauty of expression. It suggested a mental and moral beauty, and the expression was not false. There was thought on the forehead, feeling in the eye, and action about the mouth, and all good—but the whole man was very quiet; so quiet and still as to be felt, at first, as even too passionless. Such was Sir Giles Morton. He was the only child of one who had been Lord Westrey's friend. He had been for four years abroad, and had lately returned to attend his father and mother on their death-beds. Now he had accepted Lord Westrey's invitation to Lullingstone, to make acquaintance with him and his family. When Anna and Mary entered the room Sir Giles Morton was talking to Lady Westrey. Lord Westrey took Mary's hand and introduced her, and Edward, who was watching them, saw a sudden start and a changed look, which to his, a little jealous heart, said that Sir Giles admired her. This is set down as Edward's first pang—as his first *sight* of possible misery and disappointment. Lord Westrey's wards were also there.

The two girls were rather pretty, and Madame Lefranc's taste in dress being unimpeachable, they contrived to look better than other girls would have looked. Old family prophets of good had already said that they would be very handsome as women. Edward thought them beyond all calculation inferior to Mary Westrey. They seemed to be just like the rest of the world, and Mary was immeasurably above the world's standard. So Edward talked to his new acquaintance a short time, and felt himself by their side to be a man of very mature judgment, and of considerable discernment in those things which make an agreeable woman. But still, while he tried to do his best to those to whom Lady Westrey had introduced him, two things vexed him, made him hot, and nervous, and feverish, and kept his cheek warm, and his heart throbbing. They were, Sir Giles Morton, not talking to Mary, but looking at her aside, furtively, again and again, and as he looked at nothing else; and Lepard Eastner in the midst of a grand career with his sister Anna.

To his great relief dinner was announced. Sir Giles Morton gave Lady Westrey his arm, and then Lord Westrey said, " Now boys and girls, run you on before us, if you please," Lepard Eastner looked at Anna with a smile, as if he would have liked more ceremony, and to have given her his arm, and then shook his head, as if to say that it would not do to rebel, and this made Anna blush; and Edward, who hated Lepard's audacity at that moment more than ever, felt very angry, and so the "boys and girls," with the passions and feelings of men and women struggling in their hearts, walked on as their host directed them.

But dinner was not so great a relief to Edward as he had expected it would be. It seemed to him that no one talked but Anna and Lepard Eastner, and Lepard talked very loudly, and it seemed to Edward's sensibilities as if this manner of his drew attention disagreeably on Anna, and made her appear to be altogether unlike her natural self. Edward was nervously exaggerating things, but his misery was real. He felt as if every morsel was choking him; he was saying to himself that people would remark Anna as not being gentle, modest, retiring, and all that makes girlhood attractive; that Anna would get the character of being all that she was not. But dinner was over at last, and soon after the ladies retired. And after that Lord Westrey and Sir Giles Morton took a turn on the terrace; Lepard, saying that he was going to the drawing-room, disappeared; and Edward leaned back in a chair sorrowful—really suffering, so much had his delicacy of mind been wrought upon, and meditating on the possible trials of a rising man. After a time he heard his own name spoken close by the window. He started up. It was Lord Westrey's voice in conversation with Sir Giles. They passed by, and Edward stepped from the low window to the ground, and stood out in the open air. He saw them turn back from the farthest end of the terrace, and then he turned away to enter the house by the door. Lord Westrey called after him, and Edward turned back. "Here," he said, "I have been telling Sir Giles your history. It is that which you need never be ashamed of." By this time Sir Giles and Edward had exchanged smiles; and Sir Giles followed up his smile by offering his hand, which Edward took very readily; then Lord Westrey said, "That's right; I should like you to be friends;" and all the troubled thoughts that had lately oppressed his mind cleared quickly off. Sir Giles Morton's remarkable countenance wore a deepened expression as Lord Westrey spoke. He looked full on Edward, and it seemed as if every peculiarity passed away, and his face grew gradually overspread with a wondrous beauty.

An exquisite sense of happiness thrilled to the bottom of Edward's boyish heart; he felt as if a sweet flattery, which he might believe, had been whispered in his ear, and as if the charmed accents still lingered in tender music on the air around, heard only by himself. He could not answer; he turned and walked by Sir Giles Morton's side. There was the thought in his mind of the power that dwelt in his companion. Suddenly came another thought—"What if he exercise it upon *her*?"

Edward could stay no longer with his friends. He made some excuse, and passed quickly into the house. He rushed to his own room. He clasped his hands and looked upwards with a real agony in his heart.

He paced up and down, and tried to recover himself. The struggle was long, but his efforts were powerful and he succeeded. Again the youth stood calm and collected; the deep well-spring of passion was still again. He could gaze on its unruffled surface, and look into its farthest depths. He stood still, absorbed in this examination. Then, murmuring low, as if appealing to a higher power, and pleading his cause with it, he said: "If I deserve her—if I bear up against *all* that may occur, and never lose hope—if amid temptation I yet never take, for one instant, the thoughts of my heart away from her—if I never try to win her love before the time when she may give it nobly—if I keep firmly fixed in my soul the resolution that, should I lose my hopes, she shall never know of their having existed—if I walk thus circumspectly—." Once more with regular beatings the work of life went on. Again the clear strong voice of early years issued in untrembling tones; and Edward, with a light step, was in the drawing-room again. Anna was singing, and Madame Lefranc was playing the accompaniment. There was silence in the room, all but the music. It was a song in which music and poetry had united to charm, and Anna was singing with remarkable feeling. Edward stood aside and studied this sister of his. There was more in her voice than any teaching could have infused into it. It was no more the voice of the timid child who plied her needle in her father's workshop, and sung stories of woods and fields. It was the voice of that child, possessed of a woman's heart, and who had learnt a woman's lesson—to *feel*.

There was a burst of applause. "Our thanks must be offered to *you*," said Sir Giles Morton to Mary Westrey, "for having obtained us such a treat."

"I was sure you would like it," exclaimed Mary.

"You were very good about it," said Sir Giles to Anna, "for you evidently would rather not have sung that song, and yet, when *made* to sing it, you did your best."

"Oh yes!" answered Anna, "of course I would do my best. I should never deserve to sing here at all, if I did not do my *very* best; always, when asked to do any thing here, I shall do my best."

"I should like one day to hear that song again; one day, when you don't feel any real disinclination to it, will you sing it again?"

"Oh yes!" cried Mary Westrey, answering for her, "I am sure that Anna will sing it any day. We will have a select party in mamma's room, shall it be to-morrow, Anna?"

Anna made no reply.

"Anna!" exclaimed Lullingstone, in a peevish voice, a few minutes afterwards, as she passed a couch on which he was stretching himself.

"Well," she said, and stopped.

He raised himself, and said, "Here, come here. Sit by me, Anna, I want to say something to you." Then with great energy, "And I *must* say it to you, I declare that I shall not be happy again till I have said it to you?"

Anna sat down by the impetuous Lullingstone's side, and asked what he had to say. There certainly was something in his face which spoke of a discomposed state of mind.

"So you have sung a very fine, difficult, wonderful song, and every body has admired your singing exceedingly?"

"I suppose so," said Anna, with a smile.

"Well, then, *not* every body, Anna;" answered

Lullingstone with very determined emphasis, "for *I* did not admire it. I can't bear that song; and if you ever sing it again;" and he started to an upright position, and looked at her fixedly; "if you ever sing it again, Anna, you must let me know beforehand, that I may go away. It will be bad enough to know that you are singing it, but to hear it—Oh, Anna, I hate that song!"

"Don't go away," said Anna, very softly, and detaining him as he was going to rise, "tell me a little more."

He shook his head.

"No, no," she said, still holding him, "I want to know more—what, perhaps, only you will tell me. Don't go, I say."

Lullingstone looked at her. He sat down in a pacified and softened mood.

"Why don't you like me to sing that song? Tell me all that you feel."

"Because it is a theatrical song, and not fit for you."

"But so many songs are theatrical songs, and you like them."

"But this is not fit for you—you are doing yourself injustice when you sing it."

"But how? why? explain it to me."

"I can't explain it," said Lullingstone.

"But you can tell me what you feel—that will be sufficient explanation for me," urged Anna.

"Do you really wish to know?"

"Yes."

"If you were to have ten guineas for it, I should have liked it very well."

"You are a provoking boy. It is impossible to understand you!"

"Well, then, listen to me. If you had been doing it for money, I should have believed that you were just only acting. To throw meaning into your song, and to *appear* to feel all you said and sung, would not *then* argue that you did feel it, but only that you were perfect in the profession which you had chosen. Do you know, Anna," he said with great animation, "that no one on earth could have sung that song better than you did it?"

"And yet you did not like it?"

"No, Anna, I hated it, because for you to do it so well looked as if you felt it *really;* as if there could be no pretence about it; as if you realized all you sung; as if you were *in love.*"

"You are a very dear, kind foster-brother," said Anna; "And now, Lullingstone, I promise you, in return for your kindness, that I will never sing that song again—*never*, not even in idle amusement; and Lullingstone—*I am very much obliged to you.*"

"I am happy again!" cried Lullingstone; "Do you know, Anna," he went on, "I have been thinking for the last half hour what it was best to do. Whether I should tell Mr. Parker, or try to make Edward understand me, or—"

"You have done the best thing of all," interrupted Anna; "you have told me yourself—always do as kindly by me, and then you will be my friend."

"What can you be talking about?" exclaimed Lepard Eastner, seating himself by their side, "I heard something about friendship—are you offering friendship, Lullingstone? a very grave proposal from one of your years, I think. But," turning to Anna, "rather a treacherous gift is friendship sometimes. Ah?—do you understand me?"

Anna blushed, and Lepard laughed merrily, and Lullingstone got up slowly, and moved lazily off towards his father's chair.

Mary Westrey had been occupying a seat by her father's side. She had seen these last movements. When her brother approached she said: "Will you sit here, Lullingstone?" and rose up; "Are you going away?" asked the boy languidly.

"I am going to speak to Edward Julian," she said, glancing towards a distant part of the room where Edward was seated.

Lullingstone's eyes shot a sudden radiance, like that which now and then illumined the liquid depths of his beautiful sister's. She returned it with a sparkling look of love, and of woman's petting fondness. But in those beams there had been a language. The boy sat down in the offered seat, and watched his beautiful sister's stately steps as she passed down the room to where Edward sat; and then the usual expression came back to his face, and he began to talk to his father, and was again the same boy as usual.

"Anna looks well to-night," said Mary to Edward Julian.

Edward looked up inquiringly, for it was not usual for Mary to make common-place remarks.

"She is very animated to-night," said Mary again.

"She is happy where every one is kind to her," said Edward.

"Is Lepard Eastner kind to her?" asked Mary, looking towards that end of the room where they were sitting.

"Lepard Eastner, Lepard Eastner," repeated Julian, "Miss Westrey, you never make unkind remarks—I think that you never needlessly say things to hurt one—but see—she is getting up—she does not seem to enjoy his society—she is looking—"

"Very pretty, and rather confused," said Mary.

"Now, Mr. Edward Julian, let me tell you something; as a very old friend let me speak to you; Lepard Eastner is *a fortune-hunter*. He told me himself, half an hour before dinner, that he had fallen in love at first sight. He has been acting the thing out ever since. But don't be alarmed, Edward Julian; he will not propose to-night; not even during his stay here; he will only try to fasten himself upon Anna's mind, and if no easier, or more promising prize comes in his way between this and next year, he will then make her an offer, and marry her too if your father will give her as much as Lepard Eastner requires."

Edward felt quite out of breath. He could only think of what Lepard had said, and begin repeating—" He told you—"

" He told me he was the victim of love at first sight, and he told me so that I might repeat it to Anna."

" But you did not tell her."

" Of course not. Don't you understand? I am telling *you* instead. I think it a better plan!"

Edward felt that that day had been full of experience to him. But if he felt this, no less did Anna feel it. To her the great events had been her own feelings when she sung, and Lullingstone's observations.

There rose before her the pretty room in the old home, and the mind's eye was riveted on the things then really seen—Harold's fixed parting gaze. The eloquent, fearless, noble expression of his dilated eye was again upon her—it had meant something—what? it had surely promised something—what?

" There never was a purer mind, a more noble heart, a sincerer spirit—altogether a finer character than his," was the thought of Anna's heart. She had never made the admission so clearly to herself before, "I could not have sung *that* song so well, if I had never known him," was the next admission, "I will never sing it again—never in company—only in my own heart."

CHAPTER XIII.

OF THINGS WHICH COLOUR LIFE.

THREE weeks passed, and then Edward and Anna were again asked to visit Old Court Lullingstone; and again they went. It would be their last visit for the present, for October was come, and Anna was to return soon with Madame Lefranc, and Edward would be almost immediately going back to college. Anna was delighted to be among her friends again, for her next absence was to be till the following July, and the time seemed long enough for leave-takings of a serious kind. With the exception of Sir Giles Morton the party at Lullingstone was the same that it had been before. Sir Giles had left Lullingstone about a week. He had even called at Mayfield with Lord Westrey; and after that had called again by himself to see Edward, and at each visit had staid some time, and made every one delighted with him. But now he was gone, and Edward, notwithstanding certain fears which lived always in his heart, was, on the whole, sorry. He felt that he was a friend.

"Anna, when you return next midsummer, you

are going to stay at home, always?" said Lullingstone to her the first evening.

"Yes. I shall be very glad. I shall like to be always living at home," said Anna.

"You will be almost seventeen and a half."

"Very true—you know my age by your own."

"And Edward will be twenty, and thinking of his examination, and his degree; and I shall be at college. I shall like being there while Edward is there."

"Yes: he will like it very much, too."

"I shall be *so glad* to see you when you come back again. Everybody here loves you, Anna, I hope that you will not be altered."

"Only improved, Lullingstone," said Anna smiling. "You will like to feel that I am improved?"

"Like it!" exclaimed the youth. "Do you know, Anna, that I really believe that nothing on earth gives me so much pleasure as to hear you praised, and to know that you deserve it."

Lullingstone spoke so impetuously, and assumed an attitude to denote his sincerity which had about it so much that looked fierce and warlike, that Anna laughed merrily. And then, making her friend sit down, they chattered on upon subjects less exciting.

Anna would have been in a state of unbounded happiness during this visit but for Lepard Eastner. He troubled her greatly. Always by her side in the house and out of the house; and, what Anna felt as a very serious injury, always making it look as if she liked it, and was inducing him—almost commanding him to come near her.

One day his assiduities had become so teazing during a walk that, on her return, as she walked up stairs to her room, Mary Westrey saw tears in her eyes. So then putting her arms round Anna's waist she went with her to her room, and this kindness made Anna's tears actually fall. Mary said nothing till she stood within the room, and then, gently turning Anna towards her, and holding up her troubled face, and kissing it, she said:

"Now, Anna, don't grieve—these trifles are not worth grief. For your comfort you may know that we all understand—all but papa, and he has not seen it. I assure you that if he knew of Lepard's folly he would make him repent it even more bitterly than you would desire. You must take this as an entrance on the experiences of a woman. Something shall come, I'll promise you, Anna"—Mary smiled—"better worth tears and a heavy heart than this."

Anna felt a good deal relieved. But she could not be quite philosophical about Lepard Eastner, though she had resolved to be so. The next morning when she heard Lord Westrey say to his daughter that he wished to take her to Dyrbington, she had so great a dread of being thrown into his company unprotected, that she immediately sent a message by Edward to her mother to say that she would spend the morning at Mayfield. To do this, she had to run out of the room and catch Edward on the terrace. But when, on accomplishing this sudden determination, she returned to the breakfast-room, she heard Mary Westrey saying:

"Thank you, papa, I will tell Anna, she will like to go very much."

"Well, tell Anna," said Lord Westrey; and then added, "and perhaps it is as well; I shall like to take her." Mary moved towards the door, and met Anna.

"You are to go to Dyrbington with papa and me."

"Oh, I should so much like to go—but——"

"But what?"

"When I heard what made me think that I was to be left alone—Oh, don't laugh—don't look as if your heart was laughing at me, I really have had cause for vexation."

"Ah, but to return; when you heard—go on, please."

"I sent a message to my mother, to bid her send for me."

"What was she to send?"

"My horse—Wyke was to lead it."

"Very nice. It will arrive in time exactly. Papa only hesitated because he thought that Brown Bess would be too spirited for you. He can send back by the servant to say that you are gone to Dyrbington."

"Where is Edward?" said Lord Westrey at this moment.

"Gone to Mayfield," replied Anna.

"Indeed! I am sorry; my business at Dyrbington refers to him. Is he really gone?"

"Yes, certainly, I am very sorry."

"Well, if he be not at home in proper time, we will ride that way, and catch him if we can. Will you be ready at two o'clock, young ladies?"

The hour came, and Lord Westrey and his companions set out.

Edward had not arrived, so they went first to Mayfield. There, there was a pause but of only a short time. The ladies did not get off their horses, but remained at the door, and Mr. and Mrs. Julian stood there, talking to them, except when first one and then the other were called on to join the conference within. The matter under consultation was, whether or not Edward would like to have the living of Dyrbington held for him, till he were able to take it. Mr. Dyrbington had written to Lord Westrey to ask him to appoint some one, and had said that, had the vacancy occurred at a time when Edward Julian could have filled it, he should, though he knew his family only by report, have offered it to him. It seemed to Lord Westrey that, being thus in possession of Mr. Dyrbington's mind on the subject, some arrangement might be come to, if Edward wished it, and that he might in three years be Vicar of Dyrbington.

Edward had never had so difficult a question put to him to decide upon in his life. To look so far into the future! He had often looked into it, but it was to see there only Mary Westrey.

But could he think of her as the wife of the Vicar of Dyrbington. He hesitated,—he was wretchedly confused. He had to give an instant answer of plain 'yes,' or 'no,' and all the while the soft silvery tones of the voice of her he loved was heard alternately with his mother's, and made it impossible for him to speak as he was expected to speak.

At last a few vigorous words burst forth: "Lord Westrey," he said, "I am ambitious; I can scarcely answer you; to be Vicar of Dyrbington *might* suit my views, but if, on the time coming, it did not agree with my ambition I could not take it. How then in this uncertainty,—uncertainty in every thing but my fixed ambition after greatness,—can I answer you? I might say 'no,' at once, and I am inclined to say so; but then I might seem ungrateful, unkind, imprudent; I might say 'yes,' but when the time came, if it did not agree with my intentions for myself, how should I avoid the appearance of having trifled with you?"

"By saying what you have now said, you have

already avoided. it," said Lord Westrey, "I am glad that you are ambitious. For you, dear Edward, it is safe. And as for this question of the Vicarage of Dyrbington, we will consider it settled. I know a man, James Merit, he was tutor to Eastner for a short time, and had plenty of trouble with him, I believe; he will be glad to take it for three years, and then he can vacate for you, if you please. I am sure that this will please Dyrbington, and we will write to the bishop about it to-night. I have no doubt of its being arranged. I shall be back by dinner as usual. You shall then hear what more there may be to say."

Lord Westrey was standing at the door, going to remount his horse.

"We have been telling Miss Mary," said Mrs. Julian, "that the afternoon promises a less pleasant ride than she expects."

"Do you think it will rain?" said Lord Westrey carelessly; for, in truth, his mind was full of Edward.

"Do you think it wise of them to venture?"

"I want Anna to see Dyrbington."

"She will enjoy that, but still——"

"Oh, it will be nothing," said Lord Westrey gaily: and in a minute they were gone.

"He will see the coming storm on the common," said Mrs. Julian to herself, "he can turn back when there. It is as short a way to Lullingstone, as the way from here. They are in good hands, but there will surely be a storm."

There came a low moan, borne from far in the distance it seemed, and then a short sudden gust. The evergreens shook as if some strong hand had been a moment among their branches, and then all was still, and there was a feeling of oppressive heat. Mrs. Julian looked around her, shook her head, and murmured—"They will never go on"—and then went into the house.

Lord Westrey and his companions rode through Watermouth, then up two steep streets, and this brought them to that open place now long known to the reader. Mary had been saying that it was a pleasanter day for riding than if the sun had not been shrouded by such full dark clouds, but Anna felt that there was something in the air that made her tremble, and she was glad to be on her own horse, and not on spirited Brown Bess.

Lord Westrey urged them on. "Come," he said, "there will be bad weather before night, but I must see Dyrbington to-day." They increased their pace, and passed at full speed over the plain where Anna had so often wandered as a child—how long ago it seemed to be,—when Edward had shown her the sky-lark's nest laid so lowly on the ground among the heather and furze, and where, always, her first spring nosegays of violets and cowslips had been plucked. On another day she might have spoken of this to Mary, who always made an excellent listener when such were the topics; but now, they were going like people pursued, and Anna felt as she passed these scenes, and as the hurried thoughts that belonged to them chased each other through her mind, that it was as if she were flying from that well-remembered past into an unknown future. Once or twice as a child she had seen Dyrbington. She could not be said to remember any thing of it; but she liked the thought of seeing it now, and being made known to its strange occupant. On still they went at their utmost speed, bending their heads low before the gusts of wind which came in strange caprice upon them.

Anna felt that there was something in that ride and its circumstances which matched well with the life which had come to her. It seemed like a fleeing from the past, from the well-loved, well-remembered past, and a reckless hurrying into the unknown future. Often in after-life she remembered her ride to Dyrbington.

As they got towards the forest a few drops of rain fell. They came slowly, but they fell large and heavily. Lord Westrey drew up, and spoke to some one. Anna raised her head. She had scarcely seen where she was going while her horse had kept pace with its companions, and she had bent before the wind. She looked up—and there Lyas Norwood stood answering Lord Westrey's questions. A thrill passed through every nerve when Anna felt his eyes upon her. How often, in the old house, he had stroked her golden hair, and twisted her child's soft curls around his finger, and then looked in her mother's face with an expression which, even at that innocent age, she had known to be one of admiration. And then the thought of Harold—that unfathomed feeling connected with him—and with all this the thought of herself, where she was, and as she was! Confusion for a moment overpowered her. A host of thoughts and feelings sent the tears into her eyes. There they sparkled, but did not fall; for, true to her own excellent simplicity of character, she rallied at the thought of Lyas being a friend: and meeting the full gaze of his dark eyes with a smile, she extended her hand, and spoke to him: "Oh, Lyas, how do you do—it is a long time since I saw you last?"

The dark eye sparkled like a diamond. There came an expression over the man's face; no language could describe its intensity. In his own graceful way he drew up his figure, and, before replying to Lord Westrey, answered Anna. But he did not advance a step towards her; there was a motion of the head which bade her withdraw her hand; and yet a smile which told her that she had done well to offer it.

"It is long," he said—"long; yet longer reckoned by events, than by days and hours.

Not only to you, but to me;" and then he turned to Lord Westrey, and without speaking, seemed by his manner to denote that he was now at his service.

While these few words had been passing the storm had suddenly hushed. Lord Westrey looked at the clouds for a moment, and seemed satisfied that the danger was over. "We were going to ask your advice," he said. "My inquiries should have been about the storm, only nature has answered me already."

"Hark!" said Lyas. A lowing sound was heard. "That is nature's answer, my lord. She wears false smiles sometimes; you would be better without your companions."

"But having them, the question is what I am to do with them?" said Lord Westrey.

"Turn your horses' heads homewards, and speed there as fast as you came here," said Norwood.

"But I must see Dyrbington to-night. I have business with him. I really must get there if possible."

"To Dyrbington!—and are these going there with you?"

"Yes; I think that we shall get there pretty well; we may shelter there, and get, after the storm, a fair ride home. I believe that we must go on; come then, come; farewell, Lyas."

"Stop, stop," cried Lyas almost with agitation. "I know it will burst before you get there. 'Tis but the wood that hides the sight of it from our eyes. Think of where you are going; of how far—through the forest—and full four miles. Hush! there it is again! Go on yourself if you will, but let these stay with me; or, they will be safer in the open country, let me take them back to Lullingstone."

"You make me hesitate—what—what shall we do?"

"Oh, go on, papa," cried Mary.

"Oh yes; let us go on, Lord Westrey," said Anna.

Lyas Norwood looked from one to the other of the speakers. Anna's eyes were upon him. It seemed to her that his face lighted up strangely on hearing this. He was glad; in spite of his words there was gladness on his face when he heard their resolution, and he waved his hand with a bright smile when they left him, and passed into the forest path.

They rode on as quickly as they could. They spoke little. Anna thought how odd it was that Lyas should see them rush upon the danger he had warned them of, and smile. Mary liked the excitement of the ride and was silent; and Lord Westrey's voice was only heard directing them as to their way, and how to regulate their speed.

Suddenly, there was a change in the light, as if some dark object of enormous size had dropped on the tree tops, and overshadowed them; yet with the darkness there was a tinge, a very slight tinge of lurid red.

"Get on, get on; make the best of this widened path," said Lord Westrey. Anna was leading the way. She urged her horse onward, but he would not go. He planted his fore-feet in the ground, and from his nostrils burst a snort of terror. There was a feeling as if something terrible was encircling them. Anna shut fast her eyes, and bent her head. A low groan burst from her lips: she felt shrinking from the unseen danger.

Then came almost instantly on the flashing lightning the sound as of irregularly fired cannon. The horse jumped round on the first stroke of that fearful sound, he came upon his companions, and in an instant the poor beasts had drawn close together, and stood head to head.

The riders looked on each other by turns; making no effort, for they had no desire, to change the position the creatures had chosen. They stood actually cowering beneath the storm; again and again the same thing occurred, and then there came a sheet of light which seemed to wrap them round.

Yet, once or twice, between the flashes of fierce lightning, Mary thought she saw the figure of a man watching them among the trees, and that that man was Lyas Norwood.

At last the thunder had rolled away. "Now," said

Lord Westrey, "go on as fast as you can—shall I go first?"

"No, no," cried Mary Westrey; "we would rather that you kept us in sight. Papa had better ride behind and watch us—had he not, Anna?"

"Yes, I think so," answered Anna; "so, let me lead the way as before." And her horse, now as willing as herself to proceed, went forward readily, and at as fast a pace as the nature of the ground permitted.

But it was now as if the storm had found a new way of exercising its power. The gusts of wind were frightful. The limbs of the stoutest trees were bent like willow-wands. They creaked horribly above their heads. Small branches were continually falling about them, and the wide green path they were pursuing, was becoming covered with leaves, and small twigs, and autumn buds.

And then, all at once, a sudden calm would come, which in itself seemed terrible at such a time, and yet they welcomed it, unnatural as it felt, for it was a temporary respite from the actual danger that surrounded them.

The stillness had lasted longer than such pauses had done before: the two girls were hoping that the storm had ceased. But now comes a low, very distant sound—almost like the note of the far-off waves—it seems to be a great way from them, beyond the wood, beyond the cultivated country, beyond the untilled lands of Dyrbington; but they hear it plainly, and they know what it is—it is the mysterious sound of storm, and it is coming nearer to them. They know by the increasing volume of that sound that it is hurrying on: it is sweeping along with a force that nothing can resist—the woods feel it, there is a wild motion in every thing around them; its note is as strong as thunder; the blast is upon them, they bend beneath it in horror.

It seemed to pass over their heads, and again came that fearful wrenching sound among the trees above them; and with that sound another, which, small as it was, made them start, and look up. It was like the creaking of timber—where were they? But there was no time to think.

Anna heard her own name uttered in a cry that raised it above all other sounds. "Anna, Anna Julian, this way—stop!"

And rushing towards the riders from a point on their right, and a little in advance of them came Lyas Norwood.

He seized Anna's bridle, and dragged her on her horse into a thicket. His eyes, luminous with the fire of excitement, had fixed themselves on Mary Westrey, and his words, "You, too—come," pierced through her, and she plunged among the brushwood towards her friend's side At the same moment Lord Westrey checked his horse and drew back a step; and again there came that creaking noise, and then a rushing sound which increased till, crashing with a mighty uproar, there fell across the path a huge oak, a very monarch of the woods. It fell close in front of Lord Westrey, and immediately on the mark of the horses' hoofs before him.

"But for you," exclaimed Lord Westrey, "but for you, Lyas—what must have been?"

"You had better proceed now," said Norwood, after a few minutes, "I believe that the tempest has done its worst. You will soon be out of the dangers of the forest, and the sooner the better—you should now proceed."

They obeyed. They were again on their way, and after a ride of no little fear—for they shuddered at the storm, and could sometimes scarcely keep their seats—they arrived safely at the summit of the hill leading to the back entrance to Dyrbington.

The reader has visited Dyrbington before, with Lullingstone and Mary some time since. The entrance was effected in the same way. But as they dismounted to let their horses pass through the little door into the court, Norwood again appeared. Springing past them, with the agility of a deer, he set himself to do the attendant's part, and, taking the horses, proceeded to summon Reuben and lead them to the stable.

In the same old way Martha made sure of the character of her guests before she opened the door of the inner court. And after the old fashion they all stood in the spacious kitchen while Mr. Dyrbington was being informed of their arrival. Only Martha was more gracious in manner than usual; there never was any coldness in Martha's heart— and she looked with wondering welcome at such visitors on such a day; and when she heard of the dangers of their ride she thanked God, and said how the tempest had made her tremble even by her kitchen hearth; and how the fierce lightning had entered the apartment and flashed upon the wall; and how little she had thought that such as they had been encountering its fury.

And now that they were safely housed, the fury of the tempest again rose high. It beat against the old house as though in anger that its wall opposed its strength, and neither fell nor shook before it. Again and again it seemed to return to the attack, and to wrap it round in its fierce embrace with a flapping sound and a threatening howl, and again and again to die away with a stifling sigh of disappointment.

The two girls were standing by the kitchen fire, and old Martha had taken their hats from off their heads, and had freed their throats from their scarfs, and done such other services as she could. Lord Westrey was with Mr. Dyrbington. Full half-an-hour their conference lasted, and then his voice was heard saying that Mary and Anna were to come to them.

Mary knew the way to Mr Dyrbington's room, and Anna followed her as they proceeded to it quickly. All things were pretty much the same as the reader has already seen. The time that had elapsed had made no visible change on Mr. Dyrbington, and he welcomed his young guests kindly.

Lord Westrey had explained to Mr. Dyrbington how Edward Julian felt towards the living to which an appointment was now to be made. He had said that Merit would hold the living till Edward was of age to take it, provided that it should then be thought an eligible thing for him. Mr. Dyrbington had listened attentively; and having heard all that Lord Westrey had to say he had immediately acquiesced. He only stipulated that his friend should take all the trouble, which Lord Westrey was very ready to do.

"Though I never saw the youth I have thought a good deal about him—and I have heard a little, and what I heard pleased me. Besides, he is the son of one whose family once served mine in other days, Westrey—alas!" exclaimed Mr. Dyrbington, his constitutional nervousness making his frame tremble as he spoke—"Alas! I fear in better —yes, better times!"

"Edward would grace any time," replied Lord Westrey.

Mr. Dyrbington went on. "His father hoarded —yes, he was a strange man; there has been for several generations an oddness about them. I talked to him years back—yes, he married a Frampton."

Mr. Dyrbington ceased speaking. It had been a great exertion to him to say so much. Every sentence had come forth with an effort. He had drawn each breath with a gasp. And now he ceased, as if mind and body had done its utmost, and he fell back in his chair, and raised his dark eyebrows as if with difficulty, and throwing back his head cast a glance, painful from the smile that lingered on it, on Lord Westrey. Then he shook his head and went on speaking, but in a whisper, for all tone had departed, and only articulate breathings issued from his lips: "Ah, Westrey, I am old now. This can't last long. I am the last of a long race; the last of a line loaded with this world's honours, and yet, ever since——"

"I understand you," said Lord Westrey.

"Marked out, marked out as objects of Heaven's displeasure, seldom dying the deaths of other men, and ever finding some new terror on their way to distinguish them from their kind. At length on me, the last, there fell on my mind the meaning, the interpretation of all this, and then my mark fell here"—Mr. Dyrbington placed his hand on his high and noble-looking forehead—"and yet it was not madness; for madness would have been happiness, but not for a moment have

I been mad—the mark placed on me was an intellectual gift, a clearness of discrimination, a power of knowing and feeling the *truth*. Yes, I am the last! To know *that* truth, to know that we perpetrated the crime, and so incurred the punishment; to know that the curse surely fell, and as surely descended, and is now on me: to know *that*, was to be the last of my race; to plead guilty before my GOD, and die."

The words ceased, and the eye-lids closed. Lord Westrey, with a quick feeling of alarm, stepped forward and placed his fingers on the long thin skeleton hand which was still resting on the table—it was as cold as ice. The veins which stood prominent, like blue cords binding the bones together, seemed to have no life within their channels, and a thrill of horror attendant on the thought that he was really dead, made Lord Westrey groan aloud. The sound roused the unfortunate being in whose cause it had been uttered. The weary eye-lids were raised, and from the depths of their cavernous retreats the eyes smiled that smile of tender benevolence which had never deserted them.

"I was afraid that you were ill, worse, suddenly worse; are you feeling ill, Dyrbington?"

"No, my friend, no," he answered, "only nature requires these moments of rest. She has lost her elasticity, and suddenly drops prostrate: but a few minutes are enough to recover the little strength that now suffices to carry on this state. I am well now, Westrey; did I frighten you?"

"If you are sufficiently well I will call in more company."

"Ah yes, your children. I always like to see them. God preserve me from ever seeing them other than they are. I had forgotten that they might be here. Yes, Westrey, call them, do."

"Of my children, Mary only is come," replied Lord Westrey. "But with her came a friend, and one whom I thought you would like to see—Anna Julian. Still, she does not expect to see you, so put no restraint upon your wishes."

"But I *should* like to see her," replied Mr. Dyrbington, with animation. "I have heard of her, too. Westrey, you judged rightly. I am quite anxious to see her—Anna Julian; send for her. But did they come with you through this storm? What, Westrey? yes; was it possible? those two young girls, and my fair cousin Mary, Ah——" But Mr. Dyrbington could say no more. He leaned back again in his chair for a moment's rest.

Some quick emotions knocked at Anna Julian's heart as she entered the room with Mary Westrey. Darkness, age, and blight, seemed around her; in an inexplicable way she felt their existence. Then those heaped-up books—surely the scent of the grave was upon them; and that ponderous table of black oak. But above all, Mr. Dyrbington himself. Mary sprang gracefully to his side. Her warm, white, jewelled little hand was within his fingers, and she looked as if she would have placed a kiss on his cold brow had she dared. She dared not, but she looked her love and interest, and her words, "Dear Mr. Dyrbington!" said more than people heard.

Mr. Dyrbington rose; he was one of the good old school, and would not be persuaded, when seeing a lady for the first time, to receive her sitting. He returned Mary's greeting, and rose to welcome Anna. She advanced almost trembling; she had never felt so shy before—it was more than shyness, she felt quite like one in fear. But her host's smile reassured her a little, and she tried to look up at him calmly. For a moment his form was as commanding as it had ever been, and something of his former beauty passed across his face, no sooner seen than gone like a winter sunbeam on a ruined tower, but leaving a loved memory behind.

"You are welcome to Dyrbington, Miss Julian. And I will hope that you may like it well enough to accompany your friends again, when, in love and charity, they visit—they visit"—his frame shrunk visibly, he made a tottering step, and again he had sunk and fallen—dropped almost out of form and shape—he had fallen into his usual seat, and there, like a thing all crushed and broken, huddled as it were in a corner, he remained sunk, and in no attitude describable as belonging to life, till nature had recovered the effort he had demanded of her, and his heart the flow of thought with which his own words had overwhelmed it.

This, in an ordinary person, would have filled Anna Julian with alarm; but seeing that Mary and her father preserved a quiet demeanour, she too waited till, as she expected, Mr. Dyrbington recovered. Then came, as ever, that loving smile, and he beckoned Anna towards him. Mary stepped back for Anna to take her place, and Mr. Dyrbington looked at her kindly. She stood in her riding dress, her head uncovered, and masses of golden hair twisted their curling length about her face. He looked in her blue eyes till they smiled, and the conscious blush very slowly and faintly mounted up her cheek. He took her hand, and still seemed to be closely examining her features. Then he spoke.

"Were you ever here before?"

"I have been with my parents in the village, and through the grounds; but I was never inside this house till now."

"Have you been often to Dyrbington?"

"Only twice."

"With whom?"

"I always walked about with my father. He, each time, hired a light covered cart at Watermouth, and put up at the little inn in the village, where the large elm tree grows; and while my father and I walked about, my mother saw those whom she knew. I remember her seeing an old woman called Wyke, and another of her own name. They are dead now."

"That is well," said Mr. Dyrbington; "for now that you are in other circumstances, and in such company"—glancing towards Lord Westrey—"you could not see them any more."

The faint blush on Anna's cheek grew ruby red, she withdrew her hand from Mr. Dyrbington's, and retreated a step from him. She looked at him, but his face was unmoved, he seemed to wait for her to speak.

"The poor and the lowly gave me life; and this day a man, poor and low, has saved my life. I owe Lord Westrey a great deal; more than I can repay. He has done for us what no one else would have done, and what we could not have done for ourselves; and I love his family. But my first affections, my earliest feelings of admiration, and my purest joys were given and found in a rank of life, which I will never forget! Oh! Mr. Dyrbington!" exclaimed Anna, the tears coursing down her cheeks—

"Stop," he said, "enough; I had my reasons for trying you, I have tried you, I am satisfied. Now, forgive me—and if you want to have amends made you for what I have caused you to suffer, hear this—you have made me feel a sweeter joy than has visited my heart for years! But what is the meaning of your life having been saved? Tell me, Westrey."

Then Lord Westrey gave the account of their passage through the storm, and this brought him to say that the time for departure had arrived, and he went to the window to see what the weather might be. The sky was completely overshadowed with dark clouds, and the rain poured in torrents.

"Is it impossible for them to go," said Mr. Dyrbington.

"It is certainly very bad," said Lord Westrey, looking very much perplexed.

"For yourself it is too bad also; I think so indeed, Westrey."

Lord Westrey smiled, but shook his head—"Nay, *I* must go," he said.

"Well, if you *must;* then go, and leave them here."

"Leave them with you? Leave Anna and Mary here?"

"Yes! They shall be taken good care of. Martha shall arrange for them. Send as early as you please to-morrow, but don't attempt to take them back in such weather as this. You know that there is one room in the house kept aired and cleaned, the room occupied four times a year, at least, by my trusty lawyer and counsellor,—Yes, yes, Westrey—leave them."

"I will leave them, and leave them gladly, but

on one condition," said Lord Westrey. "They are not to disturb you. You are not to attempt any exertion, you are not to try to amuse them."

Mr. Dyrbington gave a sad smile, as much as to say that such powers had ceased to belong to him. Lord Westrey continued.

"They will find something to do. If I go now, they may stay with you for half-an-hour, then they are to go to the room prepared for them, and you are not to see them any more to-night."

"That will suit me," said Mr. Dyrbington. "My hours are of a primitive sort enough; in less than an hour I shall have my last meal, and after that I seldom—never, except of necessity—see any one. So your plan agrees with my habits, and things shall be as you say."

CHAPTER XIV.

THE NIGHT.

Martha had never been so truly happy since she had lived with her beloved old master. She conducted the ladies to their rooms, talking all the way.

The passages seemed vault-like as they followed Martha's not very brilliant lamp, and her voice as she preceded them sounded hollow, and awoke strange echoes through their unfurnished lengths, "Martha, be sure and don't forget us to-morrow," said Mary. "I never knew my way about here, you know; and there is such a union of the awful and the mysterious in the storm without, and ourselves within, that I could never recognize any thing to-morrow as the things I have seen to-day."

"I won't forget you, Miss Mary—forget—bless you! I shall never forget either you or this day as long as ever I live."

"How far are you going, Martha? We have been to the right and the left, and up and down stairs, and walked half-a-mile already. What a distance it seems! Dear Martha, are you really quite alone here?"

"Alone!" ejaculated Martha; "why there's master!"

"Yes, but you and master, is that all?"

"Reuben sleeps over the coach-house," was the rather indirect reply.

"And you and Mr. Dyrbington actually live alone in this immense place?"

"Why, dear Miss Mary," answered Martha rather impatiently, "who else do you think is here? Do you think the pictures take to talking and keeping us company?"

"Martha, what a dreadful idea! I am so sorry you said it. Anna, are you feeling frightened? I can't tell what's the matter with me; I really think that I must be afraid."

"There!" said Martha, triumphantly throwing open a door. The two girls entered, and she followed them. A sufficiently brilliant passage lamp, pressed into the present service, united to the light of a blazing fire, shed a warm, glad glow on the ruby-coloured damask hangings of an apartment magnificently furnished. It could not be seen without a start of astonishment. Even to one whose eyes had from infancy been accustomed to sights of splendour, it looked what it was— dazzling with gold and colour.

"I never saw this room before!" exclaimed

Mary; "Mr. Dyrbington once showed us the state rooms—you recollect it, Martha,—but we were never shown this."

"I hope he has forgotten it," said Martha, with a significant look. "You can say to-morrow that you slept in Mr. Benson's room, and you need not say that there is any thing uncommon in it. Mr. Benson *does* sleep in the room into which that door opens; you see most of these rooms open one into the other; and there you will sleep too, and all things are right and dry I can tell you."

"But what room is this? There must have been some reason for such a gorgeous display; and the furniture is not old; tell us all about it, Martha."

"It was fitted up for *her*. This was to have been her sitting room, and that where you will sleep, her dressing room, and there," pointing to a door opposite that which led to the sleeping apartment, "*that* was to have been *their* bed-room."

"*Whose?*" ejaculated Mary.

"Why master's and hers," said Martha, whispering as if she feared that the walls might hear her. "She ran off, you know; the last trouble, poor man; you have heard, Miss Mary?"

"Ah; yes, yes," said Mary; "I know. Dear Mr. Dyrbington! and he loved her?"

"Loved her! you may well say that. There's those in the parish who could tell you that.

There's those who remember how, so humble, he would stand to hear the old people—they who had always loved the house, you know,—wish him joy, and a blessing on his Missis. And the tears would stand in his eyes, and he would say how God had blessed him, and how all would soon feel the blessing of a lady once more at the Court House. And then nothing that he could get could be good enough for her. And all this room he designed himself, and would help with his own hands, and hung the pictures himself. And from the time that he came back to this day, he has never said one word about these rooms, or ever been inside their doors. Indeed," continued Martha, suddenly descending to things of a less romantic nature, "I don't know that I should have put you here to-night, young ladies, but the thing was that I had no choice. Well, that comes this way. That room where you will sleep,—here, come and see it." Martha opened the door, and a simply furnished, half-carpeted bedroom was visible, looking plain and comfortable, and having, like the other, a blazing fire.

"It looks very nice," said Mary.

"Well, you see," continued Martha, "That room was never furnished. She was to have had the pleasure of furnishing that according to her own taste. So the first time I had orders to prepare for Mr. Benson's sleeping here, I thought to myself, that to put him into any of the great rooms was impossible. It would have been more than I could have done, to clean the grand old furniture in any one of them. So Reuben and I put up the bed you have seen in that empty room, and nailed up the curtains too, ourselves: and very nice, you see, we made it. So when Mr. Benson comes he sleeps there, and has a fire—winter or summer I always put a fire there—he can let it go out if he chooses; but these rooms are empty-looking without a fire, to my eyes Well, young ladies, three times a year I have that chimney swept; I am afraid of the birds building in it; and as that and this are the same chimney, when that is done, this is done too. So, seeing you must have fires in both rooms, I had no other to put you into but this."

By this time Martha had finished laying a cloth on the table, and putting thereon plates, and knives and forks, which had been concealed in a basket beneath it. Mary and Anna sat silent. They had listened, and their minds were absorbed by the crowding thoughts that Martha's history had brought to each of them. But their meditations were disturbed by Martha's advancing to the hearth to sweep it, and to bestow some further attention on the fire.

"You'll be pleased to take care of the fire, Miss Mary; and when you go to bed take out the half-burnt coals carefully, and don't put them under the grate; in this old house I would not answer for wood not being under the stone, and ready for mischief any day; put them on the side here,— do you understand, my dear?"

Mary brightened at this immediate appeal to her care, and said, "Oh yes, Martha, I understand. I'll do exactly as you say; if this house caught fire it would burn like paper."

Martha nodded and looked grave.

"Don't talk of it," said Anna.

"I'll tell you how it is," said Mary, "we are weak and hungry."

Perhaps Mary was right. Certainly, when Martha's preparations were offered for their acceptance, there was such justice done to eggs, coffee, and toast, as might fairly bring us to her opinion. Our young friends had really had no dinner, so, heroines as they are, they must be allowed a substantial tea. This meal was taken in the sitting-room, and thence removed by Martha in due course. She then brought wax-lights to last the night, and having left a tray covered with a napkin, on which she said there was "a bit of something," in case they wanted any thing before going to rest, she, after a little more chatting, left them, under promise to be with them again at sunrise in the morning.

"Good night, Miss Mary, good night, Miss Julian. Don't be afraid if you hear any bits of noises in the night, there are plenty of rats and such like in the roof, but they never come into the rooms." Such were her parting words, and then they were alone.

The two girls seated themselves near the fire to chat about the various occurrences of that strange day. For some minutes neither spoke as they looked into the blaze; at length Anna said, "I feel so strange being here, where my mother's family were servants. Yet here am I with *you;* how easily people are changed. I too might have been a servant here; and yet I cannot fancy myself such; these things have come so easily to me."

"It is all education and association. But you were never quite like other people; you have had extraordinary parents, and have been so carefully seen after, and brought up with such a kind, good strictness, and then *your brother.*"

"But also there has been *your* brother, Mary. I think that things may have come more easily for his being my foster-brother, and for your father being my sponsor, and for my frequent visits to Lullingstone, and for your coming to see us; yes, there is a great deal in association. The things that indicate independence and wealth have been familiar to me from childhood, and I always longed for education. Even now it has not lost its fascination. I shall like going back next week. Yet, as soon as I am separated from so much that I love, I shall think of my return next year with impatience."

"I wonder why Mr. Dyrbington tried you, as he called it, about those good old people in the village; it was the only disagreeable thing that I ever heard him say."

"I was thinking of it just now. I felt so wretched, and so angry. I would rather give up every new friend in the world than one of those old ones. I would rather have a smile from one of them than the praises of the greatest people on earth. I would not have them say that Anna Julian had forgotten them, and was proud; I wouldn't give pain, now that we are rich, to any to whom it was right and natural to give pleasure when we were poor."

"That is right, Anna. I love to hear you speak so. Do you know, that a long time since, when Edward was at school, he said the same sort of thing to me, when holding my pony, as he used to do, above the sands. I have never forgotten it, or him either; how good and beautiful he looked when he spoke. I quite loved him for it."

"I am not insensible to the advantages of the station into which fortune has raised me;" said Anna, "but I love my old station notwithstanding. It had its pleasures and its hopes, its labours and its rewards. I pray that the future which is now before me may have as much happiness as—as—as I used to expect." Anna's voice faltered. Her future had scarcely dawned—why did she fear?

Mary looked up; then gave a look around her.

"Dear Anna, my contemplative Anna—I know your future. Hereafter, if we live, we shall meet as women, a little more than women, perhaps; you will be *well married.* You will have married some person whom, at this moment, we have never seen, or if seen, never thought of for a moment. You will be happy, oh, very happy, Anna; nay, don't look so sad or so frightened. I am reading your fortune; it is a very good one; don't you like it?"

"Oh don't, Mary!"

"You are not civil, Anna. The coffee did me good. I like this adventure of ours very well, and it's just a time to say things that could not sound well at any other time. I am going on with your destiny."

"No—Mary, pray don't."

"Well, then, Anna. Hereafter—you know that we shall never forget this night—hereafter Lady A or Lady B shall come and make her full confession to me."

"Oh, never!" Anna covered her blushing face with her hands. "No, Mary, if not *now*, never, never *then!*"

"Look at me," said Mary.

Anna uncovered her face and looked as she was bid.

"Anna there is something."

"Stop, Mary, I won't have you say that." Anna's face was a look of agony. Mary turned aside her head, and looking at the fire spoke in her usual soft gentle way.

"After all you will be happy. Lady A and Lady B are very happy, Anna, and smile very good sensible smiles when they think of their youth's romantic thoughts and of confidential conversations where nothing was confided. And to do so is quite right. Their husbands have been in precisely the same predicament. I am informed that school-boys at a very early age discover that they have hearts, and that youths at college fall desperately in love. Oh, Anna! don't start—yes, I have really said—*love*—never mind, you know that we have been *thinking* of it all the time! So my Lord and my Lady, having each dreamt their dream and having each awaked, a little the worse for the pushing and pulling about, and knocks and rubs that attended the operation of being brought fully to themselves again—they marry each other, and are fond of each other, and they look back with good sensible smiles, I repeat it, on such folk as you and me."

"Is that the way you intend to marry, Mary?"

"Oh dear, no!" This was very quickly, very positively said, "Oh dear, no!"

"Tell me about yourself, then."

"No, my dear Anna." Mary spoke gently and tenderly now.

"But why not?"

"Because *my* marrying — *my* falling-in-love depends on that other thing—is subservient to that other thing—"

"Of which we never talk," added Anna. "But you have said that this night is just the night for talking of untalked-of things—so say it all to me now; I want to know. Your falling in love will be—?"

"As religion permits," said Mary.

"I don't understand it."

"Why not?"

"It would make the impulse of the heart so stiff, cold, formal, a bondage, an imprisonment."

"Oh, Anna! what are you saying?" said Mary.

"Something horrible to you, perhaps—but just what I feel, notwithstanding."

"Then you don't know what religion means."

"Do you, Mary, know what love means?"

"I know what it is."

"Tell me."

"Wedded love is the ordinary state, in which, by God's will, we live with each other."

"Go on."

"It is the joy of Paradise which has out-lived the fall."

"Go on," said Anna again, more interested.

"It is God's great gift to us for our consolation, encouragement, happiness. Do you think that I could wish to take so great a bounty except from the Giver's hand?"

"But you might love and be deserted, deceived, and made miserable?"

"Yes, while sin is in the world, I might suffer so."

"And what then?"

"Then I would turn to my God with security for strength and consolation. He will heal the suffering spirit of such as have never shunned His sight."

"I should be broken-hearted, I should droop, I should die," said Anna drearily.

"You would die in that furnace of affliction, which, to a Catholic, would be a purifying fire. You would die because you had acted in your own strength."

"Mary, tell me; do you think you could love as well as I could?"

"Oh, better than you, Anna; much better," said Mary, half laughing, and kissing Anna's upturned inquiring face.

"But tell me seriously, I want to know."

"More boldly, because I should have nothing to fear; more fervently, because I could not take what God gives with any thing less than all my heart; and more solemnly, because marriage is a sacrament. My dear Anna," said Mary Westrey, her face beaming with animation, "I intend to love with all my heart."

"I did not know that Catholics were so romantic," said Anna gravely, "I thought you fancied romance was wrong."

"Your romance, perhaps, I don't know," said Mary, "but not mine. My romance is truth united by a sacrament to God. It is a treasure for the right use of which I shall answer at the Judgment. Anna, you are like a motherless child who would enjoy a treat away from the sight of one whose kindness is suspected. I am a child to whom a good parent is saying—Take it my daughter, I intended it for you—it is yours. My spirit is freer, happier, than yours; I am sustained and protected. I am safe."

Mary rose up to go to bed. Anna proceeded to light a candle for her. She performed the ceremony with great deliberation, and on presenting it, said, "Well, Mary, but we need not marry at all."

Mary laughed. "Oh, Anna, you think about it every day; you wonder, you imagine, you hope, you fear; I can see it in your face. You are restless while I am at peace. You hurry your thoughts into the future, I wait for the future to come to me—no—I won't say whether I may marry or not."

"You *will* marry, Mary!"

"Good night, Anna."

"Good night."

She opened the door of the little bed-room. "How bright the room looks. How tempting those white covers and hangings—and I am really tired. Don't be long, Anna. I leave all Martha's instructions about the fire to you for their fulfilment. I shall soon be asleep."

"Do you know that it is still very early!" said Anna. "It is not nine o'clock; but I shall not linger here very long. Good night."

When Mary was gone, Anna drew her arm-chair nearer to the fire, wrapped round her the embroidered garment, half-cloak and half dressing-gown, which Martha had chosen out of certain stores of Dyrbington property which had been supplied to her on some past occasion, and gave way freely to her thoughts.

It seemed to her that Mary had been saying things strange, yet true. She thought that the bright change which had fallen on her path in life might not be a change of entire happiness. She thought that the freedom she had as yet enjoyed —the knowledge of life and its luxuries, life and its hopes, life and its enjoyments—would not always last; could not last when the season of girlhood had passed, and the time of womanhood had come. She felt that before her there were cares and trials. That she should have to suffer, to relinquish, to submit herself to the force of circumstances—that she should have to resign the happy exercise of her own will, that she should be free no more.

Why? Her heart, heaving and fearful asked, why? The answer came. Because over such as occupy prominent places in the world, that world has power.

Her thoughts had fled back to that last day of seeing Harold. Perhaps she should never see him again. Perhaps in those coming years, under those new circumstances she should see him—see him as she had so often seen him; at his work, with his busy hammer; with strong arms bending the wood; with straining limbs, gaining by hard labour his honest livelihood—his daily bread. Why did the tears rush to her eyes? Why did she rise quickly from her seat, and lean against the high marble chimney-piece in an attitude of such sorrowful meditation? At this moment she started, for she thought she heard an unusual sound. She looked carefully and cautiously all round the room. There was nothing to be seen; but the noise came again, more distinctly than before, and as if very near her. She felt the blood forsake her cheek, and held by the chimney-piece trembling, and listening with high-wrought earnestness. Again! It was a sound like the forcible opening of a door, not by the lock, but by the means of some instrument which might force the hinges. It was an idea which presented itself clearly to her mind, and as it came, again and again, she went cold all over; and in a tremor of alarm expected every minute that the draperies would move aside and a forcible entry be completed into the room in which she stood.

P

She really could not move, her feet felt either nailed or converted into lead, she had no power to stir; but the acuteness of her hearing increased painfully, and she felt her eyes wide open, and fixed in helpless staring on the satin drapery behind which that persevering sound was heard too plainly to admit of any doubt of what it was, or where. The recollection of the long dreary way by which they had reached these rooms, of their distance from the inhabited part of the house, of their utterly helpless position, came upon Anna with sickening reality. On went the sound. It seemed to become louder and louder. She could distinctly hear that wood-work was giving way before the efforts that were being made. Somebody was close by—engaged in making a forcible entrance into their rooms—no reasonable person could doubt it —no creature acquainted with the sound of tools and the cracking, splitting, and giving way of wood, could question what those sounds indicated —and—Heaven help them—they were alone! Still Anna's eyes were fixed on the drapery behind which those sounds issued, and still she held for support by the chimney-piece, feeling that fright alone kept her from fainting, but that at the first movement of that damask she might die!

Then just as she felt wrought up to the utmost pitch of endurance, when she felt that to retain her consciousness a moment longer would be impossible, that the sound of rushing waters were in her ears, and an icy feeling was crossing through her frame, the sound ceased! By a powerful effort she recalled her energies—all was still. From head to foot spread a sudden heat, a superhuman quickness of apprehension seemed to possess her—every faculty became acutely alive, and suddenly endowed with increased power, and heightened sensibility. She listened; not a sound was heard but that of the consuming coal.

A few soft, swift steps took her to the bed-room door. The fire glowed on the snowy bed, and the soft light rested on Mary's sleeping face. It was all profoundest calm.

Still as marble stood Anna Julian in the doorway; her posture hesitating; her ear still listening.

What was she to do?

She had scarcely asked herself the question when the sound came again. But this time—why, could not be told—this time she was not, as before, overcome with fright. She listened attentively with a reasoning ear to discover exactly, if she could, whence it came. She was sure that it was behind that ruby damask drapery. Was there a window there? She would see. Softly she stepped to that side of the room. She grasped the curtain; it separated in its fulness, and she pushed one part aside. Before her there was something—perhaps a window—shutters were closed on it. She determined to see what the shutters concealed. There was no way of fastening back the curtains. She must not let them fall behind her, for she should be in darkness if she did. She got two heavy chairs, and so placed them that she could throw the drapery across their backs, and thus get light and freedom. Then she brought a candle, and by it examined the fastenings of the shutters. They were very slight, and insufficient for any purpose of protection. She removed them gently; for now that she was engaged in her work of discovery she purposely sought to be as quiet as possible, and not to awake Mary. When the shutters were unfastened and taken down, there appeared behind them, not a window, but an aperture closed by small doors, which were so slight, that through them the sound of the workman and his tools was heard with as much distinctness as if he and they had been in the same room with Anna; and also these slight doors were so shrunk, that where they had met together in the centre there was an aperture wide enough to admit of the insertion of a finger for the purpose of opening them.

Anna looked at them thoughtfully. "There is some one on the other side—they must open into a room—if I open them the light from this room will discover me—and what then?" Again she considered; and in a moment her course was fixed upon. "I must release those heavy curtains, then I shall stand here in safety behind them in the dark. Then, if I open these doors—he must have a light whoever he is—I shall be able to look into the room, and satisfy my own mind without being myself discovered. I will do so."

Anna turned round, pulled the curtains from the chairs that had supported them, closed them carefully to shut out the light, and then turned round again, and passed her hands over the doors till they found the aperture in the middle.

One door is open full three inches, a light comes creeping through pale and dim, and there is the sound of a chisel as if employed in forcing open the lid of a box. Anna's heart beats quickly, why? they are such familiar sounds! And the old workshop and her father, and—but stay! The sound of a hammer is heard. It is a simple sound—why does Anna start, and her heart beat loud and her cheek flush, and her eyes gleam so strangely bright? It is heard again—two quick hard strokes; then, after a pause, another, deliberately; and then one more, just like a tap of approbation. How slight a thing suffices to bring truth to the mind; to bring knowledge, certainty; belief that cannot be persuaded away! Anna had heard those strokes before—a hundred times she had heard them—she had often smiled at the meaning that seemed to dwell in them—one only had ever made them—she heard, and *he* was there!

For an instant she pressed her hands upon her side to quell the throbbing within. "Stop—peace

—fortitude—I *must* know! I *must* see! I am not dreaming—it is all true; it is Dyrbington—it is Anna Julian—now!" She gently forced open the door as far as it could go. She looked into a room long and narrow, and not on the same level as that on which she was, for where she stood she was near to its ceiling. At one end there was a raised platform from which a descent was made by means of five or six steps to the main floor. This raised platform was close to Anna's right hand, for she was looking across the room where she stood, and not down its length. Towards the centre of the room stood a figure with two or three large packing cases about him. They had contained pictures, and the tools on the floor by his side showed that he had lately been engaged in taking them from their enclosures. Two flaring oil lamps were burning near him, and he now stood contemplating the painting that lay on the ground before him. It was Harold!

Anna stood firm and stedfast as a rock.

There stood Harold, not as he had been last seen by her, but strangely changed into an indescribable picturesqueness. The lights cast their full glare upon him. He was standing with little more than his side-face shown to her, but his attitude was one of exquisite grace, and his appearance was so full of dignity, that that grand, noble, benignant beauty which had so often been observed in him, seemed to have heightened and expanded, since she had last seen him, to its utmost development.

At last he changed that musing posture, and looked about him with a quick vivacity. He was searching for something. On the platform so near to where Anna was situated there stood two chairs and a rude sort of desk. He ran towards them, bringing one of the lights in his hand. He was very close to Anna now. His object was to form these chairs and this desk into a temporary easel, upon which he could place the picture he had been examining. The idea was soon accomplished; he returned to the platform, bearing his treasure with him, and put it on the apparatus he had contrived. Then he placed the lamps so as to throw light upon it properly, and when done he stepped back under where Anna stood, and gazed upon it as she did also.

It was a picture of herself, standing, and gazing on the Dyrbington crucifix! The blue, earnest eyes were a little raised, the long golden coloured hair hung back from her face, and fell in rich luxuriance on her shoulders, and strayed over a dress of a colour deep, dark, and undefined, except where the light fell upon its glossy folds and showed the brilliance of its hue, and the richness of its texture. But the light on the golden ringlets, the brightness on the velvet robe were as nothing to the glory that dwelt upon the countenance of that figure—the innocence, the earnestness, the devotion of that face spoke more of heaven than earth: and on those opening lips there dwelt a prayer—some great thing that young girl was asking, something beyond man's power to give; something she knew not how to obtain, except by prayer and faith. It was a countenance such as is never lifted up to man; never to fellow-mortal has such a face of hope and love, of trust and confidence been raised; on it was the reflection of the things that belong to God; and when Anna looked upon that face she wept. She sunk softly on her knees, she glided down gently out of its sight, and she sunk her head upon her breast and wept.

"Ah, no," she said within herself, "that is not me. It may be *my* face, but *his* spirit rests upon it. Oh, am I to be called *above him*—too great for *him?* too great for one who loves so purely: above one who can feel like *that!*"

But again the spirit is hushed within her. She hears a voice. She hears footsteps; they are going from her; the light also is departing; they are gone. And still Anna remained on her knees amid the falling drapery, in darkness and in prayer.

She did not know how long she staid there. But after a time she crept out softly, replaced the shutter, and laid herself down to rest.

Martha, true to her promise, came to them early in the morning. "Had they slept well?"

"Yes," Mary said; "quite well and soundly." "Would they breakfast in the room where they had supped?"—"Yes, if Martha pleased." "Well, she had brought back their riding-habits. They were quite dry."

The morning was fair and bright. By the time they had breakfasted Lord Westrey had come for them. Mr. Dyrbington sent them his love; he was engaged, and could not see the young ladies that morning. And so, by an early hour Mary and Anna were returning to Lullingstone.

But Anna had contrived to get Martha alone for a few moments, and to say to her that there had been the previous night a noise like the forcing open of packing cases. "Ah, yes," Martha said; "I was afraid that you might have heard it. I did not know of it till this morning."

"What was it?" asked Anna.

"Oh, the young German artist opening some pictures to show to master. He is with him now: that's the reason he can't see you this morning: dear master, he's always helping somebody."

Anna said no more.

CHAPTER XV.

THE PASSAGE OF A YEAR.

THE week passed at Lullingstone. Anna saw her father and mother, and told them of the preservation of her life during the storm. She saw them a second time that week; they said that they had been to Lyas's cottage; that they had seen him: that many friendly words had passed between them, but not a syllable was said of Harold. He evidently had not been there. But Anna remembered Lyas Norwood's gaze when she had spoken her desire to go on to Dyrbington; she remembered the smile with which he had heard the decision; she felt that it was for her protection in particular he had kept near them on their way, and something said to her that because he knew of Harold being at Dyrbington he was glad —because he also knew of his son's love for her he had been so solicitous for her safety.

They were unspoken thoughts; but she could not help turning often to them.

Edward had gone back to college; Anna was

soon to accompany Madame Lefranc; her last day at Lullingstone had arrived, and though she did not feel sadness at the thought of the year before her, she yet sat in the morning-room, and felt how glad she should be to return—to be always at home, and to leave off the girl and put on the woman. This last thought made her pause an instant to examine what it meant. She thought that she knew why the idea rose in her mind. She had the experience of a woman in some things, with the years only of the girl. She had gone through changes, she had a species of trial—it was the secret within her heart of which she thought—it would be pleasant for time to pass on; she wanted to know more about herself.

Thus thinking Anna sat by herself the last day of her visit to Lullingstone.

The door opened, and Lepard Eastner came in. Anna blushed as he entered. She was alone, and the nature of her thoughts came suddenly upon her at this interruption, and so she blushed.

Lepard came near her, talked for a few minutes rather agreeably, said that he was to follow Edward the next day; that he had not liked to go till the last moment; that there was that at Lullingstone which could not but detain him until the last moment.

Anna said that she too felt the charm of Lullingstone. Not, Lepard said, such a charm as he felt. Yet, Anna remarked, few people could be more alive to its attractions than herself. Lepard sat down by her side.

"Miss Julian," he said, "you know that I am Lord Westrey's ward. My father was fourth or fifth cousin of the Westrey family. I have a small fortune, and I have received, or am receiving, what is called a good education." Anna looked up in no small astonishment at this uncalled-for relation of personal history.

"You are very young; I also am young. But we are old enough to know our own minds. I love you—I love you fervently; with an inexpressible ardour. I want to speak of it to Lord Westrey and your father. Will you let me, Miss Julian?"

There was no triumph in Anna's heart when Lepard spoke to her—only she felt dreadfully nervous, and as if she had been taken suddenly ill. Her heart beat, her frame trembled. But she heard Lepard saying, "I would rather that you did not answer me. I don't wish you to bind yourself. I love you too well to wish that, Anna. But will you recollect that I love you; will you let it be known to our best friends? and then, by and by, when you are here again, and I have taken my degree—which I shall do before Edward takes his, you know, I shall take mine in less than a year—then, Anna, you will answer me, and in the mean time I will live upon the hope of your being kind. Nay, don't speak. I will tell Lord

Westrey; you can tell your parents if you like. Don't speak; only let me speak again in a year's time. That is all I ask. In the mean time you will think of me, will you not? Now I am going. Good bye, Anna. I shall not see you again; you are going back to Mayfield they tell me. I am going to pay a few parting calls—good bye, I am gone." And Lepard had risen and was half across the room. And already his heart was jubilant at the thought of having secured the heiress, that he should be able to follow up this judicious commencement with such attentions as must finally compromise this unsophisticated girl, and make her certainly his own. But Anna was only young in years and in the ways of the world, she was strong in judgment, and of full age in the courage which that judgment required.

"Mr. Eastner," she exclaimed in an agitated voice—"Come back—don't go away, come back; I pray you to come back." But he knew too well to obey. He stood still, smiling with a kind, quiet expression on his face, and after a moment, made another step towards the door. Anna's courage rose, she could speak without trembling now.

"Mr. Eastner come back. I insist upon it that you return!"

He paused again for a moment, and spoke to her.

"Dear Miss Julian, don't agitate yourself. I

don't want an answer now. I will hear all that can be said this time twelvemonths. Good bye. I carry you with me in my heart." He was close to the door, his hand was extended towards the handle—in a second he would be gone.

Anna jumped up—she sprang towards him. There was the spirit of a roused lioness within her.

"Dear Miss Julian," he began, in the same quiet, almost commanding tone that he had before used —but, "No!" she exclaimed, "you are not to call me so. I refuse distinctly to hear now, or ever, any thing of the kind from you. If you repeat those words I shall consider you are insulting me, and I shall appeal to Lord Westrey. Do you understand, Mr. Eastner? you are never again to speak to me as you have done; I will never hear any thing of the kind from you."

"Never!" repeated Lepard. "Never! For a young lady of your age and limited experience, you are more than prudently, more than modestly decisive, I think!"

"I am decisive. I know that I am. It is right to be so. Good day, sir." Anna was passing out of the room; but Lepard caught her by the wrist, and detained her.

"Stay," he said, "you will please to recollect, Miss Julian, that nothing is ever to be said of what has just passed between us."

"Sir?"

"I say that all this is to remain a secret—that we are to keep what has passed to ourselves." He felt that he was waxing very angry, and increasingly so, for the young girl whom he still held, even with painful severity, by the wrist, was looking at him with a face full of scorn. "I say," he repeated, "that all this is to be a secret between you and me. Don't you understand me?"

"No; indeed I do not understand you. Let me go, Mr. Eastner, let me go, and dictate nothing to me; I have feelings and opinions of my own."

"Which means that you are going like a puling school-girl to complain to Lord Westrey, and that I have trusted my feelings in so delicate a matter to one who has neither knowledge of the world, nor gentleness of the heart to guide her." Lepard Eastner, saying this with most bitter accents, held Anna tighter than ever.

"It means that if you don't immediately let me go that I will cry aloud for help and alarm the house."

"Go, then. Now, who are you going to *tell?*"

"Lady Westrey," replied Anna calmly, and stepping towards the door.

But Lepard laid his hand upon the lock, and said, "Why?"

"Because," she answered, "I will have no secrets between us; so small, so slight a tie as that would be disagreeable to me—I think I may say *discreditable* to me."

"And have you *no* secrets?"

"Are you going to let me pass?"

"Yes, when you have answered me. Look into your heart, please, and tell me then, that you have no secrets there."

"Do you think that such conduct as this is bearable, sir?"

"I know that you need not bear it a moment longer if you will answer me."

Anna stood still. She stood, her eyes upon the door, but she did not speak.

"Do you think I don't know?"

"I wish to leave the room, Mr. Eastner."

"Do you think that I can't see through your absurd ambition?"

Still the same speechless Anna looked towards the door with a calm, stern face.

"Do you think that I can't see that you are laying yourself out for Lullingstone?"

Here Anna could not help an involuntary start.

"Ah, you feel that, do you? Yes, I knew that I was right. Oh, you acted quite well to be decisive—I admire such decision as it ought to be admired. I too have something to tell to Lady Westrey, it seems."

"You have kept me here nearly a quarter of an hour, Mr. Eastner."

"Well, now you shall go. And recollect when you tell Lady Westrey that you tell her *all* that has passed. Tell her particularly what I am now going to say. Lullingstone loves you already. Tell Lady Westrey that I have purposely tried him, that he is jealous of me already, that he is vexed when I make you laugh, and relieved when I leave your side, and that he, their only son—too much loved to be any thing but indulged, and too constitutionally delicate to bear contradiction—is thinking in his heart of the time when he shall marry *you*. Now go," exclaimed Lepard triumphantly, for it gladdened his inward heart to look at Anna's blanching cheeks, "now go, only remember that there must be *no* secrets between *us*. Even so slight a bond of union is not to exist between you and *me*. Go; tell Lady Westrey—tell *all*."

Lepard Eastner moved away from the door, but as Anna stepped forward, he ran past her, and with a short laugh disappeared, and left her again alone.

She sat down for a moment. What should she do? Perhaps she had better take no notice of it—perhaps she had better not speak to Lady Westrey. Lepard Eastner had only spoken so to vex her, and revenge himself. She had better take no notice, let it pass; tell no one, keep it to herself.

So there was to be a secret between Lepard Eastner and Anna Julian! How could she help it? She could not tell Lady Westrey half only of what had occurred; perhaps Lepard might be spoken to, and then he would find out that she had concealed something, and then he would taunt her with it, and she should feel actually in his power. And again; suppose it to be true about Lullingstone—suppose that in future years Lullingstone should himself prove that what Eastner had just said was true, would not Eastner be able to upbraid her, and say that she had purposely kept back from Lady Westrey's knowledge that very part of their conversation which it most concerned the interest of the family to tell? That would not do.

One thing was plain therefore—she must either tell *all* or *none*. Lepard had known that; he had been very cunning. There *must* then be a secret between them. Alas! it seemed very sad. It was a feeling of absolute bondage that it brought upon Anna. She rose from her seat endowed with strength sufficient, and was soon at Lady Westrey's dressing-room door.

A soft voice bid her enter, and then a kind greeting followed, and Anna said, "Lady Westrey, I have something at my heart that I want to get rid of. Will you take the burthen from me?"

"What, heavy at heart so early in life!" said Lady Westrey smiling. "Sit down, my dear child, and say to me just what you like to say."

So Anna sat down on a low seat by her good friend's side, and she took that friend's hand, and held it to give her strength, and she told all. She told it just as it had occurred; repeated almost word for word what had passed; and when all was over she said, "I have done right to tell you, Lady Westrey, have I not?"

"Kiss me, Anna; put your arms round me as you would embrace your mother; and as a mother I will pray to God that you may never lose that singleness of heart which distinguishes you now. You have done rightly—quite rightly, my dear child. And—recollect Anna—*I thank you*. Now put it all off your mind, just as if it had never happened. Try to think no more of it; believe that your responsibility is given over to me; you have done rightly, and you have done *all* that can be done. Think no more about it—forget it—be just as usual—are you happy now, Anna?"

"Oh yes, quite happy," looking the truth of her words; and soon after she was in all the hurry of departure, and really did not think any more of the past.

It took longer to say good-bye this time. Anna knew more people, and she was older, and so more was expected of her. Mr. and Mrs. Seaforth would not be contented with any thing less than their all coming to dinner. This therefore was accomplished, and Captain Ralph was there. Mrs. Seaforth patronized him, and paid him a thousand little attentions, and *drew him out*, as the phrase is, and was very happy in the success of her charitable labours. She nourished, as has been said, great schemes in her heart for Ralph; among others that he should marry a penniless girl of her acquaintance, to whom his own money, and the settlement which his brother would make upon her, might be a sufficient inducement. "I am sure that that would turn out very well," was Mrs. Seaforth's invariable commentary. "She will marry him for the settlement—that's of course; but Ralph improves daily—has almost given up his habit of drinking. He has a great desire to settle, and she—oh, she is a good girl, and would do well by him; and he has a warm heart, and would feel her goodness; and they would end in being a fond couple, affluent and respectable —yes, I am sure that that will answer very well."

This was said that evening to Mrs. Julian, and good Mrs. Julian thought it, probably, the best thing that could be done; her hopes were not quite so sanguine as Mrs. Seaforth's, but then she was not so much interested. Moreover, she did not know them as well. But so very energetic, and so honestly in earnest was Mrs. Seaforth, that Mrs. Julian got to regard Captain Ralph as almost a reformed, and quite as an engaged man.

Madame Lefranc departed with her pupils. The journey was not performed with as much speed as it might be in these days. There was plenty of time for quiet thought, and Anna used it.

Edward was busy at his work too. But we

are not going to write of him; he is an industrious, noble-minded, strong-headed youth, and may take care of himself. The reader is assured that he conducted himself in such a manner on all occasions as, if narrated, would ensure him his or her approval.

We must go back to Watermouth. John Julian, you are not forgotten.

Success! Had he now found out what it was? If to rise surely, even suddenly, yet with that easy grace which spoke security—if to find all things ready to his hand, as if some unseen agent had . prepared all that he could require, even before he could say from experience that he did require them—if to see his children exceed all whom he had ever seen in graces of mind and person, and yet giving promise of still further improvement—if to have of this world's goods not only enough, but to spare—if the union of such things is success, then John Julian had such things, had them in their full excellence.

But Dame Fortune had it in her heart to do more than enough for John Julian. Success is but an insufficient word to describe the tide of prosperity that flowed in upon that man. Every speculation upon which he entered did more than succeed—it became the subject of a hundred happy coincidences, and doubled and trebled its natural and to be expected gains, till it returned to its master's hands like a work of enchantment.

It seemed as if all that Julian undertook became instantly invested with a charmed life. The power of winds and waves, the accidents of time and place, the impulses of brave hearts, the ready wisdom of experienced heads; all these, and every thing that men call chance, accident, and good luck, combined, whenever and wherever John Julian was concerned, to increase his accumulated gains, and crown his already astonishing prosperity.

Before the passage of this year, of which we are now writing, was made, John Julian was rich beyond calculation; Mr. Seaforth also had had immense accessions of wealth, and still the tide flowed on increasingly. Julian was getting to be, day after day, more of a public man. He subscribed munificently to all charities. He purchased a site, and began to build almshouses for superannuated seamen. He added a wing to the hospital, and his private bounties were administered with no sparing hand.

But there was one place where he would gladly, and from the kindest motives, have had his wealth felt, but where not a guinea of his could ever find its way. This was at Lyas Norwood's. Often, very often, did Julian ask to do something for them—any thing, great or small, to show his love and interest. But no, he could never do any thing—they were beyond his reach—*he* could not help *them*. He asked after Harold, and proposed to assist him. He did not wish to ask confidence of them; he would not ask to be told where Harold was; but would they not send him something as a remembrance from an old friend? Nó; he never could get any information from Lyas Norwood about his son. He once went to make a final experiment. He went armed with a cheque transferring to Harold's credit five hundred pounds; but he might as well have offered Lyas five hundred pebbles;—not an emotion was excited by the proposal. Lyas simply said, "Julian, my friend, I have throughout believed in your sincerity; why press upon me these offers, as if that which is already believed required to be any further proved?"

Before the year passed away, it had got currently reported in the higher circles, and not unjustly received, that Julian was a very valuable character, possessed of funds of local information which made his conversation highly agreeable, and not at all like a man from the lower ranks of the people, but, on the contrary, a person whose mind was as deeply imbued with aristocratic sentiments as the most prejudiced among themselves. And all this proved of great advantage to Julian, and was a preparation for the reception of his children. So passed the year with Julian. With Mr. and Mrs. Seaforth it passed in perfect prosperity. A further gift was made by the generous merchant to Ralph. Mrs. Seaforth's hopes of her brother-in-law grew higher than ever. She went busily into the match-making scheme between him and her friend Miss Thompson; and in pursuance of it gave parties out of doors, and entertainments at home. Nothing could have persuaded that kind-hearted woman during the time of which we write, that this scheme would not meet with that success which for so long had crowned every undertaking emanating from the roof of the most successful merchant of Watermouth.

As to Ralph himself he went on in the same way. He took all his brother offered, and felt soured by each act of generosity; he could not refuse money, and he hated to take it. He nourished the fancy that he was capable of earning full double as much as was given to him, and that for this compulsory dependence he was indebted to John Julian.

At Dyrbington things remained as they had long been. There was but one work going on there, and that had now nearly reached its completion—the melting of the sacred vessels, under Lyas Norwood's care, by old Isaac the Jew. In the same way as the reader has seen, at intervals of time, the same man with the fishing-basket slung across his shoulders, the fern or long grass peeping out through the opening, and the net outside securing the whole—just as the reader has seen once, might Lyas Norwood have been seen this year again and again; till, about midsummer, the last were taken to the Jew's dwelling, and reduced in the melting-pot; they were the gilded candlesticks of the high altar of Dyrbington church, which had been thought unnecessary by Sir John, the spoliator, and had therefore been exchanged by him, and their places filled by candlesticks of pewter.

And now the representative of that bold, bad man had, almost to his own satisfaction—certainly in the conviction of his doing the best that it remained to him to do—arranged for the future bestowal of the lands once belonging to the Church upon the poor of all those parishes which had formerly belonged to the guild, attached to the chantry chapel of St. George; and the money produced by the melting of the altar furniture was to be attached to them by endowment, together with a further sum of considerable amount, as compensation for the many years of unlawful appropriation of Church property of which the house of Dyrbington had been guilty.

CHAPTER XVI.

THE WORLD'S RECEPTION.

AND now the year was spent and gone.

Lord and Lady Westrey were remaining in London, that Madame Lefranc and the three who had been her pupils might join them in the last week of June.

The ladies arrived safely in London, and met with their expected welcome. Anna thought that Mary looked more graceful and noble than ever; no word had ever been coined that could satisfactorily express what *she* was; Anna was to stay in London till she could return to Watermouth under her friend's escort.

Julian had placed a liberal sum of money at Lady Westrey's disposal to procure all that could possibly be required by his daughter; with Madame Lefranc's assistance the important affair of arranging Anna's wardrobe was commenced. Her mind was full of the excitement attendant on the novelty of her circumstances. It was a mixture of pride and pleasantness; she was very happy.

Lord Westrey declared himself, when alone with

his wife, actually astonished at the loveliness of their protegée; and Madame Lefranc resigned her charge with a solemnity which was almost amusing.

Then followed a few large parties, two or three dinners, and a ball. Anna danced beautifully. Her manner was thought delightful. She was frank and lively, unaffected and obliging; and though evidently of high spirit and great energy of character, she was gentle and feminine, endowed with the charming grace of unobtrusiveness. She was every where admired, every where talked-of, every where inquired about. People praised her beauty and lauded her mind. There was also a romance in her history which assisted in making her the fashion—and the fashion in a certain circle Anna was. There was an absolute excitement about her.

In the midst of this, at the end of that gay month of June, Edward arrived.

He came in the evening. Their last party for that season—not a very large party—was assembled at Lord Westrey's. Edward heard it all from old Thomas the butler when he arrived; so he went straight to his room and prepared himself to join it. When he was ready he entered the small drawing-room where he expected to find Lord Westrey. He went from him to Lady Westrey. She received him with even more than her usual cordiality. After a few words she said,

"Edward, your sister is in the next room, she was singing with Mary just now, you had better go and see her. She is prepared for your coming, indeed we expected you earlier. But," she added these words with a smile, "but *you* are perhaps the one who ought to be prepared for the meeting."

Edward felt and looked a little puzzled. "Why?" he asked.

"Anna is improved," said Lady Westrey. "Her woman's attire suits her wonderfully. She is really quite beautiful."

"Dear Lady Westrey, how you enchant me."

"You must take care of her, Edward, there are not many such in the world. But go now; go and seek her. I will venture to say that her thoughts are this moment of you. Go—keep her waiting no longer."

Edward left Lady Westrey. His cheek was flushed with pride and joy, and his heart throbbed from the same cause. He passed slowly through the magnificent scene around him. He felt, as he looked on so much that was brilliant, that she must be gifted indeed who could shine with conspicuous radiance in such company. And really could his own gentle young sister excite remark, and had she already obtained distinction where there was so much to wonder at and admire? Still he moved on, and his eyes fell soon upon a picture which answered the question in his mind.

Standing side by side, and listening with smiles to the praises their singing brought forth, were Mary Westrey and Anna. Anna was more than all he had hoped; he paused to look at her. "How wonderful—how uncommon is her beauty!" Then Anna turned more towards him; she was seeking for some one; he followed every glance; he watched every motion. Such a sweet smile came to her face. It delighted Edward most of all. It was the loved and tender smile of home, a smile that spoke of a heart unchanged, and a head undisturbed by the flattery around her.

People were talking of Edward. "There—that's her brother!"

"Indeed! well he looks like it: there is a resemblance; he is exceedingly handsome."

"Yes, he is; and a miracle of genius I assure you. It is altogether a kind of thing such as the world does not often see. I envy Westrey his friends. The father and mother are very extraordinary people also; quite above their former place in life. He is an antiquary, and not uneducated. There is a famous school, one of the old endowments, at Watermouth—father and son were both there."

"Indeed—it is quite a romance! And every thing going together. Such beauty, and such natural good manners. Such talent—advantages —money. Dear me! Well, it is truly astonishing. I should like to be introduced to that young man. Could you manage it for me?"

"I hope they won't be spoiled," growled some one who was fond of viewing things under a threatening aspect.

"Spoiled! what for?" said the more amiable neighbour.

"Such sudden prosperity might spoil you or me."

"But those two young creatures have been brought up to it. This did not happen yesterday, you know. The tide turned years back when they were too young to attract attention. But they have been getting what is a good preparation for the flatteries that are likely to be offered to them; they have had, in the meantime, and in consequence, an excellent education."

"That is very well," remarked some one close by; "very well, indeed; just the only thing to be done. But, after all, nothing can make up for the want of gentle blood."

"But gentle blood is not always the portion of the rich."

"No. Only it ought to be. Give me pedigree —pedigree; that's the thing, sir. That makes the true nobleman."

"Well," replied the first speaker, who seemed to have it at heart to say all the good that he could for the Julians. "Well, that's curious. Do you not know that Westrey has a well-traced pedigree of these people for three hundred years? Very curious; I assure you. Not found in the Heralds' college, that's true; never borne arms, of course; but by means of old papers belonging to himself, Mr. Dyrbington, and Lady Westrey—she was a Lullingstone you recollect—the pedigree of these young people, certainly by one side, if not by both, can be traced as I have said."

"I congratulate them," was the dry reply. The speaker did not think much of three hundred years. In an instant more came another question.

"That youth has not taken his degree, I think?"

"Not yet; he can't—hasn't kept terms enough yet; can't take it till next year. He'll carry off the first honours, Parker says."

"Parker is very sanguine where he likes," said the unwillingly convinced gentleman.

"Yes. But Parker only likes where he has a right to be sanguine," said the kindly disposed, in answer.

"Is the young man intended for the Church?" asked another.

"It is not settled. The Church was looked to naturally. Lord Westrey told us all about it the other day. The thing was proposed to Julian. There is a living waiting for him; but he was perfectly candid to Lord Westrey. He said that he was ambitious—ambitious was the word; that of course he, in consequence, would not pledge himself to enter any profession which in point of fact so ties a man's hands as the Church does. That was the substance of what Lord Westrey said, I think."

"Ah, indeed; a patriot I suppose. Well I like that. He may be a very useful man; a practical man; having opportunities of observation from connexions with a lower grade of society. Well, he will enter parliament? Can he speak?" The inquirer raised his double glasses to his eyes and looked at Edward with a plain intention of getting him by heart, and knowing him again. Then he went on:—

"Large connexions in trade, commerce, great affluence, such things form a man of influence. Good education too—solid parts—a brilliancy of genius also, I think I have heard. A capital parliamentary man—get him for one of Westrey's boroughs?"

"The talk went that way the other night."

"Ah! very good. Where is Westrey? He must introduce me to him. Not taken his degree yet, you said? Never mind; never too soon to know a man of promise." And the far-seeing speaker moved off. "By the by," he said returning, "What is the father worth, any idea? Eh?"

"Oh, I can't tell you the exact sum. But his successes only this year have been extraordinary.

It's like a fairy-tale—puts Aladdin's lamp quite out of countenance."

"Not all floating, I hope? Something safely settled, of course?"

"Oh yes. Wife and children taken care of. Westrey took care of that. He advises him in every thing, I believe."

"Then," said the lady who had declared her intention of knowing Edward, "Then if any misfortune should happen to the father—I don't at all understand trade, but one hears of such things —fortunes made and lost in a day. I am afraid it is terrible gambling," the lady shut her eyes piously behind her raised fan for a moment, and then recommenced her own trading speculations, "If any reverses were unfortunately to occur, such things do happen, the fortune of this young man, I mean of these two interesting young creatures, would not be involved?"

"Quite safe, I believe so. Westrey said something, I forget exactly what. I dare say that he is trustee. But he has no dislike to talk about the Julians. Why don't you ask him?"

"Oh, it is no concern of mine, you know." It certainly was not. Only the lady had a son and two daughters unprovided for.

And so friends, good and bad, flatterers, speculators male and female, political and matrimonial, welcomed Anna and Edward Julian to the world.

R

CHAPTER XVII.

WELCOME OF ANOTHER SORT.

EDWARD'S progress through those rooms of entertainment was slow. He reached his sister and Mary Westrey, and that was all his heart desired. In all the joy of re-union, in all the exuberance of spirits belonging to so much of mingled promise and attained success—in feelings such as these Edward Julian passed that joyous night. He scarcely left Mary's side for a moment, and she seemed to be as happy as himself. There was not any thing to excite fear. The atmosphere around him was one of hope. He would not have been man if he could have resisted its enchantment. Lady Westrey was engaged in her duties as hostess. Lullingstone had just come in—he and Edward had arrived together—and he had taken Anna entirely to himself. Edward found Mary fall to his share naturally, and in the joyousness of the moment he fearlessly put forth all his powers for her entertainment.

Edward had kept his promise to himself. He

had never sought to win her—he had abstained from every word that might possibly betray his secret; he had only given way to the happy influences around him, and yet Mary Westrey had found him out, and she knew that he loved her.

And something, so slight as not to be describable, something, a mere tone, a glance, a blush, a stammering word, a passing tremor, something, that night, before they parted, told Edward that his secret was his own no longer. He knew well that she knew it. As the thought came he could scarcely restrain the words that the bursting heart sent upwards to the lips. And when he did restrain them he felt covered with confusion; nervous as a woman.

Involuntarily he looked at Mary; then quickly withdrew his glance, but then, as quickly, sought her face again. What could he do but look at her? There, on that fair tablet must he not seek to read his fate—could he seek it any where else? He dared not speak. He felt that it would be wrong to speak. He had nothing to depend upon —he could only try to read such language as might be written there. She *had* found him out; and she made no show of misunderstanding him —was he not now bound in honour to speak openly?

While the contest was going on in his mind she spoke. And she spoke with such serenity that Edward could not help contrasting his own wretched state of disquietude with the peace that possessed her.

"I am going into the drawing-room; I am going to mamma."

Edward could only acquiesce by a look. She rose quietly, and walked with a steady step away. For the remainder of the evening Edward scarcely knew what he was about. Lord Westrey introduced him to his friends; he received such attentions with his best grace, talked of what they talked of, and answered their questions, and got on in a kind of mechanical way, making himself agreeable as a matter of course, and as he best could. But all the time he was feeling that something had to be done, and thinking what he had best do.

Should he let things alone? Mary would think she had been trifled with.

The thought was not to be entertained for a moment. Should he speak to her; write to her; do her justice by confessing the feelings of whose existence she had no doubt? But what a return it would seem to be for Lord Westrey's patronage! As yet what was he? That evil spirit of torment which is always ready to do its ill offices in the heart, rose quickly to answer this grieving question, "As yet, what was he?" The son of a poor tradesman turned into a successful speculator; the clever boy of a charitable foundation; a youth all intoxicated with his good fortune, forgetful of the common requirements of life; a creature who had been helped on in the world by a great man, and had wilfully, knowingly, and obstinately placed his affections on that man's child." This was the picture presented by the spirit of torment within. Was it his? was he like it? could he recognize that as himself?

Edward indignantly flung it aside. If I be ruined, disgraced, reduced never to rise again; if I lose my position for ever in the world's esteem—and I seem to stand there in a high enough place to-night—I must go through with this thing now. I did not intend it. My own conscience is my witness to that matter. An hour ago I had not a thought of these things being as they now are; I never intended it, but now I must go through with it; I should be unworthy of her if I did not. It is like the hazard of a life's hopes on a throw of the dice. It is a tremendous risk. But I must do it; I must do it—but how?

There again came a question upon which Edward paused. And then he resolved to tell every thing to Lord Westrey that night. He soon left the drawing-room. When he reached his own bed-room, he found his travelling clothes still strewed about, and he took them up and placed them on a chair as if they were to be resumed. He locked his dressing-case, and put things in a way speedily to be replaced in his portmanteau. "No one knows how soon I may wish to go," he said to himself. "At least the decision shall not take me unawares."

The time seemed to pass with distressing slowness. There he was alone, and in a state of harassed feeling which was very hard to bear, He had lighted his candles and thrown himself into an easy chair. He lay there staring at the opposite wall, and longing to hear the sounds of departing guests. Half-hours passed, the clock in the passage chimed them forth, and still he was there, and no sound but now and then a hum of distant gladness disturbed his loneliness. He staid there picturing the scene he had left—he went on to wonder on the things that might be. He began to question himself again. "Was there any real necessity for speaking to Lord Westrey?" "He had not *said* any thing to Mary?" He rose briskly from his chair and spoke aloud. "I will speak to him to-night—I *will* tell him all."

Then came the sounds of wheels. He opened the door that he might hear more distinctly what was passing. The guests were going. He went to Lord Westrey's sitting-room and rang the bell.

"Tell Lord Westrey that I want to tell him something to-night—to tell him something he will be interested in hearing, or I would not trouble him to-night. I shall be in my bed-room. Will you ask Lord Westrey to be so good as to send for me when he is disengaged?"

Again he returned to his solitude. Again a half-hour passed drearily. Then came a servant to his door—"Lord Westrey was in his dressing-room, and would be very happy to see Mr. Julian for as long a time as he pleased."

Lord Westrey's whole man displayed delight and tenderness. He held out his hand to Edward, and looked at him with affection. All at once the youth's hopes rose.

But he had not come there to further his own interests. He had come there *to do right.* He might lose hope, and lose Mary, but he would never lose her with any thing but a heart unconscious of wrong in her cause.

"What I have to say requires your lordship's fixed attention. Will it be agreeable to you to hear me now, or shall I wait?"

"Of course I will do as you wish. There is nothing wrong, Edward? Is Lullingstone——"

"All is right with Lullingstone, sir."

"Well, go on."

"I am not a culprit and yet I feel like one," said Edward in the voice of one talking to himself.

"You don't look like one," said Lord Westrey, "You are no culprit, depend upon it, Edward; you only don't know how to begin." Lord Westrey smiled and pointed to a chair.

Edward did not take the chair. He remained

standing, his eyes fixed on Lord Westrey's face. At last he spoke.

"I am guiltless of harm, yet I come to confess to you, my lord. My life has been an extraordinary one, I have had such experience as few find in a whole life, and that a long one. Lord Westrey, I am not—I know I am not unduly elevated with a sense of wealth—great as it is, I think but little of it, for its own sake. I am gifted with talents, but I may not set a price on them. They have not yet been proved to the world. But I have long felt that if, on taking my degree, I accomplished—perhaps exceeded—the expectations of my friends—if I made myself a place in society, if, by my father's gifts, or my own exertions—for I cherished the thought before his altered fortunes came to the furtherance of my hopes—I earned a position less only by the circumstances of hereditary rank to your own; and if—these things being accomplished—I could bring also to my aid a heart, as far unsullied as might be, that then I would bring such things as I had—talents proved, position gained, independence accomplished, and virtue preserved—it may sound to your ears, my lord, a poor inventory of merits, but it is all that I could hope to achieve—I would bring these things to your daughter Mary, and ask her to accept them. Yes, Lord Westrey, that has been the sustaining, exciting hope of my life—for I have loved her—I loved her when to do so was like the dream of a child in years and knowledge as I was. I loved her as a youth when that dream seemed to gather itself into something tangible and take to itself form and shape; and I have loved her, as I now love her, with the man's heart that throbs within. And now, Lord Westrey, you are the only human being who has heard my thoughts; and I tell you now, because, of no fault of mine, but somehow, I know not how, I have seen this evening that Mary suspects my thoughts, and that the secret of my life is a secret no longer."

Not once, not by a single movement, or by any attempt to speak had Lord Westrey interrupted Edward. He had heard all through, looking at him the whole time, and never taking his eyes off him, and now that Edward ceased speaking he still looked at him; but it was impossible to say from that still fixed look what were the emotions excited within. There was silence for full a minute. Then Lord Westrey spoke.

"Nothing has passed between you?"

"Nothing."

"You are ready to assure me that you have not—not—not, what people call, made love to her."

"Never, on my soul."

"Yet you think she knows your secret."

"I do."

"May I ask whether you have any idea of how Mary would receive a confession from you?"

Edward trembled in every limb. Lord Westrey saw his agitation.

"Don't tempt me, Lord Westrey. I have not made myself worthy of her yet. I would not put that question to myself for the world. Lord Westrey, I can't tell you what I feel—if I were to answer that question to myself as I must wish it to be answered, and if, in time to come, it were to be changed, I don't know, but I think that I should never recover it."

Lord Westrey walked briskly up and down the room. Edward, still standing, looked neither to the right nor the left. He was absorbed in his own thoughts. He knew not how time passed on. It might have been only a few moments, it might have been an hour in which things stood thus, but at last he was roused by Lord Westrey stopping opposite to him, and abruptly asking him, "Edward! why have you told me this?"

He roused himself immediately, his own frank smile came back to his face. "I will tell you," he said. And then the two smiled on each other, and again in Edward's heart up sprung hope.

"I thought that she had found me out. She rose up from where, by my side, she had been sitting, and went to her mother; I thought she might feel my speaking to her possible, even probable. I knew that I was in no position to speak to her. Then I feared lest my silence should make her feel that I had dared to trifle with her. These thoughts seemed to change my position. While the secret was in my own breast, it was my own, and belonging solely to me, I had a right to preserve it as I liked. But now it had escaped, and I owed a duty somewhere, perhaps to her, if not to her, to you. That the thought of my heart should have escaped thus, was a thing entirely against my will. At this moment I would gladly at a great price purchase back the right to think of her, and cherish my love in my heart, as a thing that being mine and mine only, involved me in no responsibility. But now that that hope has passed from my heart to her knowledge, I *am* involved in a responsibility, and I have for that reason, and because you are her father, laid open my whole heart to you."

"But girls have often strange things said to them. Things are said, and done, and looked, and all that sort of thing, just as if there was some great meaning in them, and when nothing comes of it they think, if they think of it at all, that it was an instant's flirtation—that's all—and there being no more said, no harm is done. Nothing more than that has happened with Mary, I dare say?"

"Possibly not," said Edward, almost proudly. "But if your daughter has suspected me, she has suspected *truth*, Lord Westrey. I am not here before you to confess a momentary flirtation; I have asked to see you, to tell you the truth—to tell you that your daughter has been the hope of my life; that I feel to hold life simply on that hope, and that to lose it is to be at once and for ever ruined and wretched. Within my breast that passion has lived as a holy thing. And because I would not have it misunderstood—because I could not keep so holy a thing in my heart, and suffer it to be profaned by becoming the cause of any thing underhand or dishonourable between you and me —because of this I have told you all; I have risked all that makes life what it is to me rather than run any risk of this treasured hope being polluted by ought unworthy of it. My lord, I give up nothing, I promise nothing, I unsay nothing. Good night, Lord Westrey; I hope, indeed, that no harm is done!" With a thousand mingled emotions struggling in his breast, Edward was turning to leave the room, but Lord Westrey recalled him.

"Stop, Edward, come back; with what feelings—with what intentions are you leaving this room?"

Edward returned. He saw that Lord Westrey was deeply agitated. He advanced close to him.

"You are my benefactor. I know that I owe much to you. You may think that I have ill-rewarded your kindness and patronage. If I had not done as I have done this night I should feel that possibly I might be open to that charge. But now I have done all that I can do. You know me *now*. As soon as it seemed needful for you to know me you have known me. We are on even ground, my lord. If you say no more to me I shall leave this room with every thought and intention the same as they have ever been, and when the time comes that I can offer to your daughter what she may without degradation accept, I will offer it to her; but if now *you* choose to order things otherwise, you can. There is a terrible power in your hands, Lord Westrey. I would ask you to use it with mercy and caution."

"I have wished her to marry Morton," said Lord Westrey. "Old Sir Giles wished it. He spoke of it to me, and he spoke of it to Morton. I should think that Morton will certainly propose to her—probably soon—this year, on his return. It would be a good connexion for her, one I have always hoped for."

Lord Westrey looked at Edward, but Edward made no answer.

"Nonsense, Edward! By the time you have taken your degree you will see her Lady Morton."

"May God help me," groaned Edward.

"That is, if you don't make love to her in the mean time, and so turn her head, and prevent it," went on Lord Westrey.

"My determination is taken," said Edward. "Not till I have taken my place in the world, will I ask her to hear me; and then, if she be still disengaged, and if you do not now forbid it, Lord Westrey, *then* I will."

"No man has courage and patience for such a course," said Lord Westrey. "Put it out of your head, Edward; it is a trial beyond human strength. Consider; you have much to accomplish; don't worry your mind with this thing."

Edward smiled. "A great deal indeed to accomplish; do you allow me to leave the room, bent upon victory, my lord?"

"No, Edward," he exclaimed, standing up. "No, Edward, for that would be to give you a tacit consent. I will not give any consent to the course you have marked out for yourself; but I will say this, that I admire you greatly, and that you have raised yourself in my esteem by what has passed this night."

"Then I am free, my lord?" exclaimed Edward joyfully.

"Free to do as you like yourself; free to do any thing except make love to Mary. And I say this, that you may remember it, Edward. I say that, should you ever come to me, having kept your word about Mary, and bringing with you those recommendations of which you have this night spoken, and recollect that not one has to be omitted—then, Edward"—and, rising, Lord Westrey placed his hand on the youth's shoulder, "then, if she be disengaged, you shall make love to her if you like!"

Edward seized Lord Westrey's hand.

"Nay, nay, Edward; I have promised nothing after all. Don't buoy yourself up on what I have said. To me your earnestness is the most sorrowful thing in the world. You have every thing before you, and yet you peril happiness wilfully, and knowingly, on a chance which is not worth a straw. I assure you—as your friend I assure you that Mary is certain to be engaged within the year."

"Enough, enough—good, kind, noble friend," said Edward. "You shall never repent the admissions you have made to me this night. I will go to Watermouth to-morrow. I will keep my word with the most scrupulous honour. I will seek in every thing to deserve her, and trust to Heaven for success." And Edward left Lord Westrey, and laid himself down to rest happier than, an hour before, he had ventured to think would be possible.

And before Lord Westrey went to rest, he had repeated all that had passed to Lady Westrey. She heard with so little emotion, that she might have been supposed scarcely to feel at all upon the subject.

Nearly a fortnight was lingered away, and then they travelled towards Watermouth. As Anna neared her home, the recollections of her late dissipations faded away. True to her natural character, she thought of home and parents; her childhood's home—her childhood's parents; with those blessings she never associated wealth and the luxuries it purchases: they had never been dearer to her than in the days gone by.

Other things came also to her mind. The thunderstorm, the escape from death in the forest, and Dyrbington.

There, as she sat by Mary Westrey's side in the carriage, the warm feelings of her heart burnt hot upon her cheek. What a world it was to her! How would the course of time flow for her? What events would it bring? How could it bring to her what she wished—and if not what she wished, could it ever bring her any thing to compensate for its loss? She did not know; she could not guess. The noise of those rapid wheels—it sounded to her like the shaking of the sands in Time's hour-glass. Every moment seemed to rise in value, as she longed yet feared for the future. But she was going back—there was joy in the knowledge; she was going back—back to those loved scenes, to where she felt that the uncertainty around her would one day clear away. One day! She cared not how soon that day would come. She was so full of her own thoughts that she could not speak. She put her hand within Mary Westrey's. It was tenderly clasped. Then she leaned back in the corner, and wrapped her mantle round her, and shut her eyes as if in sleep.

Two days were spent at Lullingstone. Then Anna joined her brother at Mayfield. Mayfield felt like home; there was nothing like it. But the first person she saw, as Lord Westrey's carriage turned within the gate, was neither father, mother, nor brother, but Ralph Seaforth. They exchanged salutations. Anna was all gladness, and ready to give her sweetest smile to any person thus met at the door of home. She smiled her sweetest and looked her happiest, and her improved beauty was not lost on Ralph. There was also a gleam of surprise, almost of congratulation, on Anna's face, for Ralph was looking very different from that which she had left him, a year before. He was now a smart, rather dashing sort of personage, whose costume was in an extreme of that sort of fashion called "*sporting;*" and instead of being on foot, or riding a horse from his brother's stable, as it had used to be, he was himself driving a curricle, in which a pair of well-bred horses showed their best, as he reined them up to allow of Lord Westrey's carriage passing; and he took off his hat with the air of a man well satisfied with others and himself.

The admiration Anna awakened he was at no pains to repress or conceal. Something of the sort—just a consciousness that he had been surprised into admiration, and had involuntarily showed it—crossed Anna's mind. She was but a woman—a young, though not a weak woman. This tribute Anna felt that Ralph Seaforth had paid her, and as the carriage swung past him, she leaned back and smiled, and said to herself that Ralph Seaforth was most astonishingly improved.

It was the slight thought of a passing instant. In another moment she was in the arms of her parents.

For a few weeks there was a life of home happiness, varied by the revisiting of old haunts, and the seeing again of old friends. Then a county race-ball was announced. The Westreys were to go to it. They were to take Anna and Edward. But this was not enough; Lady Westrey had set her heart on Mrs. Julian going. More than once she came to Mayfield on the subject. Julian left it to his wife's decision; but when he heard that Lady Westrey had assured her that it would be best for her children if she went, and that, therefore, she had decided to go, there was gladness at his heart, and from that moment the county ball became an object of constant interest to him. Of course, much had to be said on the subject of dress and conveyance, and as to hours of going and returning. Julian was never tired of such discussions. With unabated interest he dwelt on his wife's going with Lady Westrey to the ball.

At last Anna, fondly embracing him, cried out, "Dear, kind, indulgent, patient father, why don't you go too?—do, dear father—why not?" And then, to his good wife's great surprise, he answered, "Not now, Anna, not *this* time, my darling child, but some other time I will go with you. We will all go together one day and join Lord Westrey's party in the room. Blessings on you for your fond wishes, my Anna. Some other day your father will have the joy and pride of escorting you himself—only, not now; some other time, my child."

This intention of her father's crowned Anna's happiness in her preparations for the event. She told her friends at Lullingstone, and they also were glad; and then she returned to the delight of being now to be accompanied by her mother.

When the day came, and good Mrs. Julian and her son and daughter arrived at Lullingstone, there was quite a delicate sort of rejoicing over the beauty of their appearance. Lady Westrey had induced Mrs. Herbert to join the party, that she might be companionable to Mrs. Julian at times when she should herself be engaged by her duties to her party. This was a good thought, so Mrs. Herbert was there with the desire of doing all that could be done to make the evening happy.

Sir Giles Morton was *not* there. Mary was all smiles. Edward was full of hope, and therefore in a state of boundless happiness. Lullingstone was like any thing that best denotes youth buoyant with joy. He rushed into his mother's dressing-room, where there was an assembling of the family, before the general assemblage in the drawing-room, and there kissed Mrs. Julian, and thanked her a thousand times for coming, and declared her more lovely to look upon, than any other guest in their house. He had already engaged Anna to dance an unreasonable number of times with him, and had criticized her dress, and persevered successfully in a whim about a full blown rose, which was changed, to please him, for a rose-bud. As the time arrived for their leaving Lullingstone, Mary was standing in the hall waiting for the second carriage; she was standing by her father's side, with her arm in his. Edward spoke to her: "Will you give me the pleasure of dancing with you to-night?" "Oh yes! When?" The fashion of keeping the same partner all night, we must inform the reader, had gone out of late. Edward did not answer Mary's question immediately. "The first dance?" she asked. "No, not the first." "Oh! I beg your pardon, I thought that you were disengaged." "I am disengaged, but—" Edward could not resist taking one glance at Lord Westrey's face; he was seemingly inattentive to what was going on; his eyes were wandering about the ceiling of the hall, as he stood drawn up to his utmost stature, the picture of a noble presence, with his fair, bright-eyed daughter on his arm.

But Edward thought that, amid all the legibly written dignity, he could decipher something about the corners of the mouth which spoke of an observant ear, and of rather an aroused attention to what was going forward. But, however that might be, Edward went bravely on. "I am not engaged, but there are those before whom I ought not to accept your kindness. Sometime to-night I will remind you."

"There is the carriage, Mary," said Lord Westrey.

"Come with us, Edward—come, if you like."

Edward sprang into the carriage, and in a moment they were off. It was a very full ball. The Lullingstone party was immediately voted the most attractive in the room.

Lord Westrey was not too old to open the ball with Lady Thoroughbred, whose noble husband had been for many years the patron of these entertainments, and within whose ground was the race-course. Lord Thoroughbred apologized for not dancing. He had broken his collar-bone that morning, but of course thought nothing of it, and rather gloried in being the hero of the night, in a coat cut open up the sleeve, and tied round his arm with blue ribbons.

"Anna Julian, this is Lord Arthur Underwood," says Lord Westrey. "Miss Julian, will you do me the honour," says Lord Arthur. "And

Edward," goes on Lord Westrey, "Mary is with her mother waiting for you."

And so the first appearance in public in their own county began. Things so well begun went on with equal prosperity. Mrs. Julian found some friends in the room. Mrs. Seaforth and her husband were there, and a large party accompanied them, amongst whom were Ralph, and the lady destined by his sister-in-law to be his bride—Miss Thomson. Lady Westrey also introduced Mrs. Julian to many persons in the room, with whose sons and daughters Edward and Anna had been dancing. There was no exception to the well-merited praises of her children.

Anna's beauty, her dancing, her manner, and her conversation, was the universal theme, varied by discussions on the probable riches of her father. It was the subject of the night. And still those praises rung through the room. They were ceaseless; they echoed backwards and forwards, and were heard by every one except by Anna herself: and we think we may say, that before the night was half over there was not a disengaged man in the room who would not have married Anna. It was the belief of many that she would be engaged that night. Fathers sighed after absent sons, mothers got introduced that they might try to keep her till they returned. Half a dozen men had declared to their particular friends their intentions of proposing. Double that number had made the like resolve, and kept it to themselves.

Of all this Anna neither knew nor suspected any thing. All she knew was, that she was intensely happy. But others of her party knew it—the gentlemen understood it all. Lord Westrey, Lord Arthur Underwood, and even young Lullingstone, were aware of the feeling that was excited, and each in his way was disturbed at it. It was certainly a severe penalty to pay for having attained to so high a pinnacle of success.

Anna's friends were annoyed, because the admiration excited was among rather too indiscriminate a host of people. As the time wore on the feeling increased. Knots of men, such as a large race ball must be supposed to bring together, spoke a little too loudly, and were disagreeably overheard. Lord Westrey wished his party safe at home, and began to think of making some excuse for retiring early; but to do so, he knew, would not be a popular measure in one of his rank—it would be taken as an attempt to set an example of early hours. At last the time for returning to Lullingstone arrived. The ball was pronounced to have been delightful. Anna had never been so happy before.

But Ralph Seaforth had that night involved himself in bets, which were all lost on the racecourse the next day, and to pay which put almost all that he possessed in the hands of Isaac the Jew. The maddening excitement of the whole thing—the contrast between the prosperity of the Julians and his own ruin, made him now think anxiously whether by securing Anna he could not retrieve his fortunes. There was vengeance in it too. Anna did not know that the worst enemy she could have was in the room that night.

CHAPTER XVIII.

MANY FEARS.

This presentation of Mrs. Julian and her son and daughter to the world in Lord Westrey's party at the race ball, made an agreeable impression on many families who had often heard of the Julians, and who had liked every thing that they had been told of them. To rise to fortune, and to adorn it, was a good thing in their eyes. They rejoiced to see the children of the lucky merchant such as they really were; they were glad to acknowledge their talents, and had no fear of ever repenting when they asked Lady Westrey to introduce them. This will always be remembered to John Julian's credit; and in the strange history of his rise in life the account of his own honest, straightforward simplicity of character will never be omitted. No doubt it had its effect on his children; it certainly made him, with all his oddities, and his one concealed ambition, a man to be respected, and to gather round him the sympathies and approval of persons born to a higher place in this world than his own.

Julian was a remarkable instance of the power of an idea upon a man—an idea to which he never was unfaithful. While he lived and persevered with an unfailing intention, he had always—though wildly and even unreasonably—felt that he might—yes, he *might* see that thing done—the thing he never dared to express with plainness even to himself. No doubt the knowledge of that mysterious gold, lying like a giant asleep in that iron-bound chest, had first helped to give birth to this idea—or at least to the idea that some great change was possible, even probable. Then came the opportunity; then the trial; then the success. Success the world called it. But there would be no success to John Julian till he saw his beloved Anna at Old Court Lullingstone. He had begun now to say that the thing would come. He had begun to see that Lullingstone Westrey loved his child—he enjoyed the youth's friendship with his son Edward. He gloried in Edward as being what no mere money success can make a man; Edward would have been great in character and acquirements even if the swift sailing *Sarah* had been lost for ever; so Julian felt under a sort of obligation to his good son, and showed an honest pride in every admiring word that was spoken of him.

Julian heard the ball described with an interest no man of his years had ever felt before. Asking questions in his strange way, reminding Anna of the old house, and his dreamy talk in the quiet shop when he had finished his day's work, or of evenings in the little oriel that looked upon the sea. It made the young girl laugh to remember this. She had an odd love for the old life. It came upon her as comes the remembrance of some long past mysterious time when a tale was told, into which our young imagination entered, till we felt ourselves actors in it—there was always something vague and dreamy in that remembrance; the thought of Harold made it so—Harold, whose name had never been uttered to her; of whom she had never spoken—not even to tell of what she had seen at Dyrbington. *But she had seen him!* The thought had in the girl's mind a mighty strength. It cased her young heart in armour. It had given her great diligence in study; it had blessed her with strength—strength to wait, to hope, to believe that they should meet again. And every day she blessed Mr. Dyrbington in her heart, when recalling Martha's words about the young German artist; and she blessed God too for the money by which she thought she had been made, perhaps, not unworthy of that man.

"Well, Anna, and so you danced, child; danced with Lord Arthur Underwood and Lullingstone— more than once; tell me child?" And so Anna again and again told the tale of her night of triumph, and gave her old father joy.

After this several families from a distance asked to know the Julians. Such introductions were usually made through Lord Westrey. Every one seemed fascinated by Julian's originality, and the unobtrusive gentleness of his wife; and there was but one opinion of the charm that dwelt with Anna. No one seemed to enjoy the contemplation of the Julian family more than a man who about three years before had distinguished himself at Oxford, and whose name and character had first been learnt there by Edward. Mr. Temple, of Templehousen, was the only son of a widowed mother, and one of the Members for Watermouth. He had been for some time interested in Edward, and at the race ball he had been introduced to Mrs. Julian and to Anna. When dancing with Mary Westrey he had heard much in Anna's praise, and he had followed up the acquaintance in a way that had made Lady Westrey suspect there was a special meaning in it. His mother too, who had won the character of being proud and reserved, had certainly not acted up to this character in her intercourse with Mrs. Julian: but then Mrs. Julian was a safe person without a particle of boasting in her whole composition. The grand Mrs. Temple always made herself very pleasant at Mayfield, and she had asked them all to Templehousen. Mrs. Julian was pleased when the great lady called, because she knew how to bring pleasure with her; but she had refused the invitation for all but Edward, who had gone and enjoyed himself. And when, on another occasion, Mrs. Julian again refused, and Mrs. Temple asked to have Anna entrusted to her, Mrs. Julian had honestly said, that if she could repeat the invitation some time when Lord and Lady Westrey was coming to Templehousen it would be gladly accepted, but that Anna must not go by herself. All this Mrs. Temple repeated with much commendation, and sometimes with bluntly expressed wishes, that all her friends were as sensible and right-minded as Mrs. Julian.

The Julians, in this way, found their acquaintance extending far beyond the circle of Watermouth. And quietly and peaceably they took what came for their children's sake, with an ease and graceful self-possession which was found to be universally attractive.

But the time had now come for Edward to return to Oxford. He was reading hard, for he intended to take honours. His twenty-first birthday had passed—passed without any public display of rejoicing at Mayfield, though many had suggested such a proceeding to John Julian. But the old man's reply had been like himself. "No, no; Ned has no inheritance. For his son perhaps, in days to come, there might be something done —but not for Ned. He has won his own laurels, and there are more waiting for his gathering, I fancy, though to his mother and me he can hardly be more honourable than he is." And yet, when the day came, there was not a poor father or mother in Watermouth who had not received, secretly, a blessing from John Julian's hand. Edward thanked his father for this, and worked harder than ever to repay him for his good deeds. Lullingstone was at Oxford, doing well, and strong enough now to make Lady Westrey's heart easy about his health. Mr. Parker lived in London, but was often at Oxford with his former pupils, whose progress he watched with an affection which they fully returned. Lullingstone had been at home for the whole of the long vacation; but Edward had only paid a visit of three weeks at Mayfield, and had then gone away with Mr. Parker to read. After his departure Anna had been asked to stay at Old Court, and the fact of Lullingstone being there had made her father more than willing to spare her. It was like a return to the old school-holiday time; for Lullingstone was still a petted boy, with the fascination of a merry wilfulness when he chose to put it on; though the charm of the thoughtfulness of manhood, when, in soberer moods, he let the depths of his character be known, was a far more terrible thing to Anna than the lively freedom of the more youthful state.

Again and again she wondered if Lady Westrey ever remembered the confession she had made after Lepard Eastner had threatened her. Again and again Anna felt a sensation scarcely short of terror, that Lady Westrey saw, and knew,—and Lord Westrey too—and that no one ever supposed that *she* could object. She felt as if bound by invisible chains. It was almost as if it were a thing understood. What could she do? She could not refuse that which had never been offered; and yet even Lullingstone himself seemed sometimes *almost* to throw off all disguise. Again and again, with aching heart, the poor girl wondered—What shall I do? But in October Lullingstone went away; and on the very day he went away Mary Westrey spoke to her—spoke plainly, as Mary did when she spoke at all.

She came into Anna's room with an open letter in her hand. "Look here; here is a letter from Mrs. Temple. She wants us all to go to Templehousen. You will not return to-morrow, now—you will go with us?"

"I think I should like to go, as Lady Westrey and Mrs. Temple propose it. Thank you, Mary," said Anna thoughtfully; "I should certainly like to go."

"You would *like* it," repeated Mary with a smile; "Anna, don't like it—not too much at least."

"Mary, what do you mean?"

"Sit down, Anna. Of course you have suspected?"

"What?"

"Don't be young-ladyish. You can be sincere with me. You know it would break our hearts if you liked it."

Anna grew suddenly strong and straight-seeing. She had begun to tremble; but when Mary made it a personal matter she grew strong at once.

"If Mr. Temple likes me, why not?" was her question.

"Sit down, Anna. I don't believe you care for Mr. Temple—we none of us think you do."

"You have discussed it?"

"Yes; ten times over. Mamma refused an invitation while Lullingstone was here—she thought it would be too much for him."

"But, Mary—"

"Stop, stop, darling," kissing her; "of course we know all about Mr. Temple—old family, long pedigree, great possessions, fine talents, an only son, in the best company, sits in Parliament, and dines with the king; but—"

"Mary, Mary!"

"Stop—wait. But you are not going to break Lullingstone's heart!" Then, with a great gasp, "I've said it now," said Mary.

Yes, she had said it indeed; so Anna sat down on the couch that just held two comfortably with Mary, and said, "Thank you. But I wish I had known before what you were thinking about."

"You have known it all your life—your life with us, I mean," answered Mary. "Mamma knows that you knew it; it has been the one idea of Lullingstone's life; and you know, Anna, that if for any reason my father had disliked it, we should not have had you here; we should have loved you just the same, but common justice to Lullingstone would have prevented my father and mother having you here, as it has been our delight to have you."

"Has there been no justice for me?" asked Anna with a face of despair. "Has Lullingstone ever said he liked me?"

"Yes; to me. To me, over and over again, he has spoken of it. You know that in his health no trial that could be helped would ever be allowed to harass him. But this is no trial. If he likes it we like it—and you know you don't care for Mr. Temple."

"I like Mr. Temple. I don't want to *marry* him—I wouldn't. But, Mary—now, Mary, I will be heard. I will not have Lullingstone talk of loving me."

"Don't say so," said Mary; "it is a foolish pride."

"Not so. I couldn't—I couldn't marry Lullingstone!"

But Mary's face grew pale as death. "It has been like a thing understood," she said. "You would be his death if you said 'No.' Oh, my

T

sister! Anna, you *will* be a sister to me? How could we bear the cross of seeing our darling broken-hearted! But you don't know," urged Mary; "you have thought him boyish and thoughtless; but, oh, Anna, he has had one thought ever since you first came to us in London. When he speaks to you, you will feel differently. Anna, why do you look so wretched! You can't dislike to marry Lullingstone. Of course you will marry—marry some one. It is, for you, a matter of course—why do you weep?"

But Mary wept herself now! and Anna sobbed in her arms bitterly. But it was not long—she roused herself, and said, "I don't want to be unkind—ungrateful. But this matter-of-course way of dealing with me has been wrong. If I now show that we are too old for playful friendship—if, in fact, I refuse to come here until Lullingstone thinks of some one else, you must make Lady Westrey understand the reason. You will tell her of all we have said to-night."

"I could not. At least I could not just now. Wait—he will not be back till Christmas; of course you can explain then if you like. But oh, Anna! *think;* think of the misery you may cause. You cannot care for any one else."

"It is enough that, in that way, I shall never care for Lullingstone," said Anna. "Now, Mary, I will not go to Templehousen, and I will go back to Mayfield. I will go home to-morrow." And so on the morrow Anna returned home, with a heavy heart, and a feeling of having involuntarily injured her dearest friends, and of having to give up Old Court—give up the greatest pleasure of her life.

But she had only been a few days at home when a note came to her from Lord Westrey. He entreated her to return to them, saying that Lullingstone was extremely ill, and that he was going to start for Oxford immediately. Mary and Lady Westrey wanted her, he said. So Anna returned in the carriage that had been sent for her, and found her friends in the greatest distress.

Hour after hour Lady Westrey in her little chapel prayed for her child's life. Alas! it was to this mother like praying for his soul too. Now came the full sense of the greatness of that separation so terrible for great love to contemplate; and Anna saw Lady Westrey's wasted look, and watched her suffering as she waited for the accounts that Lord Westrey sent with a heart full of awe. Oh, this son, how dear he was! And then she blamed herself for being there, even then, and trembled for fear of another trial in which *she* might have to act the part of *Fate*.

After three days Lord Westrey came back. He brought better accounts. But the weakness which now prostrated his son was of a most alarming kind. He spoke of Edward; speaking of him, before Mary, with the most grateful praise. Lullingstone's love for Edward had now, in his weakness, become a trying gift. In fact he could not bear his friend out of his sight. "And so," said Lord Westrey, "Edward has thrown aside his books, and gives up every thing to yield to our dear boy's whims. It might cost us Lullingstone's life to change things now—indeed Edward, I believe, could not be persuaded away from him. Parker is there, and said several times that we should thank Edward for Lullingstone's life. I spoke to him," said Lord Westrey. "I felt how important this last month's reading would be to him. But he cast all such thoughts aside. He does not care for taking honours, if Lullingstone is to suffer for his absence. Besides his heart is so much with our boy that I don't believe he could read. He is there night and day." Thus talking, thus listening, two days passed, and Lord Westrey returned to Oxford. Better accounts came of Lullingstone; but Edward was said to be tired out. Then improved accounts of Edward, and plans for bringing Lullingstone home, and day after day Anna felt that there was that in the love and thankfulness that bound her family and the Westreys to each other that took away her strength, and made a captive of her will.

Lord Westrey again returned from Oxford—Lullingstone could not be moved; Edward had put off going up for his examination until Easter. "It vexes me," said Lord Westrey, "yet I am glad. Owing to his devotion to Lullingstone, he would now have gone up at a disadvantage. His tutor felt that he would be wrong to go up. All who know him are full of his praises, and now I can take his devotion to my son with a less anxious heart." But still unsatisfactory accounts came of Edward, and when Lord Westrey next went to Oxford John Julian went with him.

It surprised Anna a little when her father came back to hear so little of Edward, and so much of Lullingstone. The old man's interest seemed to be absorbed by the statue-like figure of the happy, merry youth, who had been the life of Old Court but a short time before. It was true that he had been for a few weeks at death's door, and that only Edward's ceaseless loving care had kept him from the grave. The strong love that Lullingstone had given to Edward, and the respect and admiration he entertained for him had made him gentle and obedient under his guidance; and as he grew better he confided in Edward so perfectly, that only to have him in the room with him, seemed to give him repose and peace. So the ties between these families strengthened; and Anna, as she saw that it was so, felt in dread of the trouble and difficulties that most assuredly would come.

Just before Christmas Lullingstone was brought back to Old Court. He had said that he hoped Anna would be there. Unluckily for her she was staying there at the time, and it became impossible for her to return. He was carried through the hall, and laid on a sofa in the library; not yet able to walk without help, requiring to be kept free from all excitement, and with injunctions from the medical man who had been attending him to keep him in peace of mind and rest of body, and as nearly as possible in the same temperature till the spring, by which time it was believed that, if there was no relapse, he would be restored to health. His spirits were very good, and perhaps he had never been more really interesting to a kind woman's heart than he was as he lay in his constrained helplessness, full of pleasant talk, and so good-tempered and thankful, that not to love Lullingstone in one sense was impossible.

At Christmas Edward came, making Mayfield bright. Mr. Parker, too, arrived at Old Court. General meetings at the two houses occurred frequently. And, at Old Court, Lullingstone would praise Edward till he was stopped by his friend's remonstrances, and repetitions of the doctor's prohibition concerning too much conversation. But Lady Westrey knew how much they owed to Edward, and she told him so.

The winter wore away;—Anna trying to be as little as possible at Old Court, and every one there trying to secure as much of her time as possible—her father pressing her to go—her mother saying that now a time had come when she could repay Lady Westrey in some degree for her great goodness. Was she not wanted to read aloud and sing to Lullingstone? Ah, that fatal gift of song! How her heart ached as she poured forth strain after strain, to the sick youth's delight, till at last, in a transport of misery, she said, " Oh, when will this end! Are we to live on poisons for ever?" But Mary only shed tears, and said, "Is it so very hard to love him? If you are going to marry at all, why not him? You know us all—love us—is that nothing to you? We all wish it—oh, Anna, it must be sweet to be welcome!" And once Mary asked, "Anna, tell me; is there any one else?" And when her friend refused to speak, she told her that her own father wished for it as much as any one of them. " Have you not known it, Anna?" But now Anna could laugh. " Oh no, Mary. Wise one, no!" And Mary was silenced.

On the excuse of Edward going to Oxford after Christmas, Anna returned to Mayfield. And there, one evening, sitting alone in the room that was called her own, Edward told Anna all that he had ever felt about Mary Westrey, and how Lord Westrey had now bid him win her if he could—how he had told his father that, after he had passed his examination at Easter, he should bravely try to make an interest in her heart. The wonder with which Anna listened was extreme. As Edward talked she began to see what a great and solemn thing was a long-enduring, faithful devotion to a lawful end; how it had possessed Edward—guided him—made him. And one quick thought of Harold came—of the picture —of his face of hope and truth; and then a sudden resolution to give up going to Old Court— *if possible;* and then, poor girl, her heart seemed to faint within her, and she bade Edward good-night tearfully.

Edward went to Oxford, and Easter came, and the examination. And Edward had got a double first. For this they were asked to Old Court to make rejoicing that his devotion to Lullingstone had only postponed his success; and Anna could not help being left behind. Edward came down to Old Court to receive again from Lord Westrey full leave to win Mary if he could. Then he went to Mayfield, and talked to his parents of his hope.

CHAPTER XIX.

JULIAN'S SUCCESS.

On the following day Julian arrived at Lullingstone. He came to see Lord Westrey; for Edward had told him exactly what had passed. He told Lord Westrey that his daughter should not listen to the proposals of a man dependent on his father. He would settle two thousand a year on Edward immediately, and a further sum on Mary if she married Edward. And he wanted Lord Westrey to go to a place about five miles distant, called Thornbank, which he wished to purchase for Edward.

Lord Westrey hesitated about going; he said that he did not like to do any thing which might make matters look more certain than they really were. But Julian pressed him to go. Thornbank was to be sold in a few days. He hoped Lord Westrey would see it with him. So Lord Westrey consented, and they went together.

When they were gone Mary Westrey sought Anna. Would she go with her and Lullingstone? Anna hesitated; but Lady Westrey immediately said, "Oh yes; go, dearest Anna. You ought not to stay in this morning. Is your brother going to *walk*, Mary?"

"He is going to try to walk to the holly-dell, and there Mark, in about an hour, is to bring the pony. He is so well to-day, mamma, that I think he will manage it."

"He must not over-fatigue himself," said Lady Westrey anxiously.

"I think he has seemed much stronger, both yesterday and to-day," said Anna.

"He is really stronger, but I dread sudden changes; even sudden improvements are bad symptoms for one in his delicate state. His nerves are so tenderly alive just at present, his spirits are so easily affected, and his health depends so much upon his spirits. Oh, it has been a terrible trial! It is still a most serious thing," exclaimed Lady Westrey.

Then looking at Mary's wretched face of fear and woe, she suddenly checked herself, and putting her arm within her daughter's she said, "But you need not be afraid, my dear Mary, I am sure that he is better. We have been recommended to take him to Madeira. I have thought of telling you many times, but I shrunk from doing so, for you are as nervous about him as I am, I think, my child."

"I have been very low about him sometimes," said Mary.

"But he does not require Madeira now, surely? He seems wonderfully well to-day," said Anna.

"Well, go out now."

And, thus dismissed, the two girls prepared for their walk. The three spent all that morning out of doors; sometimes walking, sometimes sitting in some warm, yet shaded nook. Once or twice Mary reminded Lullingstone that it was time to return—that he had never, since his illness, been out for so long at a time. He could not attend to her—he was too happy. But Anna, she was saying long tender farewells to the spots she loved so much—she could not, would not visit Lullingstone again, till she could see it with a less anxious heart. She would never again be forced into such a false position; henceforth she would be true to herself—honest to her own feelings; never again would she allow herself to be so compassed about with difficulties; she should that day be free once more; she would take her freedom to her heart, and never again part from it for a moment. And then, when that future came, which surely would come, she should feel that she had been as true to Harold as he had been to her. Lord Westrey and Julian during this time had made their visit to Thornbank, and were returning to Lullingstone. While their children had been dwelling upon the romance of life they had been satisfactorily engaged with its realities. They agreed that Thornbank would do extremely well: that it was neither too large nor too small, but just what they desired.

Julian had returned in greater spirits than usual. He had a stronger realization of the happiness of success. As he returned, and the carriage drove on to the terrace where he had liked, in days long passed, to walk with Lord Westrey, while his wife made her *adieux* to the ladies within, John Julian smiled, and felt how gladdening a thing it was *to be* all that he had once dwelt upon in dreamy longings. There was not a visible drawback to his happiness. The eyes of the world in which he lived were upon himself and his children—they were approving, admiring eyes; great things were promised to him—greater still were pressing round him; he was a great man—great in himself and in his children; and John Julian stood free and welcome before the walls of Old Court Lullingstone, and looked forth upon the world and smiled, happy at his own success.

"Won't you dine with us? Must you really return?"

"I must go back, my lord; Mrs. Julian expects us."

"But you will see Lullingstone before you go. We think him better. The doctors have been talking of Madeira, but I think that a little travelling may do—to the south of France, for instance; he only requires a little present care."

"I should like to see Lullingstone. Where is he?"

"Oh, in the little room up-stairs—you know the way—I must go to Lady Westrey."

Julian proceeded towards the room pointed out to him as being occupied by Lullingstone.

It was a room in which Lullingstone usually spent his mornings. It had been fitted up expressly for him in consequence of this illness. On this morning, after his return from walking, Mary and Anna had been sitting with him. There were two doors, one opening to the great staircase, by which the servants usually entered. Lullingstone's couch was drawn towards a large stone-mullioned window, which let in upon the room a lovely view of the scenery without; a table stood near, and at right angles with his couch; another like it facing the window; and, to shield his couch from the draft of the side-door, there was a high leather screen.

It was a habit with John Julian to open a door very softly. It was perhaps the remains of his workman-like ways. He put his hand on the lock, and turned it slowly and gently, as if testing its powers. So he opened that side-door. The screen hid the speakers from his sight; but he could not help hearing their voices, and he knew them to belong to his daughter and Lullingstone. For a moment he was transfixed with what he heard—"I love you so earnestly, Anna!" Julian held his breath; and then stepped back into the passage, closing the door.

"Oh, Lullingstone! But you must not talk in that sort of way, you know." Anna was a true woman. The trial was come; the time for discretion and determination; she was penetrated with the acutest sentiments of distress, but her voice was calm and free; and her slight words, in answer to the terrible truth that had been told, were as gently spoken as if she had been answering the loving expressions of a petted child.

"And why not?" asked Lullingstone, smiling, and quite amused by the answer he had received. "Why not, Anna?"

"Because it is not fair," she said, now looking up from the sweet wild violets she was tying up so busily in little bunches.

"Not fair! What do you mean?"

"It is not fair to talk of love, when you are not sufficiently strong to bear the excitement of a refusal," said Anna, gravely.

Lullingstone laughed outright. "You delightful little creature!" he exclaimed. Then, suddenly pausing,—"Anna, what was that? Look at the door." Anna looked round the screen.

"The door is shut," she said; "did you hear any one?"

"I fancied that I heard the door open. But, when I am strong enough to bear refusal, then you will not give it to me; will you, Anna?

Please to remember, then, what I am going to tell you now. I shall *never be strong enough to bear that from you;* will you promise to remember that?"

"I promise to forget that any thing of the kind has ever been spoken of—there! I forget it all—what were we talking about? I forget—it is gone! Lullingstone, it is past the hour when I promised my father to be ready. I must leave you alone. Mary promised to be only a minute away, and she has been absent a full half hour. Ah!—there she is—no! my father. I will be ready immediately;" and Anna ran off to her own room. She had well said that she would be ready immediately. She felt that she would not at that moment leave her father and Lullingstone together for worlds. She threw her shawl round her shoulders, and returned to the room with her bonnet in her hand. She found them talking of Thornbank. She put her hand within her father's arm, and drew him away. They bade Lullingstone good-bye, and then went to Lady Westrey's room to repeat their farewell there. She had no rest in her mind till she was safe in the carriage by her father's side, and on the way to Mayfield.

It was a very silent drive. Julian took his pocket-book out, and pretended to be engaged in calculations; in truth, he was so impressed with, as it seemed to him, the fulfilment of *every* hope, that he could not speak. Anna thought that he was satisfying his mind on some questions relating to Thornbank, and was glad of an excuse for not entering into conversation. There sat father and child; their minds occupied by the same thought; —one depressed to a state bordering on misery, the other raised to so great happiness that, at that time, and in that place, he dared not think of it, lest the rapture it excited should get beyond control.

When Julian had heard all that he dared hear in his unsuspected situation in Lullingstone's room, he had retired as softly as he could. Lullingstone had heard the sound of his departure; but neither he nor Anna guessed that that sound arose from one who had overheard what had been said.

For a moment, in that silent passage, Julian had stood with his head and hands upraised. So full was his heart with the sense of the extent of his happiness, that his lips softly whispered—" It is too much—too much!" But then he took courage, and it was solemn—very solemn, the way in which that man thanked God for that which he had heard—for granting to him the thought and desire of his heart—for all that He had given him. When he saw Anna again, and felt her hand upon his arm, it was as if she had grown a thousand times more precious to him than she had ever been before. He sat by her in the carriage, and felt that the desire of his soul was satisfied. He did not want to talk. His spirit sought to rest upon its knowledge. He would not disturb such happiness; his life was buoyed up upon it; it supported his very soul. Now he knew what success meant. Success—success—people had called it his before. But they knew not that the things of which they spoke were but as trash compared to that secret desire of his heart, which was now accomplished. No gratification that he had ever felt was in any degree to be compared to this. The events of the past he had never regarded but as means to an end; and now the end was come. Again Julian lifted up his heart and thanked God.

Anna entered Mayfield hurriedly. She gave her mother one kiss, and then asked for Edward. He was upstairs. She would go to him. She remained with him some time. She told him all. "You must take a note from me to Lady Westrey," she said; "and you must make them understand that it can never be. Remember, Edward, no unkind kindness—no hopes—no looking to the future. My answer is *No*—and *Never!*"

In vain Edward prayed and besought. In vain he urged her to wait—to take more time. In vain he painted the difficulty it might make for himself—the distress of Lullingstone—the vexation of his father and mother—and the unaccountableness of her conduct. He even reproached her with having grown proud and impetuous, and said that it was her duty to listen to reason. Anna would hear nothing, and submit to no persuasions. He was to take her note to Lady Westrey, informing her briefly of what had passed; and he was to make it clearly understood, that her answer was as she had said, "No—and Never!"

At last she gained her point. The note was written, and Edward took possession of it. Grieved, vexed, and angry, the young man pursued his way. As Anna gazed after him, her heart grew lighter and lighter, till she felt quite glad and gay.

How proud and happy her father was that night! She played and sung; she amused him by her lively talk; she wove together bright groups of flowers for their room; she was the crowning joy of his life, and silently his heart blessed her a thousand times.

That night, after Anna and her mother had each left the drawing-room some time, there came a gentle knock at the door of the ante-room to Anna's bed-room, which had been prettily fitted up for her use by day. In this little sitting-room, wrapped in an embroidered India robe, with her feet thrust into slippers, quilted and wadded, and leaning on a small couch, was Anna, deep in thought on the events of the day. It so happened that her father had frequently added to the decoration and furniture of this gay little apartment out of love to the child, who called it, not a little proudly, her own. A brilliant lamp hung from the ceiling; pictures adorned the walls; a pianoforte, a music stand, a guitar, and a long narrow table, occupied one side; a bookcase, filled with the literature Anna best liked, occupied another; it was a very choice spot for ease and retirement; and in it, at that hour of the night, Anna found as much as she could have found any where. "What do I want?" she was asking herself, and looking round on the many indications of taste and wealthy liberality which surrounded her. "I have every thing," was her answer; "why, then, should I not be free? If I could sell myself in marriage, what is there upon earth that would be called gain to me?"

Again the little knock came, and Anna rising, went to the door.

"Who is there?"

"Your father—can you let me in?"

"Yes, dear father—there, come in. You look as if something was the matter. What is it?"

"Nothing—never mind, Anna." He looked with a gratified air on the luxury around him. "Are you comfortable here—in this room, I mean, Anna?"

"What do you think?" she answered, smiling, and setting him a chair, and kissing his forehead gently as he dropped into it.

"My dear child—my Anna, why don't you tell me?" She was still stooping over him, and he

now took her hand and pressed it to his heart
and lips. "Do you know that your old father
could not sleep till he had heard it; so he sought
his child, that her sweet voice might tell him."

"Tell him—tell you—what is it, dear father?"
And Anna pressed his head against her neck, and
bent till her cheek touched his, and her long
golden hair rested on his shoulder, and strayed
across his breast. "Tell you what, father?"

Then Julian told his daughter how he had stood
unseen in Lullingstone's room, and what he had
heard.

The warm cheek that had touched his grew as
cold as ice, and Julian started from it. He
jumped from his seat and looked at Anna, as she
still stood drooping over the back of the chair on
which he had been sitting.

"What did you say, Anna—what have you
answered him?"

She knew by Julian's manner how it was. She
knew her father well. She knew the voice and
manner which spoke of feelings deep in that rugged
heart, which could never be expressed, but which
thus by voice and manner were betrayed. She
knew by the trembling of that giant form; she
knew by the scintillation of that blood-shot eye;
she knew by the strained posture of that generally
bowed head; she knew by the nervous grasping
of the huge hand at the first object within reach,
and by a grating, discordant sharpness in the

voice, and by the tremulous articulation of the few words he spoke—that he felt from the bottom of his soul interested in her answer. 'That he desired to hear that she had said "Yes" to Lullingstone, with that strong desire formed of the concentration of all the hopes, wishes, and plans of his most exciting and extraordinary life; and that, with this desire, there was awakened for the first time a never anticipated pain—the fear that she had said "No."

Alas! alas! She had thought her trial over; now she knew that it had just begun!

She raised herself slowly from her drooping attitude. She knew that she must be firm. "I refused to marry Lullingstone Westrey," she said, with a gentle gravity—"I do not wish to marry him. I cannot marry him. I said all that I dared say to him in his delicate state of health, and I made my answer final by desiring Edward—"

"Edward! How dare he?"—Oh! was it fiend or man that spoke? Anna shuddered.

"I *made* him deliver my note. I insisted on his explaining my meaning to Lord Westrey, that there might be no misunderstanding—that they might know that I was not presuming to trifle with them—that they might instantly make the matter clear to Lullingstone—my answer was *No—and Never!* I said it many times, and I repeat it now. Father! you have given me all that any woman can require—speak no more of this—Edward is disappointed—my mother, perhaps, will be; and I see that you are, but—"

She paused, for Julian was trembling as if struck with palsy. "It has been the one desire of my life." He gasped the words slowly.

"Oh, don't say that!—ask any thing else of me," said Anna.

"I never wanted any thing else—I have nothing else to ask. We will alter this message—you can't mean it. I thought of it when you were children. I desired wealth, to make it easy to me. The wealth came—I *so* desired it—night and day. My thoughts—all, Anna, of you, God knows it—you did not speak positively, Anna." The voice and manner were so changed, Anna could not read their meaning now. "We can alter this—you referred them to me—speak—Anna!"

"Try to bear it, father. Think of how you loved me. We will talk of it to-morrow. I don't like to seem undutiful—I can't bear giving you a moment's pain—sit down, lean your head on my shoulder. Kiss me, and forgive me."

He did not seem to listen to her. Her heart felt raw and bleeding. Her anxiety to pacify and comfort him pained her in its excess; but he did not seem to understand her. He looked at her oddly, and said, "Ah, yes; we can alter this!"

"No, father, I am not going to marry Lullingstone Westrey." She spoke firmly. He understood that. A strange look of pain passed across his face, and he tottered. Anna ran, tried to support him—the weight was too great—he fell sideways, crushing her against the couch; his mouth opened, and a small quantity of blood just stained his tongue and lips; his eyes were glazed —his strength—his senses—had departed. John Julian was in a fit. And round his daughter, like eddying waves, returned the words, "I desired wealth to make it easy to me. I *so* desired it—night and day—all for you, Anna. God knows it!"

And now the desire of his eyes had passed away from him, and he had shrunk beneath the woe. The money—the mysterious money—had purchased that for which it had been desired; and she, his daughter, for whom he had asked it, had hurriedly put the desired thing aside, or refused to have any thing to do with it; she had cast it off, and put it beyond her father's reach. Had that wealth ever been a friend to her? Had it brought her any thing but evil, fear and trial? There lay her father senseless—had it not wrought that work also? Anna disengaged herself from the weight that held and crushed her; she rang the bell, alarmed the house, and brought her mother to her aid. One servant was sent for medical assistance, another to Lullingstone to fetch Edward; and Mrs. Herbert was also sent to. The story was told to her mother by Anna, in a few words:—

"He came here to speak to me about Lullingstone Westrey. He had heard something at Lullingstone this morning. Lullingstone asked me to marry him, and Lord and Lady Westrey would not disapprove of the marriage, I believe. My father came here to ask what answer I had given Lullingstone, and I told him I could not marry him. I did not know till to-night that my father had so desired this marriage. He did not say much. It was evident to me that he was shocked, and grievously disappointed. But I could not yield. I said that I could not. He fell down; as he now is,—he fell. But, mother," she added earnestly, "if to marry Lullingstone were to save his life, *I could not do it.*"

Poor Mrs. Julian! She could only weep.

The doctor came, and all remedial measures were applied. Mrs. Herbert came, and gave sympathy, counsel, and assistance. Mr. and Mrs. Seaforth were at Mayfield at an early hour in the morning. They saw Julian. He was still insensible. The doctor still stood by the bedside. He could not give any opinion as to the result. Edward had returned, and Lord Westrey had accompanied him. Lord Westrey had sent for the physician who attended his family. He said that he should be better satisfied if there was a further consultation. The Watermouth doctor thanked him, and replied, that he was thinking of asking for assistance, and was glad to hear of such an arrangement. Then he took Lord Westrey aside, and asked if Mr. Julian had made his will?

That morning, as Mr. and Mrs. Seaforth sat at breakfast, they talked of Julian. Ralph wandered in and partook of the morning repast with them. He, too, could only talk of Julian. The shock and the great interest of the case had overcome Mr. Seaforth's usually silent habits on subjects of business.

"John Julian is an instance of the great advantages attendant upon a habit of promptness," he said. "He has been the most energetic man I ever knew. He makes up his mind, and, when that is done, he never loiters or puts off about the measures which are to follow. A very remarkable instance of this has just happened. He has just determined to settle Edward handsomely in life. He had occasion lately to leave a considerable sum of money in the hands of a London house. Well, yesterday he visited Thornbank, liked it very much, spoke to Edward about it, and found it to be equally agreeable to him. Immediately he wrote to the agent proposing to become a purchaser. He had previously ascertained that the money for the estate, when paid, was to be lodged in the hands of Williamson at B——. He, therefore, last evening, empowered me to get that money from

London for him, and keep it in my hands for the use of his son Edward. Therefore, you see that, if he never regains his mind, his son's prospects will never be at all injured, for he can complete this or any other purchase for himself."

"Wonderful!" exclaimed Ralph. "You mean to say that he actually completed a legal instrument in his son's favour last night?"

"I do, indeed. And giving Edward a large sum in the funds."

Mrs. Seaforth prepared for a second visit to Mayfield.

When she got there, she was glad to learn that Julian was a little recovered. Yet sensation had come back in a sad, uncertain way. He seemed to be in a very wandering state of mind—talking strangely, sometimes with great rapidity, and at other times slowly, and even with difficulty. Thus he went on for the whole day. Towards night he appeared to be more in his right mind. He recognized his wife, answered one or two questions, and smiled on Anna, holding—or trying to hold—out his hand to her. Dr. Davis said that he was improved; and it was arranged that the medical attendants should not sit up that night, but that Mrs. Julian and Anna should stay in the room, and that young Mark Wyke—of whom of all his servants Julian was fondest—should sleep in the dressing-room; so that, if any help was wanted, he might be called, and further assistance be easily procured. This comforted Anna; for she had had so much to do with his illness, that to wait upon him, and watch him, and if possible never to leave him, was necessary to her peace of mind.

When night came, therefore, she persuaded her mother to rest herself in a large easy-chair which had been brought into the room, and supplied with pillows for that purpose. She herself, supplied with some noiseless work, took her place nearer to her father's bed. Anna had received her instructions; she was not to mind his talking in his sleep, but, if the excitement of mind increased so as to lead to bodily action or any thing like delirium, then she was to summon Dr. Davis.

For the first three hours all was calm. Anna persuaded her mother to get some sleep herself, and at last seeing that all things promised well, Mrs. Julian attended to her child's whispered remonstrances, and prepared herself for repose. The mother slept, and slept soundly, as tired and exhausted persons are apt to do, immediately on any relief being afforded to the mind. Still Anna worked quietly, and still her father slumbered at her side. There was a curtain drawn between her and him, and the lamp by which she worked was so shaded on the side next to the bed as to keep its light entirely off the sleeper.

After a time he moved a little. Anna rose and propped him with his pillows so as to support him in his changed position. Her hands about him perhaps disturbed him; the brain grew restless again, and again he began to talk, not loudly, but with a dull quickness, which was harrowing in its meaningless volubility. At first, Anna could not understand what he said, but soon she found that he was talking of what had lately occurred; of her and Lullingstone, of Edward and Mary, of Thornbank, money, Lord Westrey, Mr. Seaforth— never seeming to dwell on any one of these subjects with either pain or pleasure; but talking on, in an incoherent, senseless way, like a thing obliged to talk—as an instrument is wound up for motion, not able to help himself, but obeying some uncontrollable impulse, by which this wearing action was continued while there remained strength to produce it.

It was inexpressibly painful to hear this. Anna stooped over the sufferer, passed her arm beneath his neck, and, kissing him, whispered—" Try not to talk, dear father; try to be at rest; try to sleep; Anna watches by you; let her see you sleep." She had no idea whether he would hear her or not. She had spoken from a desire to stop that wearing current of words, or at least somehow to change it. It did change, but that was all.

The words now ran on about old times—the times of the old house. They flowed not so fast —there seemed to be more of mind and meaning in them; there was certainly memory. That boundless sea on which he had so often gazed

—the workshop—where in such strange ways he had used to speak to the young, timid child, who yet loved to be always near him. The room, so prettily arranged, where they used to sit when work was over; the chair on which Julian always rested, and where his day-dreams had been so often sought, and encouraged. All these things passed in rapid review; not as one describing them did Julian speak, but he talked of them without any pause between the subjects, passing from one to another, and back again, in a manner which only one who had known such things in their reality could have comprehended. But Anna could disentangle these subjects as she listened; and listening, sighed, and wondered if such a state of mind ought to be permitted to continue undisturbed—if she should try to wake him, or if she should send for Dr. Davis.

But stay—he talks of other things now, things about which Anna does not understand. The old iron chest, his own boyhood; that that chest's contents *must* live, and bring to its owner his wishes. Those wishes were wealth—wealth for *her*—for Anna; and then came words about the hidden store itself. Anna shuddered—"Oh! he is not mad—he is not going mad—this, surely, is not madness!" The tears gushed, and she sank upon her knees, and hid her face on the covering of the bed where lay, like a thing struck powerless, her poor father's arm, all bound with stained bandages, from where they had bled him. She took the senseless hand; it seemed like the hand of a corpse, and pressed upon it kisses of agonizing feeling.

And now, whether or not disturbed by her caresses, she did not know, Julian's voice waxed louder, and his words more distinct—

"I read the papers, I read them often, I could read them, they were Latin, but I learnt at the corporation school—I always from a boy had kept trying to read them. I had picked up their meaning clear enough; they belonged to the gold, the gold belonged to them; they had been afraid to spend it; 'twas a fair sight, a good sight; it was looking upon power; year upon year had rolled up, more than two hundred and fifty years they had kept the papers of St. Julian's chapel; those of Dyrbington were copied; it was easy to read them; they had got the English of it; given by Sir John Dyrbington to Snigge, to reward his faithful services, and at his own request, copes, chasuble, chalice, paten, sometime used in the chantry chapel of St. George at Dyrbington, not the ones given by the Bishop at consecrating the altar, but others bestowed by Dame Dorothy, and the second set of all the utensils belonging to the chapel of St. Katherine, and power to carry out their intentions of the laws of godly framing against the chapel of St. Julian, and memorandum of the spoils of the Benedictine house on Benet's

Mount, and the same of the Augustinians in Friary court, and more, a good deal more, and money saved and hoarded, and money from things changed away through Spanish vessels, which could not have been safely changed away in this country, all good gold—put them aside in separate heaps; I knew that they were not going to be lost; I knew that they would bring me my wishes one day. Mr. Seaforth, very silent—good friend—good—good."

Like a fair statue of white alabaster stood Anna by his side. Her ears had been drinking in each word. This was no raving; there was no madness there; it was the story of the past, incoherently told, but true; it was the source of their wealth displayed. She had never heard a syllable of it before, but she felt that *now* all that she heard was true. He had paused; he had taken a few slow breaths as if resting from his exertions; and then, just in the same way, he went on—

"It couldn't die—it couldn't go down; it was blessed gold; it was obliged to live. I knew it would come back. It would come back, and give me my wish. Anna! Anna! beauty and power; I used to see them together, put to stand side by side, Lord Westrey and I, the two fathers, looking upon them; I said, Give me that—ah! gold, gold, gold—Give me *that;* I said to it, Give me *that!* It all went away; all—all! It was quite empty, that great box. I sent it all away, but I knew

that it would come back. Seaforth took it—
waited. Oh!—" again there was a pause; again,
as if for rest, the tongue ceased to move for a
while. But now Anna leaned forward, afraid of
losing a single word; longing to hear the end.

"Ah! rich—rich; very rich now; all succeeding. She is always with him. I had said, Give
me *that!* I always said it. I knew that I should
have it. The money had come, and the other
would come. Hark! hush—Anna! Love! yes,
I heard him. It is come; it is *all* come. I have
it all now; yes, all! Oh! my heart—all, all; it
is all come. Let me go—let me go to them!
Lullingstone! Let me bless them; all is come—
mine—mine; oh!—oh!—"

Like a cry of pain he uttered the last words.
Anna spoke to him, but her voice seemed to make
him more agitated. He repeated those cries; in
notes of agony they rose. Mrs. Julian started up.
"Hush, mother! He will be quiet again directly;
don't move." She sat up with staring eyes, fixed
in horrible distress upon the sufferer.

The loud cry of the delirious man rang round
the room. He raised himself in the bed. Anna
tried to draw him towards her to be soothed, to
rest on her shoulder; but he was as stiff as iron,
and he glared at her. Oh! a long, fixed, terrible,
glaring look he fastened upon her; not as a man
looks, but as a wild beast, roused by a raging
hunger, glares upon his prey. "Call Mark," she

cried in a smothered voice, for she was afraid. "No, no!" cried Julian, loudly, and his wife instinctively stopped in her passage across the room, for she thought that those words were addressed to her. "No, no, Anna! I tell you, child—dear child—ah! if you knew; it is here—" he pressed his hand against his head. "But, I won't—I can't hear it! No, no! Tell me again, Anna! I didn't hear."

Again those loud cries—now louder, sharper, and more agonizing than ever—smote their ears, and sank into their souls.

The servant heard, and woke, and drew his clothes about him quickly, and joined his mistress in that chamber of distress. But Julian seemed to see no one but Anna. Still his eyes were fixed upon her with an expression of mingled horror and inquiry; and, as he glared at her, his jaw dropped, and his mouth opened wide.

The thought came into her mind that she would pacify him by saying that she would marry Lullingstone. A bright picture of the change from death to life that those few words would make passed before her. Something within urged her. The words are on her lips—"I will marry Lullingstone, my father;"—the words are on her lips—give them voice—speak, and it will be done. He is dying—he is dying mad! Should medicine save him, he may be an idiot. He can never recover this if it continues much longer. It is all

x

in your own power—speak, and give him life and reason. The words are on your lips; speak, and it will be done!

But there passed other visions before her mind's eye. There came the recollection of Harold's last lingering look—of how her heart had pleaded for him in that room—and how she had resisted, and he had gone away without a word. No! she could not speak. Her father lay gasping on her breast; but she could not say that she would marry Lullingstone. No! not if it would save his life.

A soft step was heard by her side. It was Dr. Davis. He looked sadly on his patient—he put his fingers to his wrist—his throat—his temples. Julian never moved.

"You must go, Miss Julian—you must not come near your father again till I give you leave. Go—go directly, if you please; he must not see you."

Bursting into tears, Anna left the room. She flew hastily to her own little apartment. Scarcely a thing had been touched since her father had fallen there. She threw herself on the ground where she had seen him lie, and poured forth tears and groans unheard and undisturbed.

CHAPTER XX.

A WEIGHT OF WOE.

There while Anna lay in mingled sorrow and surprise, she thought of all that she had heard. The secret of their rapid and extraordinary rise in life was before her. Anna had often heard Mr. Dyrbington's feelings on the subject of sacrilegious wealth discussed. That there was a clinging evil in such treasures she had heard, and she believed it. But she had never suspected that her own family were guilty of sacrilegious spoil, and liable to its penalty. Now that she knew it, and at the same time was writhing under her first great trial of heart, she accounted for one by the other; and looking upon the costly elegances that surrounded her, and thinking of the habits of life upon which they had now long entered, she shuddered, and thought how impossible it must be to separate themselves from these circumstances of life; and yet, how terrible to hold them, suffering!

The night of sorrow passed. The next morning, though Julian was pronounced to be better, Anna was not allowed to see him; only, as he lay sleeping, she ventured one quickly withdrawn glance on his pale, gaunt features, on which, even in repose, there rested a look of trouble and disappointment.

Lord Westrey came to inquire after Julian. Anna was sitting in the morning room alone when he was announced. They met each other with great kindness.

"How is your father?"

"We scarcely know. He is still sleeping. He had another attack—I can hardly describe what it was—yesterday."

"Am I keeping you from him?"

"No; I am not allowed to be with him." Anna burst into tears.

"Indeed! How is that? Anna, what is the matter?"

"Oh, I cannot tell! But I have been the wretched cause of this illness. Oh, my poor father!"

Again Anna was interrupted by her tears. But now Lord Westrey would know all about it; and, sitting down beside her, in the kind way peculiar to him he talked to the unhappy girl, and learnt the whole history from her trembling lips. They had not spoken of Lullingstone till then. Anna had had no answer to her note to Lady Westrey. Perhaps Edward had been charged with a verbal one; but his return on the night of her father's first attack had been so sudden, and the circumstances under which he had been sent were so painful, that, if he had had any message, he had forgotten to deliver it. And Anna had felt that there was a restraint in Edward's manner towards her, and that hour after hour this restraint had increased; so that, in pouring forth all that was upon her mind to Lord Westrey, she really enjoyed a relief of spirits which she would no where else have found.

That good man comforted her as well as he could; and to do so was a hard task; for when she asked after Lullingstone, then the sorrows of his own heart were opened, and he required comforting in his turn.

"We all made too sure of you, Anna," he said. "Lullingstone himself, dear boy, was to blame in that. He had got too strong an impression of your belonging to us. And our wishes for dear Lullingstone directed us to you. He has not, on account of his ill health as a child, received such discipline in life as falls usually to the lot of young men. But you know what he is, dear Lullingstone! Well, we wished to see him with a wife, good, tender, amiable, devoted—you were just the woman, and he loved you. But, never mind. Don't weep, Anna. We never wished you to force your inclinations. There must be a few years of separation."

Anna started at those words, "separation" and "a few years!" Was she to lose friends just as she most wanted them? This was another trial. But Lord Westrey went on; he talked as if, now that he had begun to speak, talking was a relief to him.

"I think that that is the only thing to be done. Lullingstone is—in fact, he has suffered a good deal. But he is noble and generous. I wished to plead his cause with you myself, but he dreaded giving you pain in the first place, and to hope, however slightly, to be again disappointed, might. —in fact, I don't think that he could bear a second trial."

Lord Westrey looked at Anna—he looked hardly and askingly. She knew what he meant. Every nerve trembled with emotion. Should she yield? But her father? To yield now would not undo the past. No. *Now* it was too late! She could only bury her face in the cushion of the chair on which she leaned, and weep more bitterly than ever.

"Well, well, I must not be hard upon you. We have made up our minds what to do," resumed Lord Westrey. "Mary and her mother are now engaged superintending a rather extensive packing up. Happily Caroline Eastnor's marriage is a good excuse. It would not do to tell Lullingstone that it was necessary for *him* to remove for a time.

But Caroline's marriage is an excellent excuse. Mary is to be a bridesmaid. We all like the match exceedingly."

Lord Westrey was talking in an odd disjointed sort of way. Anna felt that there was strong proof of nervousness in his thus telling her of the marriage, and of their approval of it, when she knew both facts before.

"Is Caroline going to be married immediately?" she asked.

"No—not for a month—a month at least. Lady Westrey is going to London first. In fact, Anna—in fact, Lullingstone must have advice."

"Is he ill—worse? *How* is he, Lord Westrey?"

"He broke a bloodvessel the night before last," said the father with a gasp, and walking quickly towards the window, at once to hide his own emotion, and to avoid seeing the trouble that the announcement might give to Anna.

"Oh, God! and could I have prevented all this?" Anna uttered the words aloud, and *really* as a prayer they came from her heart—as a prayer from one who desired to know what share of responsibility was hers, whether she really had or had not any thing to answer for. There was a sad, confused, reproachful feeling in her heart. Had any one a right to cause misery, so great and so extensive? was she really the cause of it? ought she not at once to have sacrificed herself? But then she could not have foreseen the effects to be produced by her determination—and Harold? Oh! why mention *him* at that moment? It was as if her heart itself was divided, and had risen up against itself.

Harold! What did she know of him? where was he? what was he doing? should they ever meet again? did *he* ever wish that they might meet again? what did she know of his thoughts and hopes? how could she judge of his feelings? What folly—worse, perhaps—what wickedness, to sacrifice those to whom her greatest gratitude was due, for the sake of a romantic fancy, which perhaps it was improper to indulge! She was miserable—utterly miserable; she had separated herself from her best friends. In her heart she felt lonely and deserted. Her own conscience even had risen up in judgment against her, and had reproached her for a folly—which was more than folly—which was ingratitude, coldness of heart, selfishness, cruelty. Alas! this was to be indeed deserted.

"But I must bring this interview to a close," said Lord Westrey; "and perhaps it is best for us both that I should do so, though I confess that I am loth to leave you; it is like bidding farewell to old times. I always loved old times, you know, Anna; I am sorry to think of the past as the past; indeed, a past never to be recalled! We can never be all the same again. I must go off with my family as soon as possible. They sent love to you, Anna; they would have called with me to-day, but I thought that to do so would be a needless trial of feeling, both to Lady Westrey and to Mary; there is trial enough at home—Heaven knows!" Again there was a pause. Anna roused all her energies to speak.

"My mother is miserable, my father stricken, you are all going away—good-bye! Pray that God have mercy on me—farewell!" Lord Westrey took the poor girl in his arms, and embraced her with a fatherly kindness.

"Edward will write to me," he said; "don't encourage these thoughts: we shall still have happy times, perhaps. Would you like to write to me yourself, Anna, sometimes? Always do as you please with me. You have no better friend in the world. Good-bye!"

Lord Westrey was gone, and Anna was left in her loneliness. How, throughout that day, she longed to go to her father; but the commands of Dr. Davis were positive: she was not even to sit in his room. He feared even for her father to hear her voice, or to detect her footsteps. It was as if the day would never pass—alone, alone—always alone, except when Mrs. Herbert came, and she would stay and speak to her. Mrs. Herbert knew—her mother had told her of what had passed between her father and herself: she could stay and speak to *her*. But if she heard Mrs. Seaforth's voice or the voice of any other friend, then Anna fled away, and feared to be seen or heard. She felt like a cast-out creature; she could not explain to others why she was shut out of her father's room; she could not bear that people should see that she was absent from it. A nervous excitement of feeling possessed her on this subject; her tranquil mother never suspected it; her absorbed and sadly thinking brother never remarked it. There, in her own home, poor Anna, suddenly struck down with a sense of being the cause of evil, wandered along or sat in a state of miserable dejection, or, on Mrs. Herbert's breast, gave way to the dangerous relief of hours of enervating tears.

Still, her father remained the same; still, no one could say whether he would live or die. And so passed the day and the night, and another day, and then towards evening there was an improvement. He had spoken, he had been propped up in the bed, he had taken some refreshment, he had recognized her mother and Edward. He had made some remark on his bandaged arm and shaved and blistered head; he had smiled, and thanked them for their kindness; he had said, "Ah, doctor! this is a terrible illness—thank God, I am better;" and, lastly, he was again asleep. These accounts were delivered to Anna, time after time. How her heart throbbed—would he speak of her? Oh yes! surely, with returned consciousness, he would ask about her. But now he was asleep, that was the last thing to be heard that night. He had never spoken of her.

Edward joined her about half-past nine o'clock. He looked pale and fatigued; he was very silent; he hardly seemed to know when she spoke to him.

"Who sits up to-night, Edward?"

"What!—sits up? Oh! Mark. He says that he slept well last night. He wishes to sit up."

"I hope that *you* will sleep well, then, to-night."

Edward pulled out his watch. "I am going to Lullingstone. How late they are with the horse! I ought to have been half way there by this time." It was the first time that Edward and Anna had talked of Lullingstone, or any thing connected with it, since she had sent that note to Lady Westrey by him.

"Lullingstone! Edward! what—"

"To say good-bye," said Edward hastily. "They go early to-morrow."

A great coat lay thrown across the back of a chair; Edward heard the approach of a horse outside, and began to put it on. While so engaged, and never looking at Anna, he went on—"I intend to be here again in the morning early for two hours, perhaps from five to seven, then I shall return to Lullingstone and see them off."

And, so saying, he left the room. No kiss offered—not even his hand, at parting. Not another word; not even good-night. The strokes of his horse's hoofs fell like blows on his sister's heart. But she was not destined to go to bed quite neglected. Her mother stole from her father's room to see her again that night. Anna could not heighten her mother's griefs by adding to them the swelling sorrows of her own sad heart. But they talked together for a few minutes, and then parted with blessings, embraces, and prayers; and Anna lay down with a spirit consoled.

Edward did as he said he should do. Early the next morning she heard him pass her door to go to their father's room. She opened the door and stopped him on his return.

"How is he, Edward?"

"He has had a good night."

"Has Dr. Davis seen him?"

"Yes, and is pleased with his appearance."

"Has he spoken again?"

"Yes, he asked for my mother in the night, and said 'that's right,' when he was told she was lying down."

"Are you going to Lullingstone again, Edward?"

"Yes, now, immediately. They hope to get off by nine o'clock. I shall come back as soon as they are gone. You did not tell me that you had seen Lord Westrey yesterday, Anna."

"We said so little to each then on any subject."

"He sent his particular remembrances to you.

Lady Westrey, too. I shall bring you a note from Lady Westrey bye and bye. Lullingstone is better. Good-bye for the present, Anna."

Edward put his hand through the small space of the door which Anna had been holding open. She took it gladly and pressed it to her lips. Edward's hand returned the pressure of hers fondly. He said something, but Anna could not make out what it was, only it sounded kind, and that was enough. She went back to her bed shedding tears of joy.

That day Mr. Seaforth came to see Edward. He told him what his father had done. "Thornbank is to be sold to-morrow," said Mr. Seaforth, "and the money for the purchase is already in my hands. Your rental will be about a thousand a year; and the whole of your father's money in the funds, to the amount of another thousand a year, is yours by a deed of gift executed the night before his illness. Your father is able to do this without inconvenience," said Mr. Seaforth, "and I am very glad he has done it."

After about a week Julian one night sat, propped up with cushions, by a fire in his room while his bed was again preparing for him. He turned round a little on hearing a step near him and said, "Is that Edward or Anna?" It was Edward, but he answered readily, "Anna will be here directly, father;" and then he signed to his mother to go and fetch her. In another minute

Anna was in the room. She had presence of mind enough not to speak to her father as if she had not seen him lately. She only stood near him and said, "The bed will soon be ready. I hope you won't be tired with sitting up." Julian looked up at her and smiled. "Good girl!" he said, and no more. Then his attention was withdrawn from her by his being lifted back to bed. She was so happy at the success of this adventure, that she left the room almost immediately, afraid to stay lest something uncomfortable should occur to spoil the recollection of so much pleasure. After this Julian improved daily; Anna kept more and more in his sight. He seemed again to enjoy looking at her, and watching her in his old way as she moved about the room. He was pronounced to be out of danger; but so great was his weakness that he required incessant attention and care. People poured in to call on Mrs. Julian, and congratulate her on her husband's recovery; so that, within the ten days that followed on Lord Westrey's departure, a delightful change had occurred at Mayfield.

CHAPTER XXI.

A DESPERATE MAN.

Mr. Seaforth was in the counting-house. Ralph Seaforth was standing by his side. He began to talk, and spoke openly of Julian and his affairs. Edward had just been with him. Mr. Seaforth was pleased to see Edward independent. He had just been saying that Mrs. Julian could draw upon him to any amount, and he had been hearing a rather improved account of Julian. Ralph did not interrupt his brother. He had come there as a ruined man—a man who would soon see Isaac sell all that he most valued if he could not satisfy him. In a desperate state of mind he heard his brother praise those prosperous Julians, and he watched his brother fingering money which he was sure was theirs.

Mr. Seaforth pronounced the notes "all right!" Laying his hand on a heavy, square, well-corded package of gold, all sealed carefully at the edges of the paper and the intersections of the cords, he said—"You can answer for this, I suppose, Barnes?" The answer being "Yes," he said—

"Well, then, I will look over it to-morrow. To-morrow Edward will be here himself." He drew out a drawer—it was lined with metal. He placed the notes and the packet in it. He closed the drawer, fastened two locks which secured it, and then sealed pieces of wide red tape across and across the edges.

"Come," said Mr. Seaforth, rising, "we can go now." Then, looking round, he said, "Where's Ralph?"

"He has been gone two or three minutes," said Barnes. Then they left the room together. The doors were fastened after them, as usual. It was about five o'clock in the afternoon, and the time was the second week in May.

It would be hard to give the reader any idea of the state of mind in which Ralph Seaforth had left that room.

The love of gold had never been so strong within him—his necessities had never been greater. Not a difficulty was absent from his mind. As he walked from the room and the house, they seemed to accompany him like spectres. They were urging him, threatening him, laughing at him, triumphing over him. They were suggesting, persuading, expostulating with him.

He had had to suffer Isaac's threats; he had had to force himself to the task of soliciting his forbearance. The time was fast coming when his whole folly must be made known to the world.

Ralph would not have cared for the world knowing either of his folly or his vice, if it could also, and at the same time, have seen him successful. What he could not bear to contemplate was the world seeing him ruined and disappointed. *Failure*—that was *his* dread—that was the one thing to prevent which he would attempt and encounter any thing. Yet failure was sure to be his. There it was now, staring him in the face, keeping close to him, and never to be persuaded away by any contrivance or argument for a single moment. Ah, failure!—failure before a mocking world! Any thing but that!

So Ralph Seaforth thought, and still walked on. His steps took him—without any fixed intention on his part—to Isaac the Jew's.

Isaac received him not very graciously.

"I shall do no more!" he exclaimed, immediately on seeing Ralph enter; and then, turning aside in an obstinate mood, he went on with the work of cleaning and apparently mending some keys, of which a large number lay before him.

"Why do you speak so soon? I haven't asked you for more yet!"

"What else should you be here for?"

"Mayn't I wish to talk to a friend?"

A bitter, scornful laugh was the answer.

"What if I come to talk of paying you?"

"I shall be paid when I like; next month, according to agreement. I shall be paid *then*, you know."

Ralph feared and hated him at the same moment.

"You've forgotten that I am to marry that girl," he said, with as much coolness as he could command.

"'Tis impossible!" said Isaac gravely.

"But I shall disappoint you. I am going to take to work again. I am going to sea!"

"Eh—sea? I wish you would. But that's *talk*."

"Haven't I always said that I would take a few more trips?"

"Yes always *said!*"

"I tell you that I am engaged—for the Williamsons—the boat, the Nymph."

"Ah! ah!"

"Yes—for next month; and with your help may take my pretty wife off in her."

Isaac looked up brightly. His sunk, bleared, bloodshot eyes gave forth sparks of intelligence.

"There'll be plenty of pay."

Isaac rubbed his hands. "We must see—we must see!" he muttered.

"I believe," said Ralph, looking at the wretch before him—"I believe that such fellows as you are sent on purpose to tempt men to the devil!"

Isaac only laughed.

"They have been there before they come here," he said.

"In the mean time, it is well to have two

anchors in a storm—you are busy at cleaning keys, Master Isaac—are you clever at opening a lock?"

"A very hard one?"

"Yes—very hard, difficult, close, a little dangerous, but a quick way of getting back our own. Goods got by injustice to another don't prosper— 'tis a proverb, Isaac. I know the history of this gold. I look upon it as mine. Why not take it? It would make things right directly." Isaac took up a small instrument.

"This is a good friend," he said, and handed it to Ralph.

Ralph examined it. "I can hold a helm easier."

"Yet this requires less experience," answered Isaac; and, applying it to a lock on a drawer near, he exhibited its powers plainly enough.

He then replaced it on the table, and turned aside. Ralph put the instrument into his pocket. And those keys—that, and that, and that—good! The likeness is perfect. He took them and walked away.

His impressions as to what he might do were not very distinct. He felt that he would do something. He must watch his opportunity. Yet there must be speed. Whatever was done must be done that night. The next day would be too late. He walked about thoughtfully for sometime; then he returned to his brother's house. He sat with his sister-in-law, for his brother had gone to Mayfield, and was not expected back till late. Ralph did his best to be agreeable to his hostess. He so far succeeded as to be pressed to stay to tea, and he accepted the invitation.

During the evening he wandered into the office. There was Barnes still at work, looking over some accounts on which the clerks had been engaged in his absence.

"You are late, Barnes."

"Not very. I generally stay after the others. It is but a little after eight."

"Well, I'm glad that you are not gone. I want to go into the counting-house above. I dropped a guinea there, I think, to-day. I heard something drop, and, when I missed the money, I thought of it."

"I am going up to bar the windows directly," said Barnes.

"I am rather in a hurry. Can't you send Ben? I'll go with him, and report how he does his work."

"Yes, Ben may go," said Barnes, scarcely lifting his eyes from the ledger.

Ben was a youth who lived in the house, and to whom the barring and bolting of outer doors belonged. He was not often intrusted with fastening other doors, but he did such things occasionally, and, being in the office at that moment, there seemed nothing extraordinary in Ralph's proposal.

Barnes now produced some keys; among them was the key of the upper counting-house. "Here —put up the cross-bar—you know—to the window, I mean. Take a candle; you won't see how to do it properly by this light." Ben took candle and keys, and, going out of the room, was followed by Ralph.

When they came to the door, Ben was going to set the candle down on the floor. "There—give me the key," said Ralph. Ben gave the key, and held the light while Ralph opened the door.

"We may be here a minute or two while I am hunting for my money," said Ralph; "so I think that we had better take the key out—we don't want a passer-by to lock us in, I suppose."

Ben laughed, and said—"No; that he should not like that;" so the keys were taken out, and Ralph put them in his pocket. Ben bolted and barred the window. Ralph looked about for his money. "I've found it!" he cried.

"Well, that's in good time," said Ben, "for I've just finished my job."

"Very well, let us be going," answered Ralph.

Outside the door Ralph produced the keys. He found some difficulty in locking the door. "Hold the candle more this way, Ben; there, that will do." The door was locked, but Ralph's hand struck back and knocked the candle out of Ben's hand. "Pick it up—quick; we shall be in the dark," cried Ralph. The boy turned round—

caught up the candle—saved the flame from expiring; and, Ralph giving him some keys—not *the* keys—praised him for his quickness, and bid him good-night. "And say 'good-night' for me to Barnes," he said. "I shall not see him; I am going to Mrs. Seaforth again."

He went back to the drawing-room, and there remained for another hour. Then he bade her good-night and went down-stairs. He tried the office door. It was locked; all was still; the trick had succeeded, and Barnes was gone. The street door was not fastened within. Mr. Seaforth was expected home, and it would not be fastened till after his return. Ralph put his candle out and placed it, as his custom on such occasions was, on the hall table; he had, however, first lighted a small dark lantern which he sometimes used when walking home at night. He then opened and shut the street door loudly, but did not go out. He walked quickly and softly back, and proceeded again up-stairs. He had known the house all his life. He had been born in that part of it; he could traverse its passages as easily by night as by day. His brother had purchased the premises on either side of it, but love of past times had induced him to leave the old house as it had always been remembered; and this enabled Ralph to use his utmost speed and activity in safety and certainty, and, finally, to conceal himself, with the keys of the counting-house in his pocket, in an apartment not far from the door.

He had hardly reached his place of concealment in safety before he heard his brother return. Then he heard bolts and bars made fast, and soon all was silence. *He couldn't* get out now; almost his blood curdled; almost he wished that he had never attempted such an enterprise; almost he feared—but such sensations could only produce desperation in a man like him; for *he couldn't get out now!*

He waited till twelve o'clock. Then he opened the door of the counting-house, closed it, locked himself in, and stood before the place in which the money had been deposited. His lantern gave him sufficient light. He looked round the room, as if fearing to see some one watching him. Its dull recesses and gloomy loneliness reassured him. He listened: all was silent. He could hear his own heart beat. He drew a small pistol from his great-coat pocket, for he had clothed himself as if for his night-walk, and laid it on the table. Then he produced the instrument procured from Isaac, and the work began. It did not take much trouble. Soon the precious packet was before him. The notes were of no use to him. Those could be recovered, and perhaps traced. He therefore took only the gold, and put it safely in his breast, securing it with a handkerchief tied round him.

Gently and softly he opened the window. He

produced a strong rope and fastened it to an iron bar, which, being still screwed on to the window frame at one end, hung down, and afforded him a secure place for the purpose. He opened the window. By means of the rope he could easily descend to the alley into which the window looked. He returned to the table for his lantern; when there, the sight of the open drawer brought a thousand terrors to his mind. He stood still, appalled! To exchange the keys had been his first difficulty, but how to again exchange them? He must be in the office as soon as Barnes. He must be lurking by. He must enter it with him. He must watch for the production of the keys. But the difficulties bewildered him. The chances of success were infinitely against him. His hand shook—his whole frame trembled; a cold perspiration burst out upon his guilty brow. What was to be done?

The flame in the lantern burnt low. He opened it to examine the light. It was quite right; the tremor of his hand must have affected it. It was a small wax light he held in his hand. One thing would cover his sin. Why not do it? He put the candle to the papers. There were piles of letters, newspapers, invoices, old account books. In his hurry he lighted every thing—every thing—all were ignited. He let himself down from the window. It was a double rope, and had nooses tied in it for his hands, or feet, if he chose. He suspended himself, holding by one hand, and closing as well as he could the shutters of the open window. He reached the ground, and pulled the rope down. He rolled it up, secured it safely, and rushed away.

It was not an uncommon thing for Ralph to absent himself from his home for a night. He always carried a key by which he could let himself in, and his servants never sat up for him. Now he went off in the direction of Isaac's. There he was admitted; for his wretched assistant in crime was staying up to know the result. Even he shuddered when he had heard the whole.

"Now," said Ralph, "I must lie here for a few hours. But you must go out and raise the alarm of fire in proper time. It was a safe part of the house for the experiment. No one sleeps there. They must not be burnt in their beds. You'll take care of that Isaac."

Isaac went out two or three times, and as many times returned, always saying that it was not time to give the alarm yet. But the smoke was pouring from the window, and the window looking into that narrow alley sent forth its terror unobserved; for the good people of Watermouth were asleep, and the few persons whose business called them through the streets, did not pass that narrow passage so late at night.

There, in the most secret recess of those dark chambers, he sat crouching, longing for Isaac's return, listening for noises which might tell of his brother's danger being discovered; yet dreading lest the fire should be discovered too soon, and urging Isaac to go out again before he had been five minutes returned.

At last sounds were heard. Ralph jumped up; Isaac rushed to the door with him. There they stood for a moment listening; then Isaac sped forward, and Ralph returned to the dark chamber he had left, and crouched down again beside the embers of the dying fire. He heard the increasing sound of footsteps. The cry of "Fire!" mingled with loud exhortations, reached his ear; and still these sounds of terror came thicker and thicker, amid the continuous flow of rapid footsteps, and the murmuring, ceaseless notes of a speaking multitude, all passing near him, and all debating the deed that *he* had done. First he felt cowed by the sense of guilt—he was afraid; then a strange sort of terror came over him. He paced the room panting with excitement. This could not long be borne. Then a sense of personal danger struck at his heart. What if he should be suspected? What if he should be sought? What if he should be found *there?* It would be proof of guilt. Where ought he to be? Surely at the scene of danger. He would be looked for there. Already, perhaps, people were wondering—already his name was in their mouths. Why was he not there?

Ralph Seaforth placed his hat on his head,

seized his stick quickly, and ran from the house. Soon he was in the thickest of the crowd—soon he was before his brother's house.

The noise—the pressure—the very torment of tongues—the bewilderment of the danger—and the flames! The roof of the end of the house where Ralph had perpetrated his crime was blazing fiercely, so as to defy every effort that was making to get it under. But when, after the first moment, Ralph recovered some share of self-possession, he looked on the terrible and awful scene of ruin with an inward smile, and a glad satisfaction that his evil deed was covered.

He was awaked from this momentary joy by the sight of his brother, pale and haggard, by his side. Some words of recognition were bursting from the lips of each, when, suddenly, Mr. Seaforth's countenance changed, his grasp of his brother's hand grew closer, and a look like that of death overspread his face. He spoke lowly, and yet with rapid utterance, "My God! that man's account. Every document that fixes what he is worth in the world is in that room below!" He made a rush forward. Ralph held him back.

"What man? What accounts?" he cried.

"John Julian's—let me go!"

"You cannot!"

"I will—begone!" He struggled, but Ralph held him firmly. A thought came into his mind that any thing that injured Julian would advantage himself. But no power could hold so desperate a man as Mr. Seaforth was at that moment.

"You have duplicates—or he has," urged Ralph.

"We have only honour and memory. He left them with me the night before his illness."

"Save him—save him—keep him back!" cried Ralph wildly, as his brother, bursting from his hold, rushed towards the house. But it was not to be done. How, Ralph did not see; but he knew by the cries around him that his brother had got into the house. A few dreadful moments passed, then there was another outcry and another excitement among the mob, and this time mingled with loud expostulations from the firemen. What was it? Barnes would follow his master. He, too, had entered that burning grave. Then followed cries for ladders. Then an apparition of Mr. Seaforth at the window; his face—oh! what agony was there! How changed in a few minutes!

"He will be lost!" Ralph, mad with fear, threw his arms about him, striking back the people, and uttering cries more like the bellowings of an exasperated beast than the wails of a human being; yet wails they were; for in his heart had burst open the long-sealed fountain of a brother's love. He rushed forward—his strained eyes were upon that figure beckoning from the open space.

He was not working out any idea; he only looked on that form, and obeyed the inward impulse to go forward to it. But in his frantic course he suddenly paused. There was a loud, crashing, hissing, rattling, overpowering sound. The wretched man fell to the ground; and, a few people gathering round him in his perilous situation, held a senseless form among them. The roof had fallen in; and the groan that burst from that assemblage of people, and then the cries, sobs, and beatings of breasts that followed, told that the good merchant and his honest Barnes were lost amid the flaming ruins. It was true: and, when the scarcely then sensible Ralph was conveyed to his own house, it was with the sympathy of the people generally, for it was clear to all how much he had suffered, poor gentleman!

CHAPTER XXII.

TROUBLE AND FEAR.

A few days had passed slowly and sadly over Watermouth. The smell of fire still lingered in the air among those ruins. And still groups of people were seen, from time to time, standing by them in sorrowful contemplation, or speaking in high eulogy of the two good men whose useful lives had made so terrible an ending; and sadly wondering over the unexplained accident that had caused such woe.

Among such persons, on a fine afternoon, when the air and sun of May felt happily invigorating, were Edward and Anna Julian. Anna had been tearfully gazing on the scene before them, when her brother, pressing her arm affectionately, drew her gently away. They pursued their way silently for a short time in the direction of Mayfield. Edward spoke.

"So you would really have me go to London to-morrow?"

"Yes, certainly! There is every thing to take you there, and little or nothing to keep you here.

I really wish you to go. Our dear father will like to hear of your being there. I shall be so glad to hear more exact accounts than Mary sends to me. Perhaps she fears to pain me; but you, Edward, must tell me the truth—whatever it is, truth is best. Be very particular in telling me about Lullingstone."

"Anna, are you *sure* that you can give him no hope?" Edward had not spoken for some time on this subject. Now he spoke softly, fearfully, and tremblingly. But in his manner there was so much affection, that Anna could not be annoyed. She answered him, however, so gravely and solemnly, that he could not press the subject.

"Sure? Yes, Edward; I have never felt other than sure. Think of what I have endured because I was sure. Think of all that that heartfelt certainty has brought upon us. I regret our afflictions. I think that I would have sacrificed myself to save them falling upon us, had it been possible to look into futurity and have the choice before me. But if you ask of my heart if it is sure, it answers 'Yes; quite sure!' Oh, Edward —yes, surer than ever!"

They walked on again in silence for some time, after which Edward resumed the conversation.

"My father is not in a state to miss me, I think."

"Oh, no! If he inquires, he will be pleased to know you are with Lord Westrey."

"But if Lord Westrey wishes me to go abroad with them?"

"I think that you should go. Dr. Davis does not consider our poor father in any danger of death. He only says that it may take a year or two to get back the full exercise of his reason."

"Do you know, Anna," began Edward, faltering and blushing, "that I have heard to-day from Lord Westrey? He wishes me very much to accompany them. Lullingstone has set his heart on it. And Lord Westrey tells me that Mary has refused Sir Giles Morton. Of course this adds strength to my hope. He has been the only man I ever feared. You would not think it unkind to be left, Anna?"

"No, no! Give me a sister. Think of the joy, when my father recovers, of seeing you at Thornbank. Indeed, dear Edward, you should not want pressing."

"I don't," he answered with a smile.

Lord Westrey expected to be obliged to take Lullingstone to the south of France. About autumn a dissolution of parliament was expected, and it was already certain that Edward was to be returned for one of Lord Westrey's boroughs.

When Lord Westrey proposed to Edward to join their party abroad, he said, "And do your best with Mary, Edward. Get it settled." Edward's heart jumped. But he had made up his mind to ask Mary very soon—before these words of her father's.

Edward went on—

"About our father's affairs, Anna, I think we had better name a lawyer—Mr. Dyrbington's, for instance. Benson is a most upright man, and a well qualified person also—and then acquiesce in every thing he may say. My father will never again have any thing to do with business. When he recovers sufficiently to inquire any thing about it, he will be glad to find himself relieved of its anxieties."

"Oh, yes!" said Anna, "I am sure that that will be the best way. You will speak to my mother, and after that see Mr. Benson yourself."

"Yes; and both may be done to-night, I think."

"Did you see Mrs. Seaforth to-day?" asked Anna.

"Yes; but only for a minute. However, it was long enough for her to speak of her feelings about Ralph. Really, I had no idea that that man had so much good feeling in him. She praised him, even with tears. His conduct towards her has been most exemplary."

Mrs. Seaforth had immediately taken refuge at Ralph Seaforth's house, and there she was certainly treated with the utmost kindness and consideration. Her trial was heavy in the extreme, for she had been a happy, proud, and most affectionate wife. There was a confusion of mind attendant on her heavy loss, that made her peculiarly alive to the comfort of Ralph's oft-repeated promises that he would manage every thing, and do every thing for her. Without her husband—without Barnes—without the help which Mr. Julian would, under other circumstances, have afforded her, poor Mrs. Seaforth felt pressed to the earth with the accumulation of thoughts which harassed her mind. Therefore, to listen to Ralph's promises, to see Edward Julian, and hear his assurances of there being no occasion for her to trouble herself, for that, with Mr. Benson's assistance, every thing could be easily arranged, was an inexpressible satisfaction.

And this much being settled, Edward took leave of his friends, and left Mayfield for London.

And yet poor Julian was in a very bad state—a state which might have excused a great deal of doubt, fear, and perplexity. It was impossible to ascertain the precise state of his mental powers.

"He knows more than he seems to know," Mrs. Julian would say to her daughter. "He *feels*—at least he *feels*," would be that daughter's answer. And now the power of money, and the luxuries of prosperity, became very dear to Anna. She made them all active in her father's cause. She dressed for his smile, and thanked God when she saw his answering look of admiration. She showed him paintings, she brought him rare hot-house plants.

She rode her beautiful Fairy in his sight. She took him to Thornbank; she saw that he was pleased and interested, and understood that what he saw was Edward's. And then he spoke longer sentences than he had ventured on before, and showed a disposition to question and direct; how glad she was—what pure joy filled her heart!

Anna was to know from Mr. Benson how the arrangements went on which were to separate her father's affairs from Mr. Seaforth's.

Mr. Benson called on her one evening to make an unexpected disclosure. It was this—Julian had no claim to any property of any kind. Thornbank, and the money which had been transferred to Edward's name, was all that could be claimed.

"But of course," said Mr. Benson, "we all know Edward Julian; he will not touch any of it—it is your father's morally, though not legally, Miss Anna."

Anna knew nothing of money. She felt like one palsied. After a moment there came a rallying. "Mr. Benson, how much a year is there?" The answer to that question, she felt, would give her the clearest idea of their position.

"Thornbank must be sold again; it may, perhaps be managed without much loss—let me see." Mr. Benson made some calculations in pencil on the back of a letter. "An income of, perhaps—

at good interest—possibly two thousand a year. It is a good fortune!"

"I understand you rightly—that is *all!*"

"Yes; all."

"There has been a great deal more—immensely more; where is it gone, Mr. Benson?"

Mr. Benson looked embarrassed. "Mr. Julian should have kept his own accounts, or trusted them to some professional man. A man can't claim what he can't prove to be his. I have a common-sense feeling, certainly, that you have had, as you say, immensely more. You spend from two to three thousand a year here. You have ever been considered to live much within your income."

"But the money is some where. Who has it?" asked Anna, feeling confused, yet knowing that, by plain questions, she should probe to the bottom of the mystery.

"It is, I presume, absorbed in the Seaforth property!"

"Who inherits that?"

"There is no will. Mrs. Seaforth comes in for her legal portion, and every thing else is Ralph Seaforth's."

"But *he knows* that my father was rich."

"He says that he knows nothing."

"Who, then, knows?"

"The dead, and the incapable," said Benson bitterly, for he was both angry and unhappy. He was going to soften what he had said, but Anna interrupted him. She had become, as it were, bereft of feeling for the time.

"Have you looked over my father's papers?"

"Every thing. Broken open every thing that might contain any thing like a voucher for the money he unquestionably possessed. There is nothing. He has nothing to show. He can produce no more claim on the estate of the late banker than I can, who never had a penny in his hands. I have told you all that is acknowledged."

"Acknowledged by whom?"

"By Ralph Seaforth."

"What does he say?"

"He says that he can't believe that your father, whose beginnings were so small, could ever have made more."

"He can't suppose that my father would have given all he possessed to my brother?"

"He would not answer that, though I put it to him. He only replied that, with the property so disposed of, and with the money he can prove your father to have bestowed on charity, the seamen's hospital, and other things—that he can show the disposition of full eighty thousand pounds. He says that your father could not have made more."

"But why give all to Edward?"

"To secure the brilliant alliance that has got

noised abroad between your brother and Miss Westrey—that is the reason given for that."

"Do you believe it?" exclaimed Anna indignantly.

"No, Miss Julian, I don't," replied Benson doggedly; "but I can't help it. I have had opinions on the subject. I have not come to you before I was fully informed. I must not trouble you with legal phrases, or rules, or technicalities —I can only assure you of the fact. You have not a claim to prefer; you possess—or rather your brother possesses—if Thornbank is sold, about two thousand a year. This must be immediately told to him. It has taken me nearly a fortnight of very painful investigation. It is all true—terribly true! I have my private opinions; but what of them? Opinions are nothing—we must come to facts. Your brother must be written to."

"Don't write directly to Edward, Mr. Benson. I should like my mind to rest upon this subject for a short time. You need not write for a day or two. Will you call upon me again to-morrow?"

"Certainly, with all my heart," said Mr. Benson kindly. "But the sooner Edward knows the truth the better," he added; "don't make a longer delay than necessary. Send for me to answer any difficulty that may arise. Always recollect how glad I shall be to be in any way a comfort to you." And so speaking, and pressing her hand kindly, and looking with very heartfelt earnestness on her cold-looking inquiring eyes, Mr. Benson took leave of Anna Julian, and she was again alone.

Alone? Yes; alone indeed! The effect of years of trial and experience had passed upon Anna in that half-hour with Mr. Benson.

She did—as she had said she wished to do—she did accustom her mind to what she had heard. She saw it all plainly enough. There in her mind, where those facts were stored, she turned her eyes, and saw them and their consequences. She examined them one by one—she put them together and looked upon them as a whole. She saw how they would work, and then she felt what was the real meaning of what she had heard, and knew what consequences must thence ensue.

She knew all. And then she felt that it was cold, barren, unprofitable knowledge, for not one of those coming trials could be averted; there was nothing left to them but to submit and to suffer.

She knew that Edward would immediately resign his legal right to the remnant of property that remained. He ought to do so—he would do so; and they should accept it. A rapid review of their many unnecessary expenses showed her that they could still live at Mayfield, and that her father might thus be kept in ignorance of what had befallen them. That was the one gleam of comfort that belonged to this otherwise dark vision of the future.

Edward must earn his livelihood—could he marry Mary Westrey? No. Impossible!

"Oh, this is worse than all! Oh, Edward! I wish that I could save you. God knows that I would if I could—and then our dear father! But I am a poor, young, weak, powerless, friendless girl—what can *I* do?" exclaimed Anna.

More than she thought of. The door-bell rang, and Ralph Seaforth was announced.

Ralph Seaforth had a difficult task before him, but he accomplished it with a consummate skill and a desperate vigour. He allowed no time to be wasted. He begun by telling Anna that he had come to speak on business; and, strange to say, he threw such a sympathy into his manner, that Anna felt no objection to speak on the subject that filled her heart; on the contrary, after a few minutes, it became a relief to her to do so.

The first difficulties being over, Ralph explained to Anna the—as he said—impossibility of her father having made so great an accumulation of money in so comparatively short a time. He reckoned up his probable gains, and calculated the amount of his gifts, and his proved possessions. He said that it was enormous when all things were considered; that he could not have made more; and that he must have depended on his future successes when he made so lavish a settlement on his son.

Anna listened; it all seemed to be very clear; it sounded like good sense. She almost believed what she heard, and she was sure that Ralph believed what he said. There was never any one more kind, honest, and candid than he seemed to be that night.

Ralph sympathized in their disappointment. It was the most vexatious thing he had ever encountered. He had something to propose; he scarcely knew how to do it. He said that he had loved her from her childhood. When she was the child of a common artisan; and when he, too, was working for his living, he had loved her. That love had never left his mind. He had nourished it in difficulty; he had never relinquished the thought; surely the time was come when he might speak it! With what hitherto unknown emotions did Anna hear him! She *did* hear him; and neither by word or gesture, look or sigh, did she interrupt him. Something she felt constraining her, enabling her to endure: and the power that sustained her seemed not like a friendly power, but like that of an armed foe, who *must* be submitted to. Her heart was speaking to itself.

"Where is my youth?" it was saying; "gone! Where my hopes? gone! Where is the love of my young days?" She looked round the room with a bewildered, imploring air. "Have I not even *friends?*" There was a voice in her ear, "I can be all you desire. It is the only way in which I can relieve you. Every thing is at your disposal. When there is love such as mine it is unconditional. On your lips all things hang; the fate of many depends upon your words. Make me happy, and do what you please!"

There was but one power near her—but one voice to listen to—but one way to go—but one thing to do.

She looked up—but oh, with what an expression!—into Ralph Seaforth's face.

He saw that he was victorious. He could not but feel something like sorrow for her. He could not help feeling a strong exulting sense of the treasure he had won. Across that hardened visage there passed the trace of feelings, better and tenderer than had been seen there for many a long day. Anna saw it. There seemed to be a gleam of promise in it, and she smiled.

"Am I answered?" asked Ralph with a soft voice, a searching glance, and an almost tender smile.

"To-morrow," said Anna gravely.

"To-morrow let it be," was the reply.

Ralph moved to a side-table where pen and ink lay, and wrote a few words. Then he brought the paper to Anna, and saying, "At your leisure," he took her passive hand, and departed. He was gone; and, just as she had been left, Anna stood motionless as a statue. How long she stood no one knew, for she knew not herself. At last she stepped forward to look at the paper. The writing shone before her eyes in characters of glittering ruby, as if each letter had been traced in blood. She shuddered. "What is this?" she said; "I am ill! Oh, heaven grant me strength! Let me not fail for want of bodily strength now that the great trial is over—now that the soul has consented!"

She looked again at the writing. It was fair and plain enough now.

"My dear Miss Julian,—In our circumstances, to speak immediately of business is right, and kind to you. I propose to settle two thousand a year on you—the trustees to be Benson and Edward. I never wish to know any thing of the disposal of this. Let it be yours from this moment, if you please. I propose three hundred a year for your private purse. A legal instrument may place your affairs beyond not only my control but my knowledge. This is what I wish. Suggest any thing further that may occur to you. You will only be conferring an obligation on

"RALPH SEAFORTH."

It was night, and Anna, calm, quiet, and collected, assisted her mother in preparing for a comfortable night's rest for her father.

That good mother now slept in a small bed in

that father's room. A servant slept in the dressing-room.

Julian was propped up in the bed in the attitude he liked best, the curtains were drawn, the fire made up, all the comforts desirable for an invalid were collected in the room. Mrs. Julian was arranging things in their usual nightly order, and when that was accomplished she turned to Anna to kiss her, and bid her good-night.

"Good-night, my Anna—good-night, and may God bless you, my dear child! Ah, my child! *now* I am thankful for our abundance, this day more than any other day of my life—perhaps, I might say for the first time in my life, I have thanked God for our riches." Upon her burning heart her mother's words fell like ice drops; yet they fell with no refreshing sweetness; each one, like a pointed dart, pierced its way, and was absorbed in the fire within. Yet she looked upon her mother with the same cold, rigid smile on her pale face, and made no attempt to stop the current of her words.

"I, too, know the value of riches *now*, dear mother," said Anna. Then those two embraced each other once more, and parted. The mother fell on her knees and thanked God for riches—the child too fell on her knees, and then, praying God to give her strength to perform the part allotted to her, she wrote the words which purchased those riches of Ralph Seaforth.

The note was left where notes were always left, for the servant to deliver in the morning; and Anna went to bed. She slept a sleep deep and still almost as death. The usual hour of her rising passed; the woman came to her room again and again. Then somebody recollected that she had looked tired the evening before, and it was agreed that she should sleep on as long as she liked.

When she awoke, three letters were before her. But, before opening them, she wrote to Mr. Benson to say that he must write to Edward; that she had had an interview with Mr. Seaforth, and that she wished him to call upon her, to be told of what had passed. Then she opened her letters; one from Edward, one from Ralph Seaforth, and another. Edward's letter was full of his love for Mary, and his hopes. "By the time you read this, my sister, I may be happy." It was reading her final sentence. Mr. Seaforth's letter was a rapturous answer to her note of the preceding evening. And that last one was from Mr. Temple; from him to whom the whole country looked up— from him! And he had watched Anna through her whole career. First of all at a distance, admiring her beauty, and attracted by her gentle manners; and then nearer, as an acquaintance, and almost as a friend. And now, what said this letter? It said that he was her lover, and it asked her to be his wife.

"Too late!" said Anna, casting it from her—"too late!" But then, suddenly correcting herself, she said, "No—not *too late*. No. I should never have married *him*. In my prosperity there was *but one*. In my prosperity I would never have married any other. I have no thought that I should have married him if our prosperity had remained the same; but I would never have married any other. I would have remained faithful to that dream of my happy, peaceful childhood, before my poor father so earnestly desired riches, and so terribly received them—received them for *me*," she shuddered; "for me! Can I ever forget the night when, in his delirium, he revealed that history?—for *me*—that *I* might know their power, that *I* might feel their curse! The deceitfulness of our riches—two thousand a year—and I am so poor that I am obliged to sell myself. But I will do it bravely."

She went to her mother.

"Mr. and Mrs. Seaforth are coming here this afternoon, mother. I wish to ask Mr. Benson and Mrs. Herbert—may I, mother?"

"Yes—of course, my child! Do as you please. But why?—is there any reason?"

"Mr. Benson will talk to you about dear Edward; and, mother, could you permit another marriage?"

"My child! Anna!"

"Yes, dear mother; your own Anna! Mr.

TROUBLE AND FEAR.

Seaforth assured me yesterday that he had loved me from a child, and I believe him, mother. I should like to be always near you; and I don't care for young men; I prefer one who has always known and respected us—in fact, mother, I wish it."

"You wish to marry Ralph Seaforth?"

With what a voice that mother spoke! Good Mrs. Julian! what a host of emotions suddenly woke to life at that moment—what a bewilderment of surprise and disappointment, vexation and fear, was hers!

"Yes, dear mother!" was the child's reply; and she looked placidly into her parent's eyes, and took her hand and pressed it tenderly, as if to implore her patience and consent.

"Good God! Anna!"

Anna started, and let go her mother's hand. She never before had heard so strong an expression fall from her mother's lips. It seemed to strike her. Its power and weight seemed enough to grind her to powder. Her nerves shook, she trembled; she looked into her mother's awe-struck face, and yet she gathered strength to speak, and to speak firmly.

"I wish it—I do; I really do! I am sorry to disappoint you a second time—but—"

"*Disappoint*, child! no—but—Anna, what is the meaning of this?" and Mrs. Julian sunk into a chair, and wept, and sobbed, and wrung her hands in an access of distress.

The firm, undaunted, persevering, determined spirit of the father, was in the child at that moment. The weakness of the previous moment had passed away, and she was strong once more.

"It means," she said gravely, "that I wish you to receive Mr. Seaforth this evening as one to whom I have promised myself, and with your knowledge and consent. This evening I also wish Mr. Benson to be told of it, and Mrs. Herbert must hear it also. I wish Mr. Benson to know from you that, as my father is not in a position to make the usual settlement on a daughter at her marriage, you consent that I should receive from Mr. Seaforth the very liberal allowance which he has proposed for my acceptance."

"Say it again, Anna. Do you wish it?" said Mrs. Julian abruptly.

"Yes, mother. I wish it very much. It combines a good deal—more than any other connexion could give me. I really do wish it. Now, please not to look so astonished, mother. If you are a little disappointed, please to make the best of it. It will all look very cheerful and pleasant soon, I assure you. We will send Edward out into the world to make grand connexions, and display his talents, but my sphere is home; you and my father are my world; I am never going away from you. I like Watermouth and Watermouth people, and the names with which we have been intimate all our lives. What should I do if I were out of sight of the spreading sea, and too far away from the dear old house to go there whenever I please? No, no, dear mother! I am going to be *Mrs. Seaforth*, and to live *here;* and, if it is a strange thing in your judgment, you must yet believe me when I say that it is my choice, and that I have the most certain knowledge of giving and possessing happiness in the thing I am going to do."

Anna had sunk upon her knees by her mother's side, and her head had rested on that mother's lap, as the words, which had seemed to come most naturally from her young heart, had been poured forth. And now good Mrs. Julian laid her hand lovingly on that beautiful head, and said, "In this, and in every thing else, may Heaven bless you, my darling child! I will say, and think, and believe just as you wish."

Anna prepared for her friends by dressing herself very beautifully. She sat with her father till the ringing of the first bell announced Mr. Seaforth and his widowed sister. And, as Anna sat by her poor father's side, he played with the fanciful chain of gold, set at intervals with brilliants, which hung from her neck, and admired it like a child, and, stroking her glossy dress, said, "I like this—I like this; always wear this, Anna;

wear such things always—why don't you always dress like this?" And so he went on admiring her in a childish fondling way, and smoothing her rich gown, and playing with her ornaments, and saying things which told how much still his mind ran on money and money's worth. And once, after a pause in his play, he looked with terrifying earnestness into her face—that is, with a look which might have terrified any one but Anna—but she had learnt to meet such sudden indications of a disordered mind with a mild smile, which generally restored the invalid to his better senses—he looked into her face and said, "I can give you this. Oh! this is what I toiled for—and *thought*—oh, Anna! Looking on the bright face of that great sea for hours, hours, hours—there I used to see my fortune. Like a glass it was—I saw all there before it came—yes, long before—and it came for *you*—for you, Anna, I always thought of *you*. Take it, and use it. I like to see you thus; beautiful, and admired, and richly dressed; always let me see this. Oh! I am happier now—I have been so ill—I am tired of all these dull things. I like this," taking up her jewelled chain. "Give me things like these, not for myself—for *you*. I shall then soon get well, and—and—" A strange dulness of expression came over Julian's face. Anna rose, and, resting his head against her fair neck, whispered,—

"And what, dear father? Your own Anna

loves you so fondly that she can do any thing for you. Tell her all you wish."

"Yes, yes! my dear Anna, so you will—I know, I know! But, tell me, Anna—are you going to be married?"

"Yes, dear father!" said Anna firmly. And, as she saw those trembling lips wreathed into a silly smile, she kissed them, and added, "I am going to be married very soon—almost immediately."

"And where is he—where is he now, Anna— why is he not here?" A ray of intellect again lighting up his inquiring eyes, but only for a moment.

"Who—father?"

The fading light kindled again; "Lullingstone," he spoke quite plainly.

"He is ill—he has been very ill; they are gone abroad for his health."

"Going? *You* going, Anna?"

"No, my dear father! No; I am not going. I am never going to leave you. I would do any thing rather than leave you; I will never leave you as long as you live, father."

Julian's powers of comprehension were clouded again, and he understood nothing of what she said. Even her tears were unheeded, and her thousand kisses woke no return. But still he held her chain in his hand, and still he seemed to admire its brilliance; and again his eyes wandered over her rich dress with an expression of childish delight, and Anna thanked God that she had the power of purchasing for her father a continuance of the possessions, the love of which had taken such a close hold upon his soul. It was but a small trial to meet Ralph Seaforth after this.

She entered the room with her mother. She went up to Mrs. Seaforth, and received her thanks and the expressions of her joy, and returned her warm-hearted embraces with gladness and satisfaction. And, while they were speaking together, Anna heard her mother say the first words that had been spoken to Ralph in acknowledgment of their engagement. Her brain reeled as her ears drank them in; but she thought of her father—that thought brought strength, and she advanced to her mother's side. Anna stood by her, and met Ralph's rapturous glances with a steady smile; she was so calm and collected, that Ralph, even at that moment of success, was awed. When Mrs. Julian ceased speaking, she said, "Thank you, mother," and gave her hand to Seaforth.

Mr. Benson and Mrs. Herbert arrived; Mr. Benson, in a private interview with Anna, was made to understand in five minutes how things were to be. He was a man of business, not of love. Matrimony had never occupied his thoughts for its own sake; he only knew it as it was connected with deeds of settlement. This marriage would include a general settlement of family affairs, besides the usual individual settlement; there was enough of law in it to occupy his thoughts for many a day, and certainly they were so far occupied that night, that he never thought of the suitableness of the connexion, but said all the common-place things he had ever heard of as proper to such occasions ; and left early, because he really longed to produce his ideas on that "rough sketch," which, in spite of his civil speeches, had been dancing in the air before him all the evening.

The next morning came. She was to see Ralph Seaforth again—see him alone—see him as an accepted lover. The horror that seized her was intense. She knew that such a moment was not to be always escaped; but it must not come *that* morning—not *then!* Something she must do to prevent it. To endure so much that day would be impossible—she should die at the first sight of him. So she wrote Ralph Seaforth a note, saying that she did not feel equal to any excitement, and that she had mentioned their engagement to her father, but that he did not, as yet, properly understand it. That she wished to devote herself for a day or two to enabling him to master this new idea, and that she would be glad to defer meeting Ralph till that was done. Then it was scarcely fair, perhaps, for them to be in the same town and not meet; she suggested his going away for a few days. Now, this suggestion happened to be one of the most agreeable that could have been made to Ralph. He felt that he should prove but an awkward lover, and rather dreaded the promised interview with Anna. But the possession of her note was most delightful to him.

He answered it immediately, by assuring her of the pleasure it would always give him to conform to her wishes, and telling her that he would start that very day for London, whence he should write to her, and where he should expect to hear from her. All this took place so speedily, that Anna had scarcely time to understand her happiness at having achieved a short respite from her lover's attentions, before the coach to London, which left Watermouth twice a week, passed the house. Anna happened to be in the garden; she looked at the heavily-laden vehicle; some one waved his hat, and then kissed his hand to her; it was Ralph Seaforth. She returned his attentions, and then he was gone. So there was a respite. It was not to be *that* morning!

Julian was sitting in the sunny window, looking out listlessly; his gaze falling on a brilliant group of flowers with that pleased childish-look which things, rich and gay, always brought upon his face. Mrs. Julian and Anna were both in the room.

"She's going to be married," said Julian.

"Yes!" answered Anna, looking up at him; the colour in her face deepening, and extending

to her throat, and to the roots of her hair—
"Yes!"

"Who to?" said Julian, laying his huge hand upon her head, and keeping it in the same position. "Who to? you know—tell me—I like to hear—Who to?"

There was an uncomfortable simper on his face, and an agitated tone in his voice. Anna feared to hesitate.

"To Captain Ralph Seaforth!" she said steadily.

Julian thrust her from him, and uttered a horrible cry.

Mrs. Julian and Anna rushed to him. They tried to pacify him, but they could not. The confusion was dreadful. Julian now spoke quickly, and in a voice so loud and terrible, that it sounded like a savage roar.

"No—no—no!" and then he uttered anguished cries. "I was afraid; I have always been afraid! Years ago—I heard him—Save me; save!" And then again came those terrible cries, and he beat his breast, and threw himself about, till the two women drew back and dared not go near him, but stood at a distance and watched for what might come. He exhausted himself with lamentations and anger.

Anna heard him with an awe-struck attention. Was she going to do for him the very thing that he would rather die than let her do? Had he still knowledge and strength enough to wish—to be able to meet any thing rather than *that?*

Happily, as night came on, he slept.

That night Mrs. Julian besought her daughter to give up her engagement. And she parted from her in surprise, in misery, almost in anger, at her daughter's unreasonable determination — as she called it.

CHAPTER XXIII.

TROUBLES AND FEARS.

DREARY days—days of trial—days of fear and helplessness, and happiness for ever gone. Another of them rose on Anna, and Mayfield. Her mother sent for her breakfast to her own room. After the last night's interview with Anna she would not venture on the morning meal with her alone. And another, and another day, and her mother, kind and gentle, but still estranged, saying that she could not understand her, and vexed and disappointed at being obliged to say so. No letters from Edward, but a letter from Ralph Seaforth, full of protestations of love and constancy, which Anna put aside gravely; and one from Mr. Temple, which Anna read and burnt immediately, and whispered, "Too kind—too tempting!" over its ashes. She was doing it bravely, as she said she would do it. Yet, she said to herself, "If I could only hear from Edward I should then be strong again—only hear of his having asked Mary, and of her having accepted him! I should be rewarded.

I should get on easily then." But she did not hear; and it really was rather odd. She did not answer Ralph Seaforth's letter immediately. She had put it off from day to day. She could not bear to write to him.

"But it *must* be done!" said Anna, one lonely afternoon. "Now—I will do it now—directly; it shall go by this night's post." She got writing materials, and sat down before them.

"Dear Mr. Seaforth!"—The pen was laid down. She leaned her head on her hands, and was motionless for many minutes. Then she started up; the door had opened, and there stood Edward.

She sprang from her seat, her face all animation —"Edward! my dear Edward! What brings you? Why have you come? Is all right?"

Edward closed the door softly, sat down, and looked up at her eager, inquiring face,—"I am refused, Anna! Mary won't have me." Edward jumped up and caught his fainting sister in his arms.

She soon recovered. "I am a poor nurse. I have not called any one. I did not think of your being so shocked, my dear, darling Anna. But don't look so ghastly. I shall have to comfort you, Anna. Are you ill? You frighten me! Speak, speak, Anna!"

"I can't speak," sobbed forth Anna. "Let me lean my head against you. The whole world is bewildered, I think. But, Edward, you will ask Mary again—won't you?"

"Impossible! she behaved so nobly. She never had any idea that I loved her, except once, she told me, long ago now, in 'London; she thought I was boyish, or silly—so she called it. And she walked away from me. I recollect it well enough."

"But now, that she does know?" urged Anna.

"She was plain-spoken, and quite positive. She was determined never to marry, except with all her heart. She was certain—romantically certain—that she could never be happy in married life, unless all the strong love of her heart was her husband's. She must live in a sort of devotion to him; holding him as God's greatest earthly gift to her; she could not ever feel real love for me. I said that I loved her just in that way. But she said no—oh no! I could not; it was quite impossible. With her, wedded love must be a passion elevated into a principle, and consecrated and blessed in the sacrament. 'I know,' she said —'I know that I might marry faultlessly, and feel much less—scarcely any thing—of what I have described. I should unite myself to a hundred virtues if I married you, and lead an indulged and a happy life; and be able to perform my duties with cheerfulness and contentment. But, *some hearts want more*, and *mine* would want more. Marriage is not a necessary event to me.

But if I enter upon it, I must enter it as a state of life so blessed and so happy, that—that there is but one thing better!'"

"And what can that be?" exclaimed Anna.

"To be called away from it by the exclusive love of God—the life of the religious she meant. Oh, Anna!" continued Edward, "I knew it was hopeless; I wanted no more words. She is up—somewhere—out of my reach. I cannot soar to her. She cannot come down to me. The dream is passed. Certainty is come—"

"But how did you part?"

"I saw Lady Westrey. I could not see Lord Westrey. I could not have borne up before him. He knows what a trial I have gone through. He once said it was too much for human nature."

"But Lady Westrey?" said Anna.

"She was very kind and very positive. 'Meet the truth, and accustom yourself to it; make friends with it, Edward. You had better not see Mary again; never see her again, if possible—'"

"What a dreadful thing to say!" said Anna.

"Dreadfully true, dreadfully true!" repeated Edward. Then, suddenly catching sight of the letter she had begun, he said in a quick angry way—"What in the world are you writing to Ralph Seaforth for?"

It recalled the whole truth to Anna's mind. She burst into tears. She could not control her emotion, and Edward heard all—every thing.

Then he thanked her—solemn, tender, awe-struck thanks they were. And then he said—"How right it all is! I ought to be glad that Mary has refused me. Oh, Anna! I *will* be glad; but *I* must write that letter, and I must tell our dear mother directly. Will you go away—go to her and tell her that I am here; and send her to speak to me?"

Anna could not stop her tears, now that she had once given them leave to flow. Edward, with gentle violence, put her out of the room, and, when left by himself, wondered at her courage. But he did not know all her courage, or all the sacrifice that she had planned, for she had never mentioned Harold.

In less than an hour Mrs. Julian was standing in Anna's room. "You are a dear, good, silly child. You must not think of your sorrowful trial. Edward has already written. It is all done. You are free, Anna; and we are all going to be happy. Go to your father. He cannot forget it. I don't know what to do about that. He has been quite violent about it several times. Edward thinks I should take Dr. Davis's advice; so I have sent for him."

Anna went to her father. The same old questions—"Are you going to be married, Anna?" and "Lullingstone?" The same outbursts of excitement.

When Dr. Davis came that evening, every one

in the house felt that there would be comfort in what he said. He was very peremptory. "You must all go away. Where can you go? Some total change of scene and circumstances; and yet he can't bear a long journey." Then, turning to Anna suddenly, "Miss Julian, take care of your brother. He is unlike himself. He is ill. He has over-read and over-excited himself. He is suffering from a sudden want of power. I don't like those cases—take care of him." Then, going back to Julian, a sudden thought struck him, "The Chantry-farm at Dyrbington! I frequently send patients there. An excellent soil, and sure to do Mr. Julian good."

Anna felt that her father would like it. "I wish that we could go directly."

"You *must* go directly! I shall send there to-night. And you, or your brother, order your things off by daybreak. You shall dine at the Chantry-farm on chicken and cold beef to-morrow, at two o'clock!"

Anna laughed, thanked him, and set about making the necessary arrangements.

Julian made no objection to moving. He was evidently pleased with the drive. He knew the road, pointed out things as they passed along, and Anna thought that Watermouth and Seaforth associations were gone, at least for a time. He knew the Chantry-farm, and said he liked staying there for change of air. As he sat at his tea, at the same table with them, in the little brick-floored parlour, he was happier, and looked less sick and more like himself. He took a few steps on the gravel-walk the next day with no other help than his stick, and seemed better for the absence of Mayfield luxuries. Then he would have a chair under the apple-tree, and look towards the great Dyrbington elm-trees, and remark how beautifully the tower pressed up among their foliage. Anna left off the bright dresses and ornaments she had worn to please him, and sat by his side in quiet-coloured muslin gowns. And Julian never missed them, but talked of the glowing harvest fields, and played with the bullfinch in its cage. She had left the guitar at home, and she gave up the idea of having the piano; but she sung to him as she sat, with needle and thread, busily at work. And he beat time, and smiled, and listened, just as he had sometimes done in the old workshop, when she was a little child.

"Oh, he is better—he is better! He is getting well, and we shall be happy again!" So Anna exclaimed to her mother with a delighted heart.

"Yes, Anna; and your father is better for something more like old ways about him," answered Mrs. Julian. And Mrs. Julian was right.

Still, no letter came from Ralph Seaforth; no answer to Edward's letter to him. It made them a little anxious. Dr. Davis said that he was still absent from Watermouth.

"Certainly," said Mrs. Julian, "it would have been satisfactory to hear that he was intending to behave like a gentleman."

Edward answered, "Oh, certainly!" but he never expected so great a satisfaction from Ralph. His silence added to Edward's trouble, and made him anxious and expecting.

"Take care of your brother, Miss Julian!" was still Dr. Davis's parting remark. And then Anna would sigh over Edward's pale face and his slight form, and remark that, though it was the middle of summer, his hands were always cold.

CHAPTER XXIV.

ST. CUTHBERT'S.

FATHER BERNARD sat alone in his small chamber, which was faintly lighted by an oil lamp; some books were before him, as if for reference, and by their side lay manuscripts, and pen and ink. But Father Bernard was not writing; his arms rested on the table, and his forehead was bent on a crucifix which he held between his clasped hands, and which a chain secured round his neck. All at once he raised his head quickly, and turned it aside listening—a foot was heard upon the threshold—he placed the crucifix in his bosom, and went to the door.

"Who is there?" said the priest.

"Will you buy a Bartholomew trout, master?" said a voice from without, and a low chuckle told, as plainly as the words themselves, that the person asking admittance was no other than Lyas Norwood.

Father Bernard smiled. "And why do you laugh?" he said gently, as he closed the door after admitting his guest.

"Because I think that, being a man of muscle and make like yourself, you might do things differently."

"With a more defiant air?"

"Yes; you are a man—and who is more?"

"I am more," replied the priest, with a grand, sweet smile. "Were I only a man, I might boldly defy my fellows. But I am the servant of God, and the minister of holy things, and my warfare is against sin, and my weapons not of this world. We fly, as did our Master, from place to place; yet we have courage to suffer torture and death in that Master's service. He who suffers well has a better courage than he who rashly slays."

"I was wrong," said Lyas; "shall I test your courage?"

"Test my duty," said Father Bernard.

"Come with me to-night to Dyrbington."

"For what?"

"Ah, you hesitate!" cried Lyas.

"For what?" repeated Father Bernard, with voice and manner unchanged.

"Listen, master!" said Lyas, raising himself up, and looking with solemn dignity on the placid countenance of the man he addressed. "Listen, master! If there is world to come—if it lasts for ever—if there shall be no death there—if its happiness or sorrow will depend on the manner of each man's life in this world—then are all souls alike in the eyes of one who dedicates himself to prepare men in the life that is now, for the life that shall be then?"

"All souls are the same to us—yet our deepest anxieties are for those who have sinned."

"But to him who *thinks* that he has sinned— though, may be, he judges himself wrongly—to one who, blaming himself till he lies in misery which no friendly words can reach."

"Where is he?" cried Father Bernard, advancing towards Lyas. "Take me to him. You shall bring a blessing on your soul—quick—let us go!"

"But the danger?" said Lyas, not scoffingly, but with considerate slowness. "This is not a thing to remain hid in darkness. We may do it in deep night, but it shall be told in broad day; and that which you have done beneath the cloud, you will have to acknowledge before the sun in heaven."

"No matter Let us go! If I should have to be removed, may another and a better come. Let us go! Besides, men do not like putting these laws to their worst use. Heart and head are getting over prejudice. No harm will come—let us go!"

"But why risk any thing—perhaps for the poor tent-dweller who saw light first beneath the shadow of the stones and trees, and may look his last on life in as easy a place—why risk any thing? You are growing old—there are many who want you here—your life is precarious enough—there needs but to cry through the streets an evil deed with your name attached to it, and this refuge of yours may be food for fire, and yourself torn to pieces by a mad populace."

But now it was Father Bernard's turn to smile. "Is Lyas Norwood taking a lesson from the world he affects to despise?" said he; "and saying that with his lips which his heart denies?"

And then they turned from the room together. The night was unusually dark for that time of the year; but the two walked briskly on, for each knew the way, and had traversed it almost as often by night as by day. They reached Watermouth. They took short and unfrequented ways, and got down by the docks and shipbuilders' yards. And at one point they began to go up a steep ascent, having on the right the high blank sides of storehouses, and on the left a low parapet wall, which guarded the passengers from the dangers of the deep precipice above which the road had been raised.

The shadow of the high walls kept the road in darkness; but, looking over the parapet, it was not difficult to distinguish the shadowy outlines of things below—not that there was much to see, for it was a mere rubbish-place, where stone, and timber, and unused carts reposed at their owners' convenience.

Suddenly Lyas Norwood stopped, and, touching his companion, he made him a signal to stop also. Voices were heard rising from the depth at their side. Lyas leaned over the low wall, and Father Bernard remained close by him. A moment was spent in listening, then the voices came again.

"You must—you shall—you have helped me before; why not now?"

"Give it up!" grumbled a harsh voice.

"Give it up!" exclaimed the other, which Lyas Norwood now recognized to be Captain Ralph Seaforth's. "What, *now?* Have I made the thing a fortnight's boast to give it up? I won't!"

"You can pay the money well enough now; thanks to the work the flames did so well," urged the other.

"Don't speak of that—ah! I tell you, Isaac, I can't even yet bear to hear of that—don't speak of *that*, Isaac; oh, no! not if we are friends— don't speak of that!"

Lyas grasped the priest hard—"We shall hear something directly," he said. "Stay still—that was the voice of guilt; in my time I've known it well."

Father Bernard made no reply, for Isaac's voice in answer was immediately heard.

"Well, let that be; but you have money. You can pay them, or pay me. I would have helped you to carry off the girl if it had been in the way of business to have got my just debts paid by it; but *I* can get well paid, and *they* can get well paid; there's enough for all *now*. I won't help you to carry the girl off—I won't, I say!"

"They speak of Anna Julian," said Lyas. Father Bernard made a gesture to move on; but Norwood held him fast, saying, "There's more coming—hark! What did they say?—we missed that—nay, Master Ralph grows angry; the truth will be out quickly now."

A part of the conversation had indeed been lost here, but in another minute the words again rose plainly.

"Cease your boasting words," growled Isaac,— "cease! You can't frighten me—you can't; you know you can't; I have the secret."

"When I let you go," whispered Lyas to Father Bernard, still holding his arm with the force of a vice, "go on at a steady pace to—hark—!——"

"While I can hang you for burglary, and wilfully setting fire to the house, and being the means of the death——"

"To Dyrbington Court, and stay about till I come," said Lyas, and paused again to hear the Jew's concluding words, "You can use no threats to me!"

Pushing Father Bernard from him, Lyas Norwood uttered the single word "Go!" and himself immediately disappeared. For a moment Father Bernard knew neither where nor how his companion had gone; but then he became aware that he had leaped from the parapet to the bottom of the precipice, and was grappling with the men below.

Not choosing to go while this struggle was going forward, the priest leant over the wall as far as he was able, and strained his ears to discover what might be taking place.

That Lyas was in the hands of two men made desperate by iniquity: that the struggle going on was one of life and death; that he was being overpowered, and that his calls on Isaac to assist him as the best, the only means of saving himself, were unavailing, and only met by that unfortunate being calling on Ralph to strike hard and home, and so free them both from so terrible a witness against them; to hear and know all this was like the passage of a picture before the eyes to the mind of Father Bernard. One moment he hesitated, hoping that, unequal as was the combat, Lyas might be victorious; one moment he hesitated, but that was all. His loud clear voice rung through the night air.

"Help him, Isaac! Isaac, it is your only way of safety! Another has heard you—another now sees you; give up the guilty—it is your only hope!"

The contest ceased. "God of Israel!" exclaimed the wretched Isaac; "what voice is that?"

"It is the voice of one who knows all—who must have justice!" was the reply.

"I obey—I obey!" cried Isaac; "go not up against me! I did but shelter him; I did but seek to secure my own!"

But now Lyas spoke. He raised his head and looked in the direction where he supposed that Father Bernard must be. "It is all safe now," he said; "go!—go quickly!"

And stretching up the hill at a pace calculated to make up for the detention that had occurred, Father Bernard, as directed, pursued his way. He walked at more than his usual brisk pace; but notwithstanding, just before reaching the summit of the hill that led down to Dyrbington, he heard a quick trotting sound behind him which made him stop, and, almost at the moment of his looking round, a hand was laid upon him.

"You have walked well, man; and it made my heart beat to overtake you. But it has been done, and just at the spot intended. Now, come with me."

Lyas opened gently the small door which led into the yard and court at the back of Dyrbington-house, and taking his companion by the arm, led him straight into the kitchen.

The next day it was known that Mr. Dyrbington was dead.

In the middle of the night Mr. Benson had been sent for. He had gone immediately on receiving the summons, as he had often promised Mr. Dyrbington that he would do, and he had gone accompanied by a physician. They were received by Reuben, and upstairs they found Martha and Lyas Norwood. They were in Mr. Dyrbington's bed-room—but he was a corpse.

The limbs of the dead had required no straightening. He had laid himself out, and he was there in his bed, stretched to his full length, with his arms close to his side, and on his up-turned face a smile—such a smile as had not been there for many years—such a smile as, perhaps, had never visited that face before!

But he was dead! The spirit had fled—only cold clay remained, yet on it a most supernatural beauty.

Though he had before looked even older than he really was, he now looked full twenty years less than his real age. The lines of anguish about his face were all gone, the large high forehead was fair and smooth, and about the closed eye was a look of peace. Those who gazed on him felt that there was a magnificence about him —that they gazed on the noble dead. They felt impressed and sad; and when again they thought that this was one whom the world had so long gossiped about, whom some had pitied and others had derided, but who now lay in independence of all that might be said, in a stillness that spoke of a rest which had been long unknown to him—then their hearts softened, and they wept.

"When you did not come soon enough to hear his words, then he wrote them," said Lyas Norwood to Mr. Benson, giving him a paper.

The paper contained but a few words. "I am dying—I am happy—let Lord Westrey manage every thing. Good-bye, Benson—farewell, Dyrbington! I shall lie in our vault, in the Chantry Chapel of St. George—let it be opened for me, and then built up for ever."

"Has Mr. Dyrbington left no will?" asked the physician of Mr. Benson. He did not see how quickly and sharply Norwood looked at him, and watched for the answer.

"His will is in my possession," replied Mr. Benson. "I will call at Lullingstone to-day; in the mean time"—he looked towards Lyas—"In the mean time, I shall not leave the house," said Lyas, with gentle dignity. "I ministered to him in his life; I was in some degree his confidential friend, as you know, Mr. Benson—I think that you will find no more suitable a person than myself to assist his servants, now that he is dead."

"It is just what I should have suggested," said Mr. Benson.

Mr. Benson went immediately to Lullingstone, where happily Lord Westrey had arrived the previous day.

He returned within a few hours; Lord Westrey was with him. When Lord Westrey arrived, Lyas Norwood had an interview with him. No one knew what had been said, but there seemed to be something extraordinary in Lord Westrey's manner after it was over.

But Mr. Benson had business to transact with Lord Westrey; and as both himself and Lyas had to be at Watermouth at a given hour, on Ralph Seaforth's business—for Lyas had given him in charge for having set fire to his brother's house—he was glad to enter upon affairs immediately.

"I was desired by the late Mr. Dyrbington," he began, "to inform you at once, Lord Westrey, that you are left his sole heir. You know something, no doubt, of Mr. Dyrbington's secret life here. The property he has left is not quite so much as might be expected."

In fact, there was nothing but the land about Dyrbington. The money was left to the poor. And much more than the money in the funds was left to the poor—that sum, large as it was, he considered as only enough to repay for the possession of the Chantry farm and St. George's.

All that he had been so long laying up Lord Westrey was entreated, in a private note, to apply to the use of the sick, the aged, and the indigent. Not an ounce of the magnificent plate that had been a traditionary wonder to the neighbourhood was to be found—the jewels—the tapestry—the paintings—all were gone! Mr. Dyrbington had accomplished the work on which he had set his heart, and then he had died.

"But where is all this money?" exclaimed Lord Westrey. "Strange to say," replied Mr. Benson, "it is in the house. Knowing Mr. Dyrbington's peculiar ideas on the subject of church property, and that he had laid up in the house this large sum of money for the use of the poor, as an equivalent for that of which he considered that they had been deprived, I desired my confidential clerk to come here, to be ready to take back the money. It has already been packed by me, under Mr. Dyrbington's eye, in small iron-bound chests fit for the purpose. Myself and Lyas Norwood have alone known of the great sums that Mr. Dyrbington has laid up."

Then Mr. Benson opened a metal-lined cupboard, and astonished Lord Westrey with its contents.

The good and trusty clerk, Simmons, was at the door in a gig, drawn by a good horse, and the treasure was delivered to him to take to Watermouth.

Mr. Benson said, "Lyas, will you go with me?"

But Lyas refused—"I shall meet you at the court," he said. "We will try to get justice done now. But it is sad to my heart to go from the peace within"—and he pointed towards the room where the dead lay—"to the trouble without. But, in a few hours, I will again be a watcher beside him." At his quickest pace Lyas disappeared.

When he reached Watermouth he found the whole town in a state of excitement. Already many circumstances had been remembered which appeared like evidence against Ralph; the horror rising on all sides was boundless; by the voice of the people he was condemned already. But the excitement grew greater and greater, and the expression of the people's feelings reached almost to the height of a popular tumult when it was known that *Ralph Seaforth had escaped*—he was gone!

Lyas went directly to Mr. Benson's office. He met that gentleman immediately within the doorway. "Oh, Lyas!" he exclaimed, "there must be a curse about that Dyrbington treasure. Simmons is not arrived. I sent off a man on a fast horse. He has this moment returned—there are no tidings of him."

"I will go," said Lyas. "I will go the road-way to Dyrbington. It will be odd if I can't find out something!"

He went off at a run. He traversed the whole way and never found him. He returned, tracking the marks of the wheels. He came to a place where the wheels had made many turnings, and had then proceeded in another direction, on what was called the Great London Road.

"If this had been his own doing, there would have been fewer marks. His mind would have been made up before he arrived here; he would have turned immediately."

As Lyas murmured this, he remarked that the grass at the side was trampled; he heard a groan; he sought further—lying beneath the brambles and long grass of the ditch was the unfortunate clerk.

The man was dreadfully bruised; one arm was broken, and his back had received so severe a wrench as to disable him from standing. Lyas made him a little more comfortable by changing his posture, and then left him where he was. In as short a time as possible, he returned to Watermouth, procured help, and removed the sufferer to Mr. Benson's house.

As soon as the man could speak for a few minutes together, he made a deposition, stating that he had been met by Ralph Seaforth; that, knowing Ralph must have escaped, he had attempted to recapture him; that a severe fight had taken place between them, and that Ralph had overcome him by breaking his arm with a short iron bar, with which it was suspected Isaac had found means to supply him. Ralph had then severely treated him, and cast him into the ditch.

After that, he had jumped into the gig and driven off furiously on the London Road.

"He is rich enough now," gasped the wounded man.

"Rich!" exclaimed Lyas: "surely he has gathered to himself a double curse! Rich!—if such be riches, may I be poor for ever!"

Ralph Seaforth was followed to London. It was ascertained that he had embarked on board a vessel bound for the East Indies.

The vessel was wrecked; a few lives only were lost. Ralph Seaforth was not found among the saved; and it was certain that the vast sea had swallowed up the treasures of sacrilege. The Dyrbington gold was gone for ever; and the people of Watermouth heard, with a shudder, of the fate of the gold and the man!

In Mr. Dyrbington's room lay the happy dead, in the unclosed coffin; and looking on the uncovered face of majestic peace were Lady Westrey and Mary, Lord Westrey, Lyas Norwood, and the priest of St. Cuthbert's—and one more, and he was Harold. The crucifix lay on the dead man's breast, and as the burial service proceeded Harold answered the priest. And then quietly, and almost secretly, with few words and noiseless footsteps, all dispersed. And a few days afterwards the vault in St. George's Chapel received another occupant, and was sealed with strong masonry, for he was to be the last.

Then Lord Westrey asked some of the neighbouring gentlemen who had attended the funeral to return with him to the house, and be present at the reading of the will.

The will was soon read.

"In addition," said Lord Westrey, "I have this paper, in my beloved friend's handwriting, sent to me from his death-bed. It contains these words—"

"I know all—do justice, Westrey. Consult Mrs. Margaret Lullingstone. Of course, I have seen Mrs. Margaret, and I should like all of you to see her also."

Every body was anxious to see Mrs. Margaret, and Lord Westrey, who had stood up as he finished speaking, immediately left the room, and in a moment's time re-entered it, with one whom all seemed to know, but whom scarcely one had ever seen. They now looked at her with a respectful interest. She was of considerable age, but not a grey line was to be seen in her dark brown hair, which she wore turned back in a roll round her forehead. She was erect in her figure, and the black silk mittened hand which rested on Lord Westrey's arm, was evidently placed there for ceremony, not for support.

Mrs. Margaret glanced round on the gentlemen assembled, who rose to meet her. She did not know one of them, though they knew her. She kept her hand on Lord Westrey's arm, and, looking up at him, began to speak.

"Several years ago, shortly after your lordship's marriage with my niece, Miss Lullingstone, I made acquaintance with a strange old woman who lived in the forest with her son and grandson, and who was well known in the neighbourhood. Your lordship must have seen her often. Before I left Lullingstone, I recollect Mary and I often passing her in our rides and drives through the forest country between this place and your own."

"I remember her perfectly," said Lord Westrey. "Every body here must remember her: she was Lyas Norwood's grandmother."

"When," continued Mrs. Margaret, "I retired to St. Cuthbert's, it happened on a day of obligation, when I was going to have mass in my chapel for myself and my household, that this woman came to the door and desired to be admitted. But our habits are strict; the old woman was refused admittance. After mass she threw herself at the priest's feet, having waylaid him purposely, and in Spanish poured forth a wonderful story to him. He told me the substance of this story, and brought me a ring with the Dyrbington arms upon it, as a proof of its truth. She declared herself to be that Spanish lady whom the late Mr. Dyrbington's uncle married, who lost her husband in consequence of injuries he received in a quarrel with his brother, who was Mr. Dyrbington's father. She said that she knew Lullingstone well, having been hospitably entertained there on first coming into this neighbourhood. She certainly gave strong proof of her knowledge of Old Court. She said that she wandered through the whole country after her husband's death as a beggar. She knew that the Dyrbingtons had inquired about her, but a deep and bitter vengeance had kept her from acknowledging herself. Her child, a daughter, had been the companion of her wanderings. After some years she determined to take her child to her uncle, then living here, and throw her on his protection. She said that she met him, and spoke to him, and that he struck her with his whip, almost riding over the young girl, and they fled into the forest from his threats. There some of the forest settlers were kind to them; and, when she recovered from the long-felt effects of delirious fever, she found her daughter, to whom she had never told her real parentage, willing to marry a man who was of a kind and generous disposition, and who never for a moment failed in the kindest treatment of herself. The offspring of that marriage we know very well—Lyas Norwood. Lyas is the child, I firmly believe, of Mr. Dyrbington's first cousin; and, in the female line, he now represents this house."

There was a pause. "My dear madam," said Lord Westray, "will you favour us with some further details? You saw this extraordinary person frequently afterwards, I believe?"

"Yes," said Mrs. Margaret—"frequently. She

was often, without doubt, deranged in mind; but in her sane moments her story never varied. And she brought up her grandson to reverence this house, and got him Catholic baptism. But she never told Lyas Norwood who he really was. His parentage by his mother was never made known to him. Only he was told never to beg, or lay himself under obligation to any one but Mr. Dyrbington. He was told to apply to Mr. Dyrbington for the expenses of her and his father's funeral; and, as most of us know, his request was complied with.

"Can you tell us no more, dear madam?" said Lord Westrey.

"No more that would interest your friends, I think," replied Mrs. Margaret. But several of those assembled entreated the lady to sit down with them for a few moments, and gratify the desire they all felt to know all that she would tell them.

"It is long since I spoke to so large an audience," she said, smiling and seating herself; and then she desired those around her to be seated also, and continued to speak without reserve—
"On the night of this aged woman's death, I was sent for to their forest-hut. The friend and priest of my house sent for me to the dying bed of Manuela Dyrbington. I had kept the ring with the Dyrbington arms on it. She now gave me a small case, which looked as if it had once con-

tained a relic, and which bore upon its gold back her maiden name. She said it had been her father's. She told me never to divulge to any one the secret of her descendant's lineage, unless extraordinary circumstances should open some prospect, not only of their recovering their place in the world, but of their adorning it. I kept the promise. But when Lyas Norwood wished to remove his son from this neighbourhood, when I knew that he was at my house consulting Father Bernard on the matter, I sent for him and for Harold, and, providing for the possibilities of the future—for his son was a youth of extraordinary talent—I ventured to call on Mr. Dyrbington, and asked him to assist me in placing Harold under the protection of a monastery abroad, where he could procure such instruction as might develop his remarkable powers. Mr. Dyrbington took the whole expense of his education, and lived to be rewarded by the youth's success."

Mrs. Margaret only paused to allow her hearers to express their interest in her story, and a little of the astonishment that crossed their minds on finding that fearful, secluded, forgotten St. Cuthbert's should have been so quietly busy with the affairs around them.

"I still kept the secret," she went on, "until Lyas had been to my house and asked for Father Bernard's assistance during the last hours of my kinsman's life. Then, with Mr. Dyrbington dying, and with Harold a Catholic, I determined to tell all I had heard, and bring to him such evidence as I possessed of the story's truth. I saw Mr. Dyrbington. I told him all. We prayed together in those solemn moments; we gave thanks together to God." She paused, greatly affected. No one disturbed the silent prayers that all felt her to be offering. But she soon recovered herself, and spoke again.

"Mr. Dyrbington wrote the words you have read. It remains for Lord Westrey to act."

Then Lord Westrey spoke, "It only remains for me to bestow, by a legal instrument, all that remains of this property on Harold. Lyas, who knows every thing, refuses the property—refuses in favour of his son, I mean. Gentlemen, you will agree with me as to the justice of this measure?"

Every body agreed with Lord Westrey; and Mrs. Margaret, with a look of almost gentle triumph on the sweet face, where the many years of her life showed so softly, left the room. None but Lord Westrey and Harold ever saw her again. But when, not very long after, the earth closed over the unwritten life of this woman of silent action and secret prayer, they all paid that last respect which made people say that she was more thought of in her death than in her life.

When Lord Westrey had completed his arrangements at Dyrbington, he walked to the Chantry farm. Harold walked with him. It was not the first conversation they had had together. For some days Harold had known the change that awaited him. He had spent those days at St. Cuthbert's, and there Lord Westrey had had many and prolonged conversations with him. The young man was devout in religion, and an enthusiast in art; or, we might say, he was devout in both, for he painted because he prayed. Only religious subjects could satisfy his soul. He had worked hard; but all work resulted in some expression of that religion which filled his heart and brought strength and peace to his soul. But all the while Lord Westrey talked, he thought of who would be a good wife for this young man, and he thought of Anna Julian. It seemed but natural that the hero and heroine of such romantic stories should marry at last. Then came the recollection of her having refused his son; then a wonder why? Then the recollection that Harold had once lived with the Julians in their old house; and, finally, a suspicion—but they were arrived, and Julian rose totteringly from the bench under the apple-trees, and did not seem to recognize any change in Harold, only holding out his hand and saying, "You have been gone a long time;" but then he sank down with a faint cry, for Anna had dropped to the earth by his side, and at Lord Westrey's feet, quite senseless.

Lord Westrey took her in his arms, and carried her into the house. Harold spoke to Julian. "It is nothing," he said smiling; "She is only surprised at seeing us." "Ah, yes—yes!" stammered Julian, "so many things have happened lately, and I am grown confused, Harold. And Edward is ill, and we live here, at Dyrbington; we lived here hundreds of years ago, Harold. And it is all right—but the gold is gone. The chest is empty now. And Anna will marry, won't she? But you loved her, Harold?"

His heart trembled when he heard the old man talk thus. But Lord Westrey had returned at that moment, and just in time to hear the last words. "Go to her, Harold," he said; "I believe the right thing will happen now." And Harold was in the house in a moment.

CHAPTER XXV.

THE END.

A FEW weeks passed—weeks scarcely marked by any thing but the failing of Edward Julian's powers. Lord Westrey had been so struck with his wasted looks, that, remembering how much he had risked to nurse Lullingstone, he now sent to London for Lady Westrey and his children to come home, and determined not to leave the neighbourhood until some change took place in Edward. Edward rejoiced over Harold's return; over the discoveries that had been made; and, above all, over his engagement to his sister. Mrs. Julian looked on with content and approval, and only Edward's alarming state prevented Anna from being happy.

Edward—Edward—no wonder his name hung upon their hearts, as it were, growing heavier every day. Weaker and weaker—paler, thinner— his voice lower, his breath more laboured. Day after day the terror grew upon them and chilled their hopes, and they could not accept of happiness in others because Edward was so ill. At last there came a night when he said, "Let Harold help me up-stairs to-night. I shall never go up these stairs again. Mother, dear mother—why do you weep? I have suddenly, within the last two hours, grown too heavy for your gentle arm. Don't weep, mother. You may love Harold with a double love. If you will all promise me to be very happy, I shall die so calmly, so quietly, I think. There is no strength left for any struggle of the flesh. Be all of you quite happy, and there shall be no sorrow of the spirit either." And, so saying, he signed to Harold to come to him; and Harold helped him up-stairs. It was impossible for him to rise when the morning came. He had prophesied rightly. He was never to mount those stairs again. The knowledge that it would be so struck on Anna's heart and on her mother's with a stupifying effect. Death! They had not thought of death! Death to their house—to its pride, its manhood! Death to Edward! Ah, yes; death to Edward! And more—judgment and eternity to Edward—but who could think of that? He did not think of it. He only felt that he had worn life out; that he was weak and fainting under the burthen of the few remaining hours; that he, like all who are born to earth, must die and leave it.

The incapacity of those around him—the stillness, the silence! How powerless they were in the presence of the great fear that had entered their house—the fear that now had grown to certainty, and that kept them waiting, unable to do any thing but wait—wait—wait! with no one to speak to, for Harold had been sent for by Mr. Benson to go with him to London; and the hours passed by without a circumstance or a thought of consolation; all was cold, calm suffering. Edward, still and pale as a corpse, up-stairs, motionless on that little bed, passing away, drooping in the morning, wasting at noon, and sinking with the day—dying. It was the one idea that filled their minds—dying! It filled their minds, but was allied to no action. How helpless they were! And the moments passed, and the breathings, that it might not now be difficult to count to their end, grew fewer—and no one spoke.

At last a great struggle was pictured on the dying youth's face, and he grasped his mother's hand closely, as if warning her not to refuse him. "I must see Mary Westrey!" he said, "I must see her!—see her alone, or I cannot die!" He looked quite wild for one short moment, and then sank back—they thought he was dead, but no! He revived to look at them—alas, how imploringly!—to gather up all his stock of strength to say, "I must!"—to look at them so pleadingly that it was like suffering madness not to yield.

The mother drew back, pale, almost fainting; her heart chilled at the thought of the impossibility of complying with that strong desire. But Anna stood by him, pressing his worn hand in hers, with her stedfast gaze on his face—a gaze that comforted him; for he saw in it that he should see Mary Westrey—that, if it came within the compass of human power, he should see her.

Anna stooped, and kissed her brother's cold, damp forehead, her heart trembling as she saw the rising fever in the brightening eye and the colouring cheek. "I must!" whispered Edward; "Anna, I must!" She left the room.

What could she do? She stood still on the staircase. Lady Westrey and Mary had only arrived the day before. What could she do? Like one in a dream she stood there. She only knew that she could not see Edward again until she could say, "I have sent—she is coming." But if Mary should send a refusal by the messenger? "I must go myself—I must go myself" —said Anna.

At that moment a sound—a sound she might not have noticed any other day, or under any other circumstances—a little sharp sound, the movement of the latch on the little orchard-gate, met her ear. She felt, she *knew* it was Lord Westrey who opened that gate. She rushed to the entrance, she was crimson with excitement; every thing now seemed to depend on how she spoke to him. She met him at the door and could not speak—she burst into uncontrollable tears; and not for many minutes, not until he had led her into the little parlour, and spoken the kindest words to her, could she say, "Lord Westrey, he must see Mary; he says he can't die till he has seen her!"

"Impossible!" exclaimed Lord Westrey.

"No, no; you don't understand! It is all over; all lost! He has nothing to say to her. But he must see her—he must, indeed! You won't—you can't refuse." Still Lord Westrey hesitated. "Listen to me," said Anna, making a great effort to be composed, and with all her strength stifling the sobs that strove within her—"Listen, Lord Westrey! Edward has had one strong idea in life. He achieved every success that could bring him upon equal terms with that idea, and qualify him to ask for its fulfilment. He failed, and he is paying for it with his life. But there has been a sense in which Mary has always admired him. He knows that. Let him have the consolation in dying, which, if he had lived, he would never have asked—let him see her, hear her voice once more, know by her smile that he never degraded himself in her eyes—that she approves him. He must have it, Lord Westrey."

Still Lord Westrey never spoke. He looked at Anna as if pondering on what she had been saying, but he was silent. Anna went on—

"One thing more. We have been brought up very well, very carefully, very morally; but, somehow, I feel now that we have been brought up without religion. Edward has never had any strength but that of his brave heart and his high sentiment. Let his sentiment be his consolation, then—let him see Mary! It is too late for any thing else—let him see Mary!"

There was an unutterable melancholy in these words. Anna spoke them as from an almost broken heart. Certainly they produced on Lord Westrey the most painful impression of a solitary spirit—a soul departing in its weakness and ignorance—trying to rest on the one high hope which through life had been its sole idea of strength, reward, and consolation.

"He shall see Mary," said Lord Westrey. "I will fetch her myself. Tell him that I will return in a few hours. I will go back directly."

The day wore on. The bright spot on the sick youth's face grew brighter and brighter; his eye more full of light, and of a terrible expectancy. He never spoke. But Anna felt that the expression of that face, as he turned it towards her, was more than she could bear much longer. Hours wore on; they could neither of them speak. His mother said something about sleeping—sleeping! would he ever sleep again?

Then Anna found herself listening—listening with that intensity which seems to absorb all other powers. She lived to hear—not to hear what was passing in the little world around her, but to hear what she longed for—the desire of her heart, the hope of that life upon the couch before her—that life that sank no more as it had been sinking, but was burning itself out with the fever of expectation, the flame of its hope. And the sound of the latch on the orchard-gate made her jump, as the voice of a cannon would have failed to do; but Edward only said, "Go to her, Anna!" Anna looked from the window; a dark habit showed among the flowering shrubs. "She will be here directly," she answered, and went to meet her, as he said.

In that little red-brick floored parlour of the Chantry farm stood Lord Westrey, with his fair daughter by his side. Mrs. Julian held Mary's hand, and thanked her, weeping. Old Julian, in a chair, seemed stupified with grief. His shattered mind had now admitted the idea of danger to Edward, and he kept telling Mary not to mourn too much—to be consoled; and so, in broken sentences, he showed how his hopes had rested. Then he shed tears abundantly, and spoke of his son's goodness, his cleverness, his beauty, and how rich he would make him; and, getting confused, he talked of Harold, and wondered why Anna might not marry him, for he had long loved her, had always loved her; had loved her when they all lived together in the old house that looked out upon the sea.

Anna only gave one kind glance to her poor

father in his chair, then, exchanging a look of intelligence with her mother, she put her arm in Mary's and led her away. Lord Westrey followed them into an adjoining room. There Mary, who had not spoken yet, and who looked almost sternly still, placed her hat and gloves on the table, and took the handkerchief from her neck.

"I may be a long time, papa."

"As you please, my child."

"You remember what I have said?"

"Every thing shall be as you wish."

"Then let us go to him, Anna;" and the two girls, without another word, went to Edward's room.

Anna looked into Mary's face, wondering how she felt, or if she felt any thing. But there was no language written there that Anna could read. She entered the room with her usual firm step and easy grace; no emotion in her countenance, nor tremor in the soft accents of her tender voice. She never asked him how he felt, or spoke of her sorrow to see him ill. But she said, "I have a great deal to say to you, and I should like to say it to you with Anna in the room."

Mary sat by his side, and took his hand in hers, and met calmly his glittering, earnest, tearful eyes.

"Don't tire yourself with trying to talk, Edward. It is I who must talk. I want to talk about myself."

And she did talk of herself; of her childhood, her youth, her womanhood. And as she talked, and let his hand still rest on hers, and kept her calm eyes on his face, he grew quiet and at peace. A great interest awoke within his heart, but it was not love of Mary. All that love went out—paled away, faded, died—absolutely ceased to be, as he listened to her; and that other interest rose, and for the first time in his life he really knew her as she was.

She spoke to him of the outward life that he had seen and known; and she showed him that secret life which he had scarcely ever thought of, but which had always been her *real* life, and in which alone her true self could be seen. She told him how the world scorned her and her mother's faith—how impossible it was, belonging as they did to a man of Lord Westrey's position, that they should show to the world openly a faith that was not his—how it had seemed to become the part of the good wife and the good daughter to worship God in secret—and how this long habit had so become by use second nature, that they lived the life naturally, and gave the world no cause to gossip of its existence.

Then she asked him to understand how the treasure of their faith grew more precious for being kept in secret. And she told him how, very early in life, she had desired, as it were, to make amends to God for the irreverence and rebellion by which He suffered from the world in which she lived—how she and her mother hoped, by their adoration and their frequent acts of gratitude and reparation, to bring down the blessings of faith on those dearest to them—how all her affections got absorbed in the love of God. She still went on, and told him of how deeply her heart got pierced with the thought of the condescension of Almighty God, who trusted His honour, and offered Himself to the worship of weak women like themselves, and that she could not help wishing to return Him something as compensation for such distinguished love. She explained to him what the Mass was, what blessings flowed in the Sacrament of Penance. She told how, secretly in London, they had had Mass, and received the Sacraments in their own house—in a locked-up room which was a superior sort of garret; of how she acted as the sacristan of this holy place; of how the Blessed Sacrament had occasionally been reserved there for the sick, even when he had been with them in London; and how her heart had always seemed to live in that great Presence, even when she was visiting with Anna, and going with her from place to place.

Then she went on to say how thankful she had felt to be able to make amends for other people's irreverences towards the true religion, and, either through ignorance or profanity, towards the sacred Host. How it had come to be the greatest pleasure of her life—how she had learned to love Him in the blessed Sacrament till no lesser love could possibly be entertained—could ever for one instant inhabit the heart which was filled with His worship, and only lived to adore Him. And Edward understood all she said. The love that had been within his heart was dead, was gone for ever. But, in its stead, sprung up a wonderful interest in the faith that had won her in this perfect way, and he said—

"Oh, Mary, I am dying, and I have no faith! I wish I could believe!"

Mary's heart went up in prayer. Then she went on:—"I have more to say about myself, Edward. You know now why I could answer you and Sir Giles Morton only in one way. Let me tell you how God's grace fell, and made my heart daily, hourly, more wholly His. It did not change me outwardly. It did not withdraw me from the duties of the time and place that were still mine—but it made me hope, long, determine to be His for ever."

Now Edward listened like a little child, for Mary told him how all that God had done for us was ever recurring to her. And she spoke of Bethlehem, and Calvary, and the Church that He had planted, and the Priesthood, and the Sacraments, and how His precious blood was applied to the soul, and flowed for ever for the Church. She numbered up all that He whom her soul loved had done, and told him how the desire grew in her mind to give herself to Him without reserve, to let Him triumph over all earthly affections; how His grace had made her love the cross, and long to leave the world—to embrace its weight, its seeming shame, for the sake of the precious drops that flowed from His sacred wounds—for the dear love of that heart that broke for man. She spoke solemn words, and Edward, weeping, said them after her.

"Oh, my God, would that I had always loved Thee! I detest the time in which I loved Thee not. How could I live so long without Thy holy love?" Again and again the dying youth said those words, "How could I live so long without Thy holy love?"

"Father Bernard will come to you," said Mary. "I got my father to send for him, and meet me here." But, for the first time, her voice was not listened to by him to whom she spoke. He only said once more, gazing forth strangely on the world he was so soon to leave, "How could I live so long without Thy holy love?" Crossing herself, and trembling, now that her task was done, Mary and Anna in the next room found Father Bernard, who went to Edward immediately.

Before another sunset Edward was dead. The last of the male line of Dyrbington, the spoliator, in his trembling age—the last male hope of the line of Snygge, the destroyer, in his broken youth

—Mother Church had received them both. St. George and St. Katharine had found their own—and forgotten St. Cuthbert's had not been preserved in vain.

Harold and Anna after a few months were married. She had embraced the true religion. They lived in the old house. The chapel—that room where Anna had seen her husband with the picture—was restored. The priest lived at the Chantry farm with Mr. and Mrs. Julian.

Almost immediately after their marriage, Lyas Norwood bade them farewell, and would not tell them where he was going, but promised that, if they would be patient for a year, they should hear of him if he lived. They did hear of him. Harold even went to see him. In the monastery, where Harold had formerly found both kindness and protection, there was a lay brother of extraordinary zeal, and of a true simplicity. He was remarkable for many things—for his cleverness with his hands—for his unflagging spirits—even for a certain low, merry laugh—and for his stories of fine English trout caught about Bartholomew tide. The fine young English squire knelt down, and his father blessed him.

After Mrs. Margaret Lullingstone's death, Mary Westrey was declared her heiress. But when she came to St. Cuthbert's, it was in company with some holy women from the convent where she had made her vows, and they blessed the neighbourhood, and served God in community. She lived there in union with God, and in great peace for some years; the world speaking of her as under an extraordinary delusion; and continuing to do so long after a small black cross told where the corruptible waited for the incorruptible, and the mortal for immortality. But, when the world spoke of this retired community as morbid fanatics, one was generally excepted from the general condemnation—one was certainly full of good works and holy in their eyes. Alas, for the world, so wise in its own conceit! It never knew that the devout Sister Katharine was once Mary Westrey of Old Court Lullingstone.

Years passed on—sons and daughters were born to Dyrbington. Lord Westrey died, and his noble wife, and Lullingstone too, unmarried. The house of Westrey was no more. Old John Julian saw the end, and time seemed to leave no mark upon him. Mrs. Julian became a Catholic, and Julian attended the Church's services; but what he felt, or how much he knew, no one could tell. Father Stukeley's crucifix had been made into the centre of a grand processional cross; and the design and the idea had been Mr. Dyrbington's. John Julian had watched the putting together of this loved relic of the old times he had so often dwelt upon, with evident delight, and many expressions of devotion. When the Bishop came to bless the newly arranged chapel it seemed to give him pleasure, and he had knelt to get his blessing. Then the old chair on which he had so often sat gazing on the sea, was polished and made beautiful to look upon, and placed in the chapel for the Bishop's use; Anna and Harold trying to explain things to Julian, and unutterably glad in their hearts when he seemed to understand their words. It was at last determined that the old man might receive conditional baptism; and after this it was wonderful to see how much all his pleasure seemed to centre in that little church, and how much more he seemed to understand of religion than of any other subject. Things went on in this way for above a year. Then, one peaceful summer afternoon, John Julian was missed—his wife and daughter never allowed him to be long out of their sight—he was found as some supposed sleeping, as others said in a fit, on his knees, leaning against the rails of the altar of St. George. He was carried from the church, and recovered for a moment only before he closed his eyes and died.

THE END.

GILBERT AND RIVINGTON, PRINTERS, ST. JOHN'S SQUARE.

www.ingramcontent.com/pod-product-compliance
Lightning Source LLC
Chambersburg PA
CBHW022122290426
44112CB00008B/768